RUTLAND COOKERY SCHOOL

Recipes, Tips and Techniques

Robin Stewart

CONTENTS

Introduction 5

Measurements and Credits 6

Tales of a Chef 7

SKILLS & MASTERCLASSES
Knife Skills 12
Bread Making 15
Fish 23
Game 29
Stocks and Sauces 34
BBQ 40

CUISINES
Plant-Based 51
Modern British 59
French Bistro 67
Taste of Italy 75
Spanish Café 81
Taste of Morocco 89
Kyoto – Taste of Japan 99
Indian Curries and Indian Street Food 105
Taste of Thailand and Thai Street Food 119
Taste of China 131

BAKING
Baking for Afternoon Tea 139
Macarons 145
Patisserie 149
Danish Pastry 157

INTRODUCTION

The idea of opening a cookery school and sharing some of my knowledge, garnered over 40 years in both top restaurants and hotels and in commercial recipe development, was an embryo of an idea many years ago. And now I've finally done it, I wish I had done it years ago!

With enthusiastic encouragement from Oakham Town Council, I finally realised my dream in December 2017 and opened a small cookery school at Oakham Enterprise Park. Three years on and the response has been fantastic, with many courses sold out months ahead and some customers returning up to a dozen times!

The motto of Rutland is *Multum in Parvo - Much in Little* and I like to think that we are the same. We only cater for a maximum of 9 people but offer over 30 courses and cover much more than just how to cook a recipe.

Teaching technique is a large part of what I do, along with a thorough understanding of the ingredients, flavours and, in the case of the cuisine workshops, culture behind the dishes we prepare. I love to travel and experience other cultures and their cuisines and at the school my workshops often include photographs and videos taken during my visits of a particular type of food or dish being cooked. I strongly believe that it is only by understanding the ingredients and flavours that you use, that you truly learn to cook.

One of the main outcomes for the majority of people attending my workshops, is a boost to their confidence. It's tempting to say that cookery isn't 'rocket science'. It isn't of course, but it does help to understand the 'why' when you cook an ingredient a certain way or use a particular technique. A little knowledge helps you to cook with more confidence, question recipes (which you should do) and develop your own style and creativity. This book contains some of my favourite recipes from the school and of course many of my hints and tips.

A NOTE ON MEASUREMENTS

It is generally accepted that European cookery books will use a mix of grams and millilitres. If you are using a pair of scales that can be tared (set to zero) after each additional ingredient, then just using grams is both accurate and more convenient. However, for the sake of argument, I have followed the norm and used both, with one or two exceptions where I feel the greater accuracy of grams is important to that particular recipe.

Grams and millilitres are actually interchangeable up to a point – 100g of water is the same as 100ml. This is due to the specific gravity of the liquid and works for thin liquids including wine, stock, coconut milk, milk, single and double cream. It changes where the liquid increases in density, golden syrup for example.

I have used spoons in many recipes because it is more convenient than weighing or measuring small amounts. But you must use proper measuring spoons. These are easy to buy and you will then be confident you are following a recipe correctly. 1 tablespoon = 15g / ml and a teaspoon = 5g / ml.

That said for many of the recipes in this book, especially the cuisine recipes, a few grams more or less will make little difference – feel free to amend / adapt as you wish, this is cooking! It is more important to be accurate for the pastry recipes.

CREDITS

This is the bit where I say this book wouldn't have been possible without.... Well, actually, it was during an enforced break when we had to close the school temporarily in 2020 due to Coronavirus, that I finally had the time to create this, but my family has been suggesting for the last two years that I should combine my love of cooking and photography. I definitely couldn't have done this though, without the support of my wonderful wife, Karen. She has had the dubious pleasure of trawling through all my ramblings to ensure they actually make sense and liaising with the printers on the layout and design of the book. She is also an integral part of the school as she looks after the customers (very well!) and ensures all the administration is up to date.

I also want to credit my daughters, Jessica and Olivia, who have been unstinting in their support and encouragement, even though they now know what they will get for Christmas! I would also like to thank my very old friend Chris Goslar and his company, Chroma, for designing, printing and helping me navigate the realm of 'self-publishing'.

TALES OF A CHEF

Chefs, generally, are very generous when it comes to sharing recipes and techniques. In fact many chefs will welcome some additional input for a few days, or perhaps a week, and this in turn will enable one chef to see what another chef does and how they do it. This is known as a 'stage' and I have done many. I don't know if this is unique to chefs or not, but I was reminded of this camaraderie that exists between chefs the other day when watching a cookery competition on television with my wife, Karen. At one point, the chefs started to help each other, and Karen turned to me, surprised, and said, 'but they're competing against each other?' It was no surprise to me, 'They're chefs' I explained. 'It's what we do. We are a team first, no matter what the circumstances'.

My career in catering started out 'front of house', working at the age of 16 on the QE2. A rather different world to the Essex of my childhood! I have a vivid memory of one of my customers enjoying a world cruise, Salvador Dali, the master of surrealism looking rather surreal himself with his trademark long, thin and heavily waxed moustache.

A couple of years later I was working 'back of house' in the kitchen at the Knightsbridge Carlton Tower Hotel and I had found my calling. I remember the very best quality ingredients coupled with teamwork, camaraderie and a sense of humour that would appear to be the default setting of most chefs. A well-staffed kitchen meant that once our preparation for the evening was complete, we could decamp to the 'snug' in the local pub for a swift 'half' before Monsieur Gaume, the Executive Chef, returned for evening service. We pushed this a bit too far once when the sous chef had to deal single-handedly with an influx of room service orders. He was not a happy man!

I worked at the Carlton Tower twice, with a season at Gleneagles in between. Gleneagles was a very strict, traditional kitchen, after the creative but relaxed Carlton Tower. The Gleneagles kitchen door was guarded each morning by the sous chef, notebook in hand ready to inspect you; shoes (black) had to be polished, hair short (tied back was not acceptable), necktie and chef's toque firmly and crisply in place above spotless chef's whites. If not, your name went in the book for the chef's attention later.

My second stint at the Carlton Tower ended when a talented young sous chef, Ian McAndrew, placed me at the Dorchester Hotel with Anton Mosimann. Here I took part in a competition similar to today's 'Ready, Steady, Cook!' at the Confrérie de la Chaîne des Rôtisseurs, a gastronomic society founded in Paris in 1950. There was no fixed menu and no opportunity to practice, just a basket of ingredients, some time to plan your menu and then get cooking! The aim was to include as much technique as you could as well as cook delicious food. I finished 2nd in the London finals and 2nd in the UK finals.

Most of the sous chefs at the Dorchester were much older than Anton Mosimann and had been there for many years, but they were still quite capable of a playful side and one sous chef who must have been approaching retirement age, enjoyed a game of cricket in the kitchen when Monsieur Mossiman had gone home. The size of the kitchen meant this was perfectly possible and he would line up his batsman with a long baker's paddle and his bowler with a ball made from tin foil and that was it. Game on! That was a great way to finish a hard evening shift.

As a member of the Dorchester team of chefs, I went to the Culinary Olympics in Frankfurt and won an individual gold medal. An exciting time for me! Shortly after this, Anton Mosimann drove, with me as his assistant, to St Moritz to cook a special dinner at the Dracula Club and I was introduced to my next chef, Pierre Gilgen, at the Kulm Hotel. A beautiful old kitchen with floor to ceiling windows and an oil-fired range that had been converted from coal. There were no controls on anything — it was on or off, and that was it! I must confess to burning one or two dishes in my first week as Chef Poissonnier, which rather irritated my new boss. A popular dish was the rather old-fashioned truite au bleu. This dish relies on a live trout, killed to order and poached directly in a simmering court bouillon, at which point the slime coating the fish turns pale blue. We had a big galvanised tank in the larder that held live trout. When I had one on order I would rush to the tank, grab the net, get my fish, quickly gut and clean it, rush back and poach it. I did this once and the fish jumped completely out of the pan, now that is fresh! To say it made me jump is an understatement.

One kitchen I was privileged to work in, was the Michelin 2* Connaught Hotel. A hot, demanding kitchen where teamwork and camaraderie went hand in hand driven by an exacting and passionate Frenchman, Michel Boudin. The tougher the kitchen, the deeper you have to dig and help each other. Once more, a kitchen also infused with humour and practical jokes and I have wracked my brain for one that might be printable! There are the traditional ones of course that happen in all big kitchens — 'go and ask the store man for a long stand', only to wonder why 10 minutes later you were still *standing*. (Actually, sceptical by nature, I never fell for that one). As head chef for Corney and Barrow, at their flagship restaurant on 118 Moorgate, I did once send one of my young chefs to a sister restaurant on London Wall for a tin of chicken lips. I received a call from Chris the head chef there, 'I have one of your chefs here after a tin of chicken lips'. 'Oh yes', I replied, 'Do you have any?' 'No,' came the response, 'I've suggested Paul in Cannon Street may have some'.

Kulm Hotel 1982

In 2000 I decided to leave the world of long, unsocial hours and move into commercial recipe development. Whilst it didn't give me the same feeling I had as an 18-year-old entering the world of 5* London kitchens, I did learn a lot, not least Asian cuisines and the presentation of dishes/products to very discerning retail development managers.

I had been used to managing costs and purchasing for some time but working in a factory environment takes it to a whole new level. Working in percentages, rather than grams, fractions of pence and calculating accurate nutritional results was new to me.

My first project was developing Chinese chilled ready meals for a premium retailer and this learning curve introduced me to new ingredients and an appreciation of a great cuisine.

It was while developing and running training workshops for others at the factory that I discovered another love — that of sharing my knowledge and experience with people and helping others to understand food and, of course, cook it better. From there, I think opening a cookery school was inevitable, it was just a question of when.

Connaught Team 1983

SKILLS & MASTERCLASSES

KNIFE SKILLS

All books need to start at the beginning and as a chef, the beginning starts with learning to use, and look after, a knife. You may have noticed I said 'a' knife. It is a myth that you need the 'right knife for the right job'. True, sometimes a specialist knife is beneficial in the kitchen, but at home three knives of varying sizes will be enough. Chinese chefs manage incredibly skilful and complex tasks with just one – a cleaver.

It doesn't matter how expensive your knife is, if it is blunt it is worthless. Keeping it sharp is essential and chefs do this by using a sharpening steel continuously throughout the day. Knives lose their edge with very little use. You can actually hear when this happens, the knife will cease to 'swish' through things and start to 'crunch' instead. It doesn't matter what you use to sharpen your knives. At the school, on the knife skills workshop, I teach learners how to use a steel, but a little pull-through set of sharpening wheels will work too, albeit not so well, in my experience. But anything is better than nothing. Do remember though, that both of these tools are for *maintaining* a sharp edge. You will spend a very long time indeed trying to sharpen a totally blunt knife with a steel! For that you need to use an oil or whet stone.

So, the rules for using knives in the kitchen:

RULE NUMBER 1. Keep your knife sharp. No, I mean it! Even the most expensive knives will go blunt if not sharpened regularly. If you wait until it slides off that onion, you have already neglected your most important tool in the kitchen for too long.

RULE NUMBER 2. Learn to chop an onion properly and everything else will follow.

RULE NUMBER 3. Practise, Practise, Practise! The amount of time spent in the kitchen preparing food, relative to cooking it, eating it and clearing up afterwards, is disproportionate and I'm sure you can guess which is the quickest bit — yes, it is the eating. The longest part is the preparation. This is directly influenced by your skill with a knife. I wish I had a fresh truffle every time someone said to me 'the recipe said 20 minutes, but it took me 40!' I am rarely surprised by this. Most chefs work at warp speed compared to home cooks and it is all down to knife skills and a sharp knife. But these are not skills acquired in a few hours, they take practice.

HOW TO CHOP AN ONION

Cut the onion in half lengthways — from the tip to the root. Lay one half cut-side down, and hold it with a claw-like grip, with your fingernails tucked away from the knife but just digging into the onion. Make sure your thumb is slightly behind your fingers, towards the back of the onion.

Holding the knife up against your first knuckle, slice down the onion (from the tip to the root), using the full length of the knife blade, but stop just before the root. Repeat, still keeping the knife against your knuckles, move back along the onion as you slice, moving your fingers back at the same time.

> **TOP TIP**
>
> Always leave the root section intact – it stops the onion disintegrating under your hand.

A few strokes horizontally produce a finer chop, but it is not essential at home.

Complete the task by slicing downwards across the onion to produce your dice. How fine this is, depends on how far you move your fingertips along the onion. Chefs measure mentally depending on what is required.

That's it. But is does take practise!

If you want to know how to avoid tears whilst chopping an onion (from the vapours, not from cutting your finger!) use a very sharp knife and learn to work quickly. Or get someone else to do it!

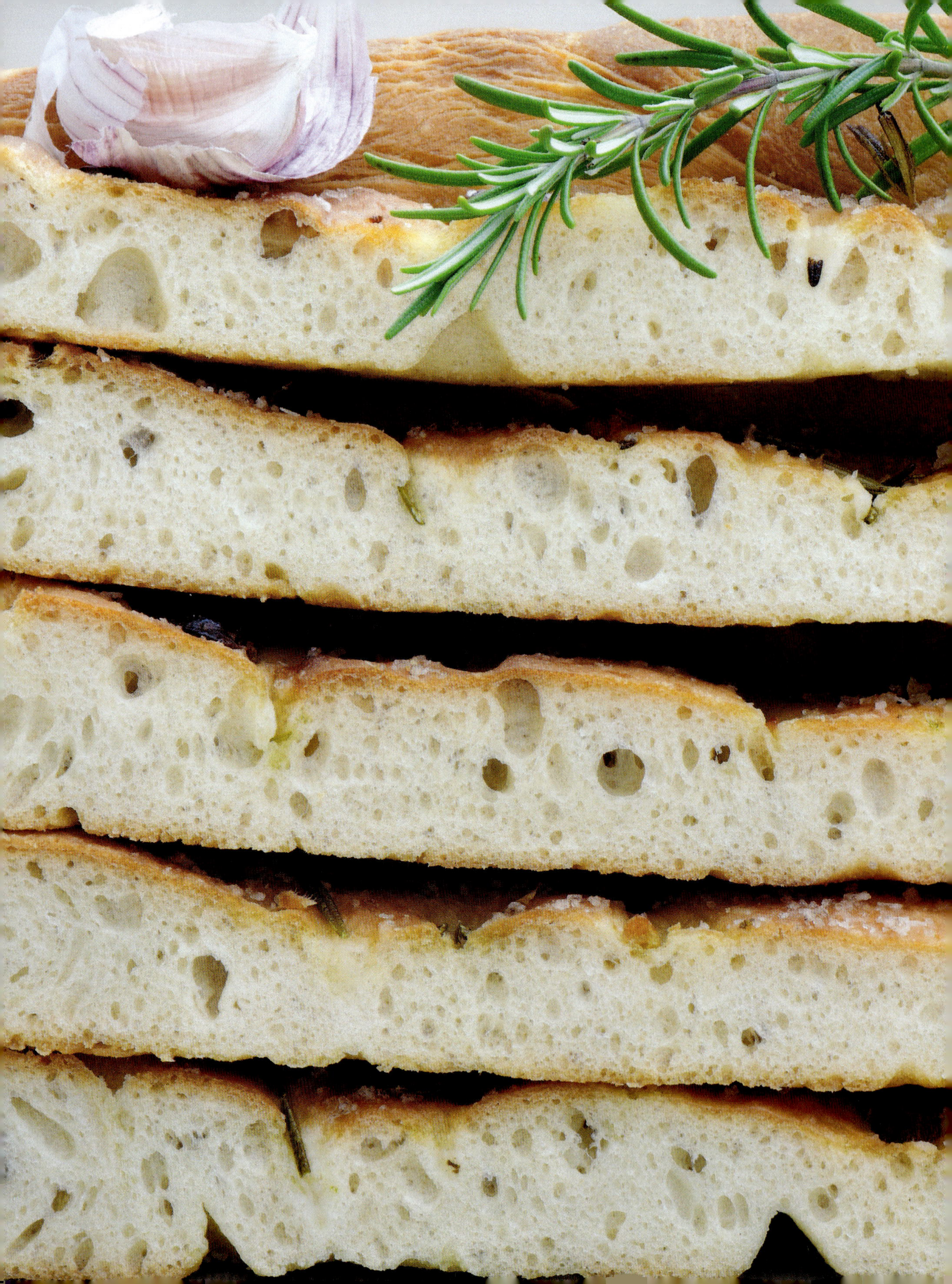

BREAD MAKING MASTERCLASS

Bread consumption has halved since the 1950's yet the incidence of people reporting problems digesting bread has increased exponentially in that time frame. Given that bread has been a staple food for a millennium, why is this?

Bread used to be made slowly for the simple reason that there was no way to make it quickly. Wild yeasts work their magic slowly and so the baker would have to give the bread time to 'ripen' naturally, a process that takes from several hours to a day – or longer if you wish. The reason for this is that the bulk of the flour consists of starch, which are carbohydrates in glucose form bonded together into long chains. When making bread, during fermentation, these long chains are broken down into smaller pieces by yeast, enzymes and lactic acid bacteria. It takes time for this to happen. So, bread which has been made in a hurry, like most supermarket bread, still contains a lot of the original long glucose chains, the raw flour, and less of the smaller chains. These long chains are harder to digest and this makes most factory bread harder on your internal system.

The Bread Masterclass at Rutland Cookery School has steadily evolved into a comprehensive day on all things to do with bread, flour, gluten, yeast, bacteria, and production processes.

We make five types of bread: a very simple flour, water, yeast, and salt focaccia, two types of sourdough, challah and a very wet ciabatta dough. This really helps learners to understand how gluten, yeast (wild and commercial), bacteria, water and fats affect the dough and final crumb and crust. We make all five breads by hand. For learners it is very important to feel the dough change as you knead. Once you are proficient by all means use a stand mixer and dough hook but, to begin with, it helps to knead the dough by hand. We use plastic bowl scrapers for initial mixing — it prevents sticky fingers until the flour has had a chance to absorb most of the liquid.

If I were to highlight the most common cause of problems when people make bread, it is the fact that often additional flour is added to make the dough easier to work with. This then makes the dough heavier. The trick is to keep a little mound of flour on the table and just dip the palm of your hand onto it each time the dough starts to stick. That way you add the minimum amount of extra flour and the dough won't stick to your hand.

Working with moist, even wet doughs - as we do with sourdough and ciabatta - is a revelation to many, not least the light, springy loaves with a fine, crisp crust that result.

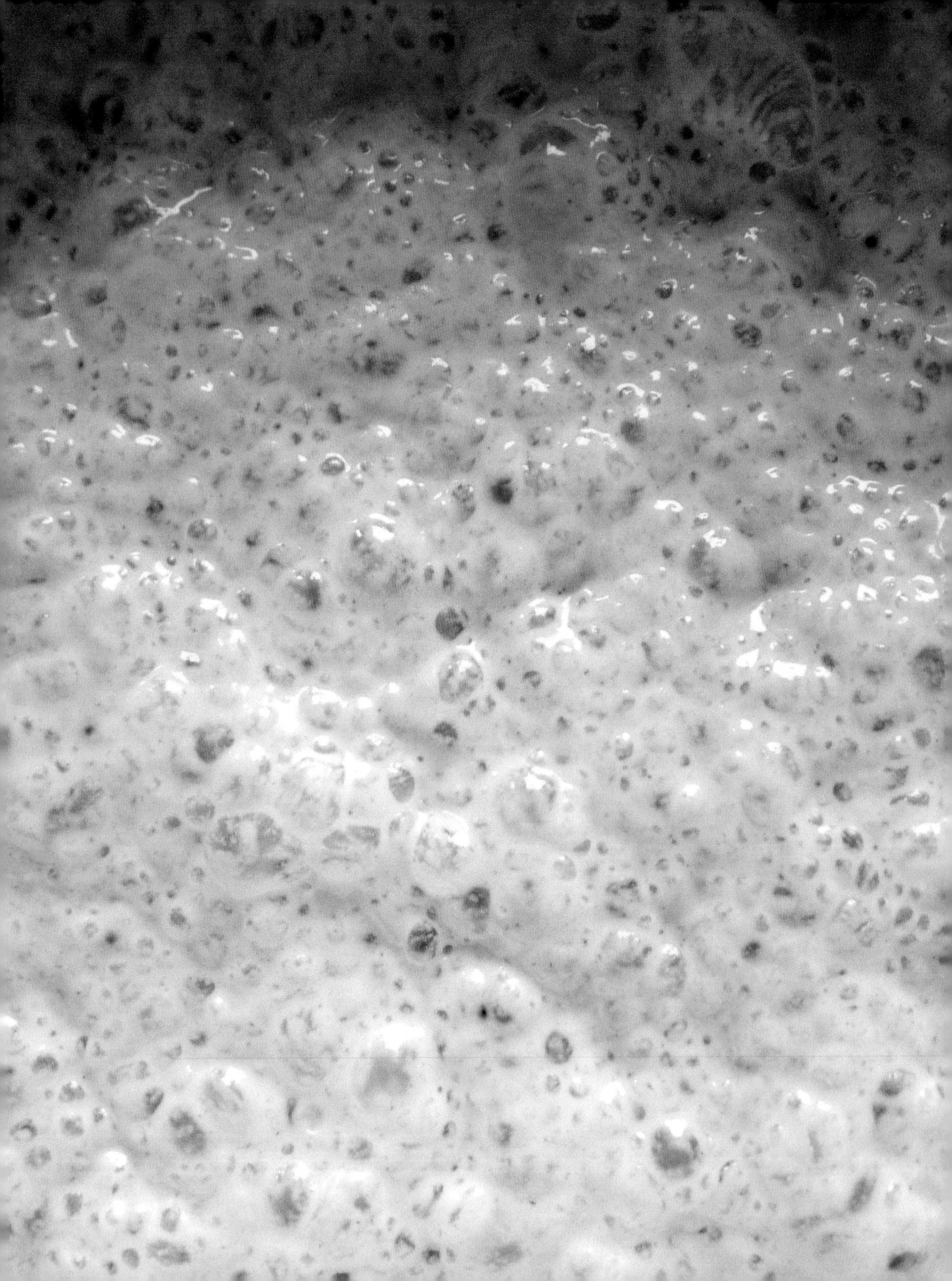

SOURDOUGH STARTER

Sourdough has become an extremely popular bread because it is made with wild yeast and takes longer to ferment, thereby making it more digestible for people. I teach how to make a sourdough starter on the bread workshop. The starter might appear a little daunting at first but working with wild yeast and the process of fermentation is simply magical. Do be patient and persevere!

Starter: (poolish)

DAY 1   75g strong white flour, 25g rye flour, 125g water

DAY 2   NOTHING

DAY 3   NOTHING

DAY 4   add 50g strong white flour and 50g water

DAY 5   add 50g strong white flour, 50g water

DAY 6   NOTHING

DAY 7   add 100g strong white flour, 50g water

DAY 8   discard 250g starter and add 100g flour, 50g water

DAY 9   follow instructions in the recipe below for making the pre-ferment (poolish)

DAY 10 follow instructions in the recipe below for making the dough

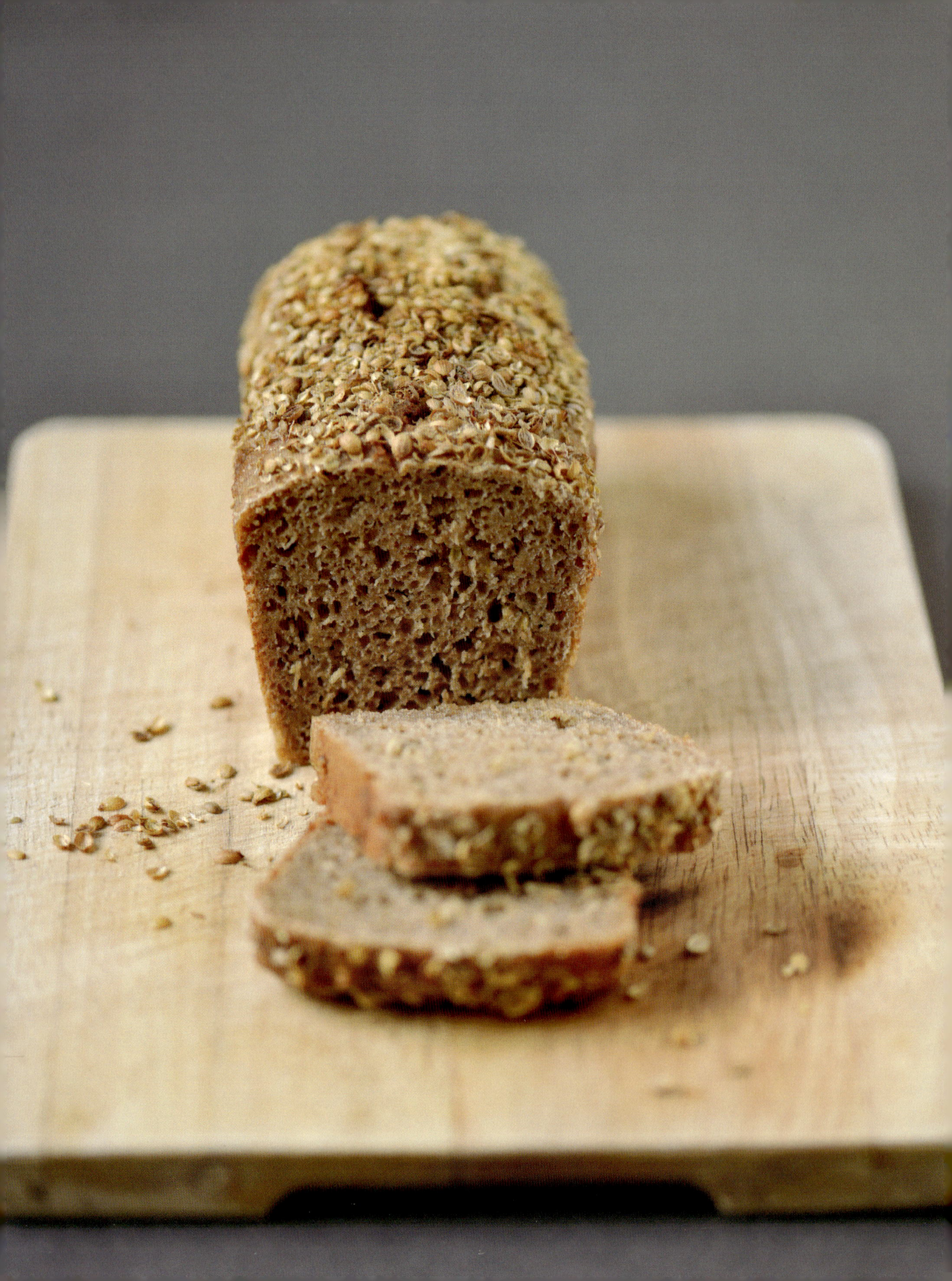

BORODINSKY

PRE-FERMENT (N.B this needs to be started the day before)

65g sourdough starter

100g wholemeal rye flour

175ml water

MAIN DOUGH

100g rye flour

3g sea salt

5g cracked coriander (give seeds a quick whizz in a blender), plus extra to sprinkle on top of the loaf

12g molasses (black treacle)

12g barley malt extract

This Russian bread has several legends attributed to its name. I am going to stick with the one I like best, even though it is apocryphal. The widow of a Russian general who perished in the Napoleonic wars, established a convent at the site of the battle of Borodino. She eventually became the abbess and the nuns reportedly came up with this recipe to serve at events of mourning, thus a dark solemn colour with rounded coriander seeds representing deadly grapeshot. Originally developed with an all-rye sourdough starter, I changed this to the same starter we use in the San Francisco sourdough for ease of use for home cooks. Two starters for the price of one!

FOR THE PRE-FERMENT: The day before, mix the ingredients for the sponge together with a spoon, cover the bowl with a tea towel and leave overnight.

TO MAKE THE BORODINSKY DOUGH: add all the other ingredients to the sponge and mix to a soft dough (use a wooden spoon and beat very well) — it won't be anything like wheat dough, not stretchy or elastic, rather resembling a brownish concrete mix or mud!

Prepare a small loaf tin by lining with parchment and greasing it thoroughly with butter or oil. Place the dough in the tin, don't worry too much about smoothing it level, it will settle as it proves. Sprinkle with the cracked coriander seeds, pressing lightly into the surface of the dough and cover with oiled cling film. Leave in a warm place for 2-3 hours, it needs to nearly double in size, or better still, in the fridge overnight.

When the loaf has risen appreciably, or doubled in volume, put in the oven preheated to 200°C and bake for 30 minutes.

Remove from the oven and turn out onto a wire rack. If the loaf doesn't want to come out, leave it in the tin for a while. Cool completely before wrapping in cling film or a polythene bag. Rye bread slices more easily if it has had a day's rest after baking.

CHALLAH

- 200g strong white flour
- 4g dried yeast
- 25g caster sugar
- 1g sea salt
- Zest of 1 lemon
- 1 medium egg, room temperature
- 25g soft unsalted butter
- 60ml milk
- Mixed Seeds
- Beaten egg to glaze

I have been making challah for decades. We used to coil the dough around large flowerpots and serve as a centrepiece with tufts of herbs, rosemary, thyme and bay coming out of the top. Traditionally of course challah is plaited, and each plait has a meaning. We make a three-plait challah on the bread workshop, representing peace, truth, and justice. The word challah means 'portion' in Hebrew and Jews were biblically commanded to give 1/24th of their dough to a priest.

This dough is enriched with butter and egg, although less so than a brioche, and it helps learners to understand how adding fats to a bread dough changes the texture of the crumb. The lemon zest gives a wonderful fragrance.

TO MAKE THE DOUGH: Mix all the dry ingredients (including lemon zest) thoroughly with your fingertips. Then add all the wet ingredients. Use a plastic bowl scraper to mix the wet into the dry ingredients.

Turn out onto your table and start to knead. The dough will be sticky to start with but do not add more flour, just keep flouring your hands as you knead it.

Knead until the dough is smooth and silky. It should take about ten minutes by hand and you do not need to worry about over-kneading — it isn't like pastry.

Place the dough in a lightly oiled bowl and cover with a piece of oiled cling film (if you don't oil the cling film the dough will stick to it). Leave to double in size at room temperature. You don't need to put it in a warm place. Bread proves equally well in the fridge; it just takes longer. A longer prove (overnight) is actually beneficial; you will have a loaf with more flavour, and it will be more digestible.

TOP TIP

Knead with one hand only and use the other to turn and fold the dough over as you knead. The object of kneading is to stretch and strengthen the gluten in the flour – don't just press or squeeze the dough!

TO SHAPE THE DOUGH: When the dough has doubled in size, tip it out onto your table and roll into one long sausage 750mm long. Divide this into 3 and plait (see pictures).

Place on a parchment-lined baking sheet, cover loosely with oiled cling film and leave to double in size.

Preheat the oven to 160°C (fan)

When the bread is ready to bake, brush carefully with a little egg wash, sprinkle with seeds — sesame, caraway, cumin, poppy etc. and bake for 25 minutes.

This loaf colours quickly. Be prepared to turn the oven up or down a little as required but do bake for the full time.

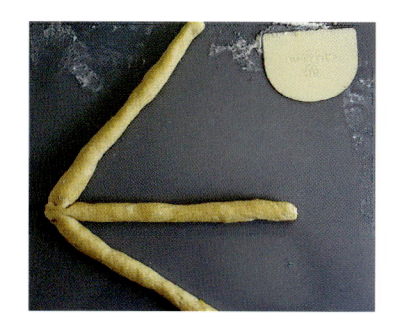

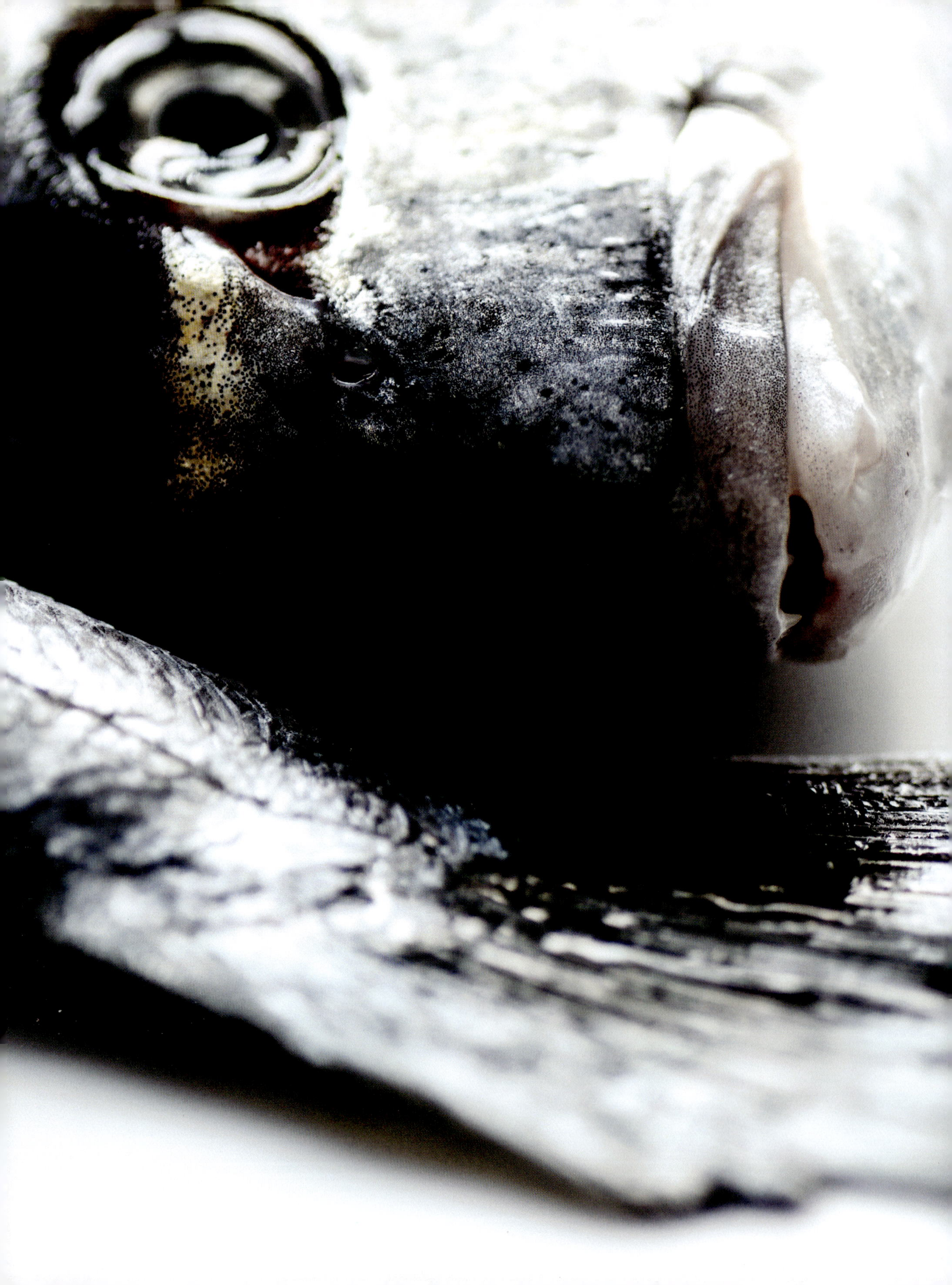

FISH MASTERCLASS

The preparation and cooking of fish is a subject close to my heart. As a young chef, fish was always delivered whole and in the days before farmed fish that meant it was wild and caught by trawler, or rod and line. Sea bass was seasonal, as was salmon and salmon trout, and the size was usually pretty big. No single portion seabass in those days! Turbot, brill, cod, mackerel, sole, herring, halibut, everything came in whole to be prepared in the larder section of the kitchen.

Cooking fish is not so much about a recipe, as about techniques and understanding those techniques. In the professional kitchen we simply never cooked from recipes. Skill, understanding, and knowledge are built over time and we just cooked. At the school therefore, I prefer to teach techniques first and specific recipes second. The logic is that understanding technique means you can cook the same fish multiple ways, but one recipe is just that — one recipe. I often use the analogy, 'give a man a fish and you feed him for a day but teach him to fish and you feed him for a lifetime.'

At the school we always start by discussing how to buy fish, how to gauge freshness and how to fillet. Everyone has two fish each to fillet — practice makes perfect!

Fish dishes shouldn't be over-complicated, it is important to let the fish shine through. White fish can be quite delicate and should be treated accordingly. More robust, oily fish will tolerate, and complement, stronger flavours. At the Connaught Hotel we made a rich red wine sauce to serve with roast turbot. The sauce is called matelote, which we made with eel to give the required rich fish flavour. These used to be delivered live in sacks, were the size of a man's arm, and had to be dispatched (killed) and skinned before use. An eel that size is a strong fish and took some dealing with, I can tell you!

The two fish recipes below cover a couple of core techniques: pan-frying with a crispy skin and grilling / baking. The sauces in each recipe are incredibly simple but complement each dish perfectly.

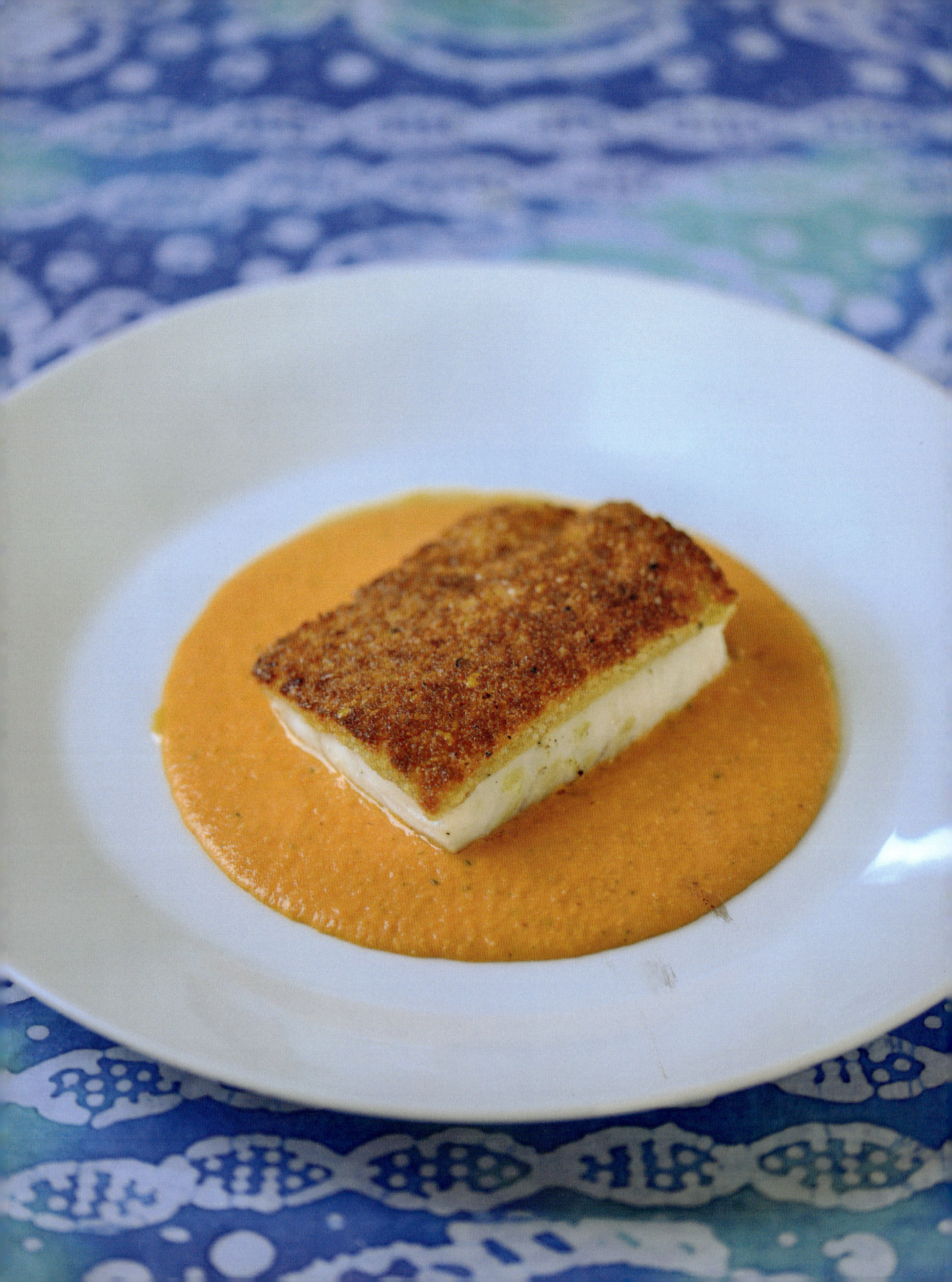

BAKED COD, TOMATO FONDUE, PARMESAN CRUST

Serves 1

1 piece of fresh cod loin about 120g

PARMESAN CRUST

20g butter, softened

10g grated Parmesan

20g breadcrumbs

Black pepper

TOMATO FONDUE

15g butter

20g chopped shallot

1 sprig of thyme

1 large tomato, chopped

Pinch of salt, sugar, and freshly ground pepper

TO MAKE THE CRUST: Combine the softened butter, Parmesan, and breadcrumbs together. Season with freshly ground black pepper (no salt is necessary as the parmesan is salty). Place this mix between two pieces of cling film and gently roll flat, slightly larger all round than your piece of fish. Place in the fridge to chill and set firm.

TO MAKE THE FONDUE: Melt the 15g of butter and sweat the shallots gently (cook gently with a lid on to trap the moisture), until softened. Add the chopped tomato and thyme. Cook until the tomato has mostly turned to mush. Season to taste (if your tomato is acidic, add a little sugar), blend in a liquidiser and pass through a strainer to remove the skin and seeds then keep warm.

> **TOP TIP**
>
> Keeping the tomato a little undercooked makes for a fresh tomato flavour in the sauce.

TO COOK THE FISH: Remove the crust from the fridge and unwrap. Season the fish and place it upside down on top of the crust and carefully trim the crust so that it fits the fish exactly. Carefully turn the fish and crust back over and place, crust uppermost, on a piece of lightly oiled tin foil.

Preheat the grill, and when hot, place the fish underneath. Grill until you have a deep golden crust, then bake in the oven at 180°C for approximately 6 minutes.

TO SERVE: Spoon the warm tomato fondue onto a warm plate and carefully place the fish on top.

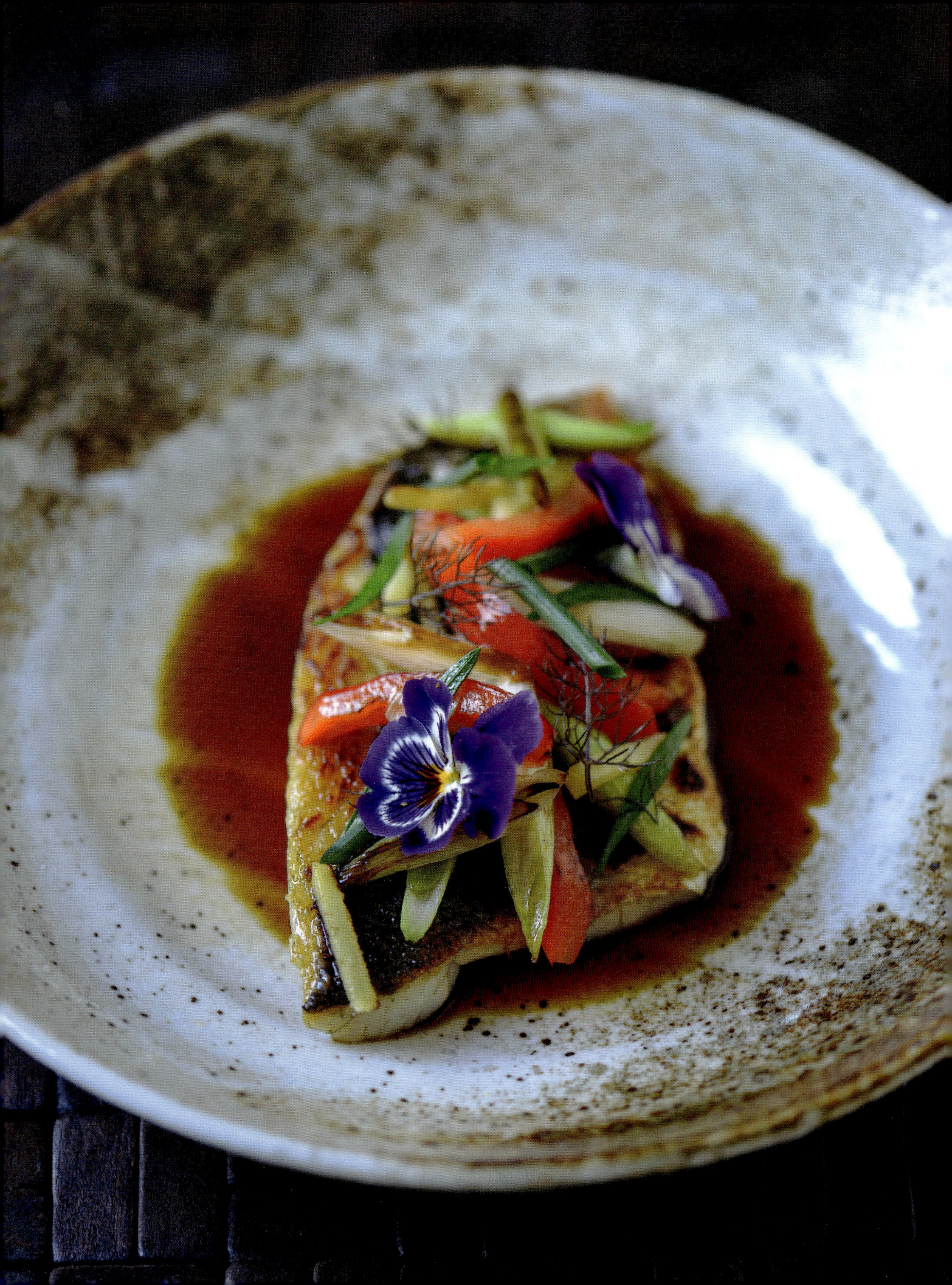

PAN-FRIED SEA BASS WITH SOY, GINGER & RED PEPPER

Serves 1

- 1 fillet sea bass
- 1cm fresh ginger
- 1 spring onion
- 1/4 Red pepper
- 1 small clove garlic
- 1/2 teaspoon vegetable oil
- 1 teaspoon soy sauce
- Fresh flowers and herbs to decorate

TO PREPARE THE VEG: Peel and finely shred the ginger. Cut the spring onion, on the diagonal, into 2-3cm pieces. Cut the red pepper to roughly the same size as the spring onion. Peel and finely slice the garlic.

TO COOK THE FISH: Heat a non-stick frying pan over a medium heat. Pat the fish dry with kitchen paper and season with pepper only. Add the oil to the pan and swirl to cover the centre (where the fish will go). Then place the fish gently in the pan, skin side down. Leave the fish to cook for a few minutes on the skin side only. Do not move it around during this time or the skin will not crisp up! You want a crisp, golden skin.

As the fish begins to cook, you will see the flesh change colour. The fish will cook first where it is thinnest, around the sides. When there is just a narrow strip of raw fish in the centre, carefully turn the fish over. Don't flip it! Turn it by carefully sliding a wide spatula under the fish and, supporting the top of the fish with your fingers, slowly turn it over. Leave for just one more minute, then turn the heat off. Carefully remove the fish and place skin side up onto a warm plate.

TO SERVE: Heat the same pan again until it is very hot. There should be enough oil left in the pan but, if not, add a teaspoon more. Quickly stir-fry the red pepper, spring onion, ginger and garlic — don't overcook, they must be crunchy. Spoon the vegetables over the fish and drizzle with the soy sauce. Decorate with fresh flowers and herbs.

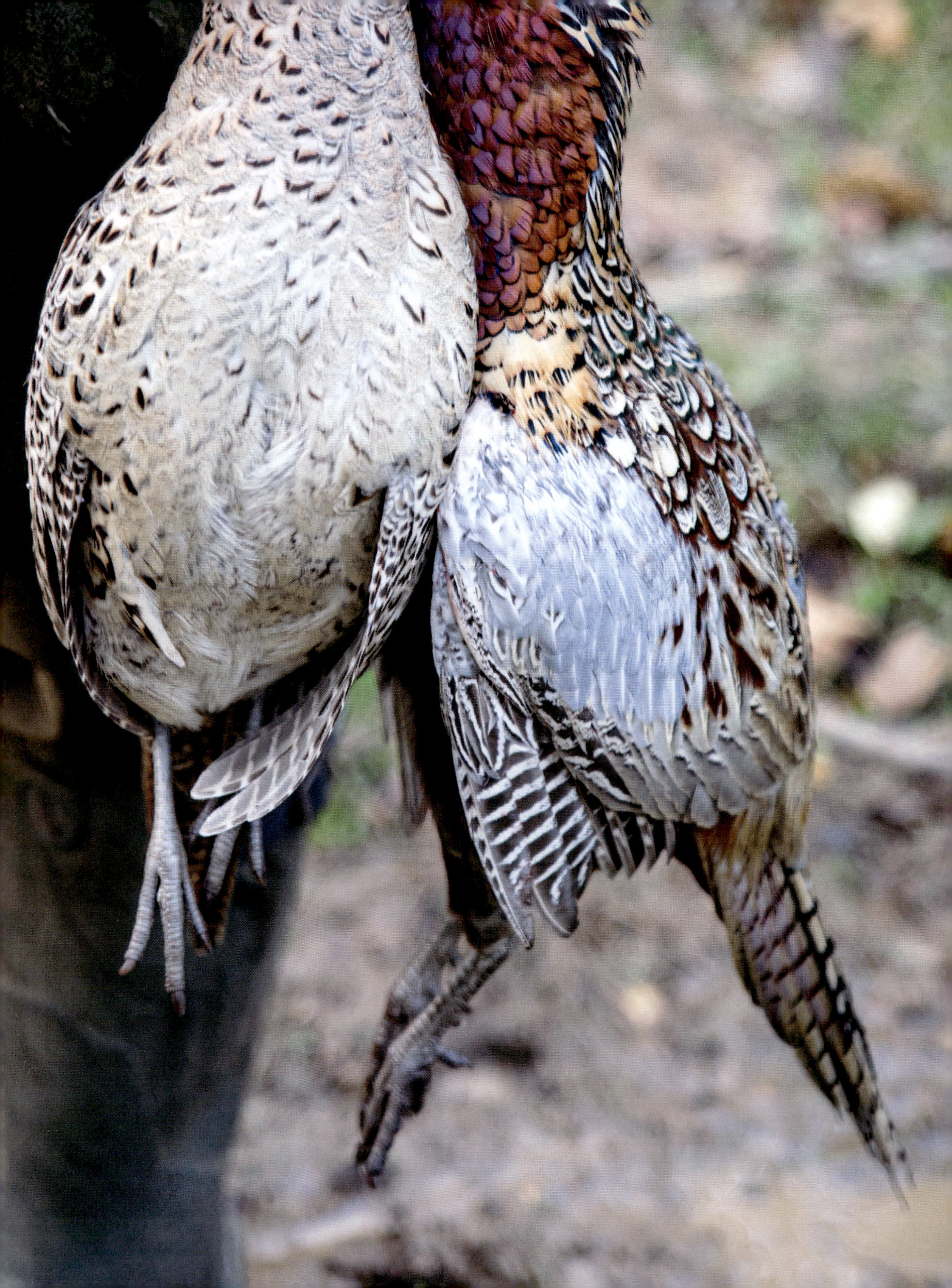

GAME MASTERCLASS

Living in the beautiful county of Rutland, game is readily available. I found many customers were saying that they had been given a brace of pheasant, or a partridge, by a friend and didn't know what to do with them. Hence the game workshop!

I buy game at the fur and feather auction in Melton Mowbray. Availability is variable and the content of the workshop varies accordingly, but we always manage to have either rabbit, hare, or muntjac, plus a selection of birds. The workshop usually includes plucking and jointing of two birds each, plus I also demonstrate how to skin and joint a rabbit or hare.

Wild rabbit is, understandably, a very lean meat with a delicate, gamey flavour which works equally well paired with tomato-based stews and rich, creamy sauces. It is particularly prevalent in regional dishes from the north of Italy, with the abundant countryside providing the perfect breeding ground. Rabbit is also prevalent in the UK and it is a crying shame that this meat is not more popular. The saddle is, in particular, a lovely cut of meat but bear in mind it is essential not to overcook it - a common mistake. The cooking time will appear too short. It isn't. The meat must be slightly undercooked and allowed time to rest. This applies to all game, other than braised dishes such as jugged hare, or haunch of venison casserole.

If you are cooking rabbit, it is beneficial to using the trimmings, or fore legs, to make stock for the sauce (see section on stocks and sauces). If you don't have these, then use fresh chicken stock or a stock cube.

Mallard is a lovely dark red meat. There isn't so much meat on the legs, it is best to confit these (there are instructions for this in the French section under Duck Cassoulet). The breast must be cooked no more than pink — it will be very dry if overcooked. The merlot sauce we make with this, is not only delicious but also the simplest sauce recipe I know.

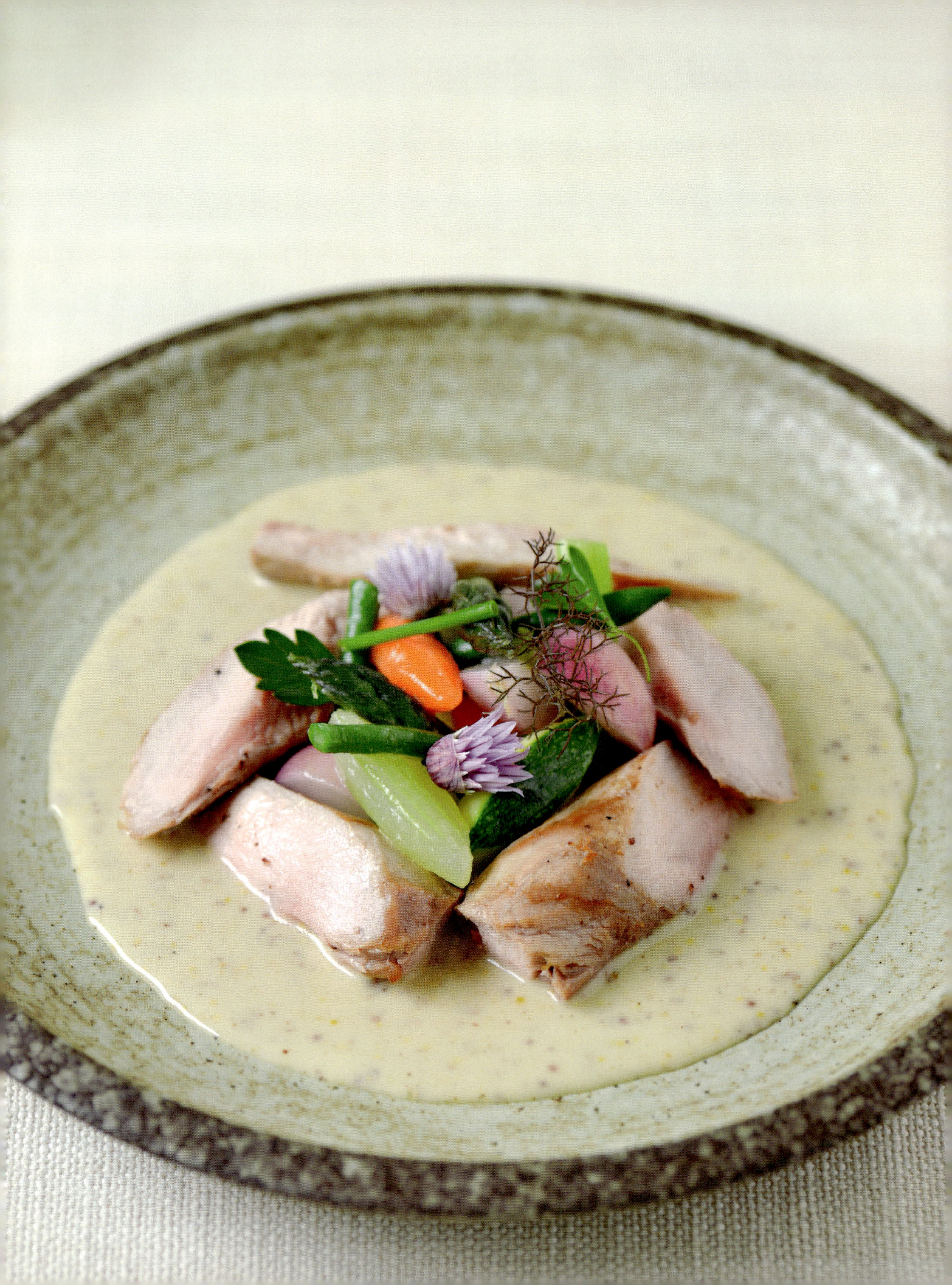

SADDLE OF RABBIT WITH MUSTARD SAUCE & SPRING VEGETABLES

A small saddle serves 1, a large saddle serves 2. This recipe is for a small rabbit.

- 1 saddle of rabbit, cleaned and ready to roast
- 10g butter
- 10g flour
- 1 shallot, finely diced
- 50ml white wine (or cider)
- 150ml rabbit stock (or a chicken stock cube)
- 1 tablespoon single cream
- 1 teaspoon grain mustard
- Selection of spring vegetables

TO COOK THE RABBIT: Preheat the oven to 200°C. Heat an ovenproof pan on the hob and add a teaspoon of oil and a teaspoon of butter. Season the saddle all over, brown in the oil and butter and then roast in the oven for 6 minutes. Remove the rabbit from the pan and keep warm.

TO MAKE THE SAUCE: Tip the rabbit fat out of the pan and add the butter. Cook the shallots in the butter until soft, add the flour and stir in well. Add the wine and stir in to make a smooth paste, then add the stock gradually, changing to a whisk as the sauce thins. Strain the sauce into a clean saucepan, add the mustard and cream, season to taste and keep warm.

TO COOK THE VEGETABLES: Choose a colourful selection such as carrots, courgettes, spring onions, radish, asparagus, green beans etc. Cut them neatly and of a similar size. Cook them in a large pot of boiling water, one vegetable at a time until just cooked and set aside. When all the vegetables are cooked and you are ready to serve, warm the vegetables in a little butter and a drop of water, and season.

TO SERVE: Pour the sauce onto a warm plate. Carefully remove the loins from the saddle (don't forget the two fillets on the inside - the chef usually eats these!). Slice the loins on the diagonal and arrange in a circle. Spoon the vegetables into the centre and serve.

TOP TIP

The vegetables can be pre-cooked to save time. To do this, make sure each vegetable is only just cooked (or even slightly undercooked) remove with a slotted spoon and drop into a bowl of iced water to stop them cooking any further. When all the vegetables are cooked, drain, and mix together, ready for use later. By keeping the vegetables slightly undercooked, they can then be warmed up in either the microwave or with a drop of water and butter as above, without them overcooking.

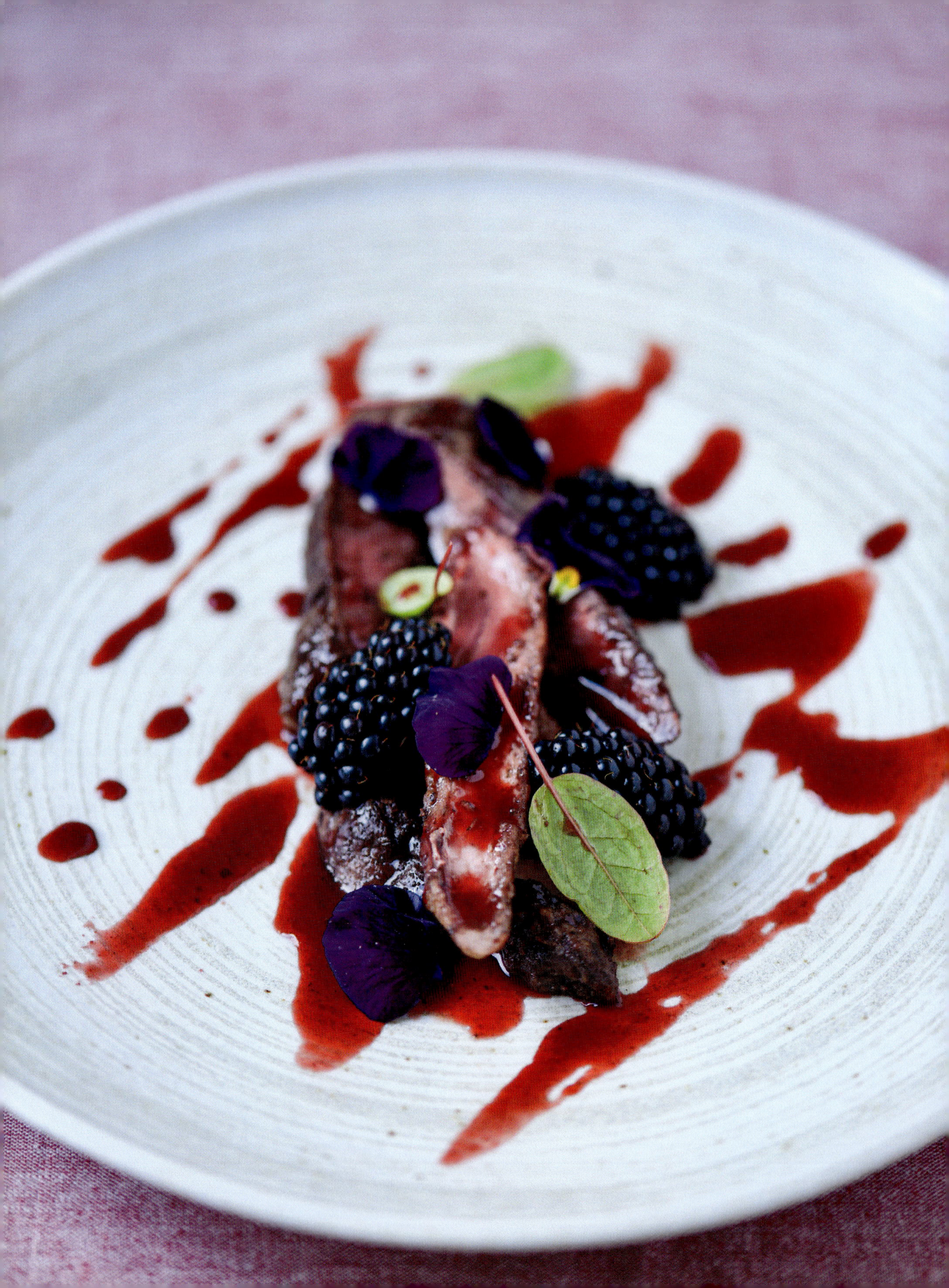

MALLARD AIGUILLETTES WITH MERLOT SAUCE

Serves 1

- 1 duck breast, without skin
- 1 tablespoon plain flour
- Pinch of nutmeg
- Pinch of cinnamon
- 2 teaspoons olive oil
- 120ml Merlot red wine
- 2 teaspoons crab apple jelly or redcurrant jelly
- 3 or 4 blackberries

TO COOK THE DUCK: Cut the duck breast into three even pieces lengthwise (aiguillettes). Season the flour with the nutmeg, cinnamon, salt and pepper. Heat a small frying pan and add the oil. Dust the duck strips lightly in the flour and fry for 3 minutes, turning frequently so they brown evenly. Remove from the pan and keep warm.

TO MAKE THE SAUCE: Discard the oil from cooking the duck and add the wine and jelly to the pan. Boil until you are left with just 2 tablespoons of liquid, by which time it should be thick and syrupy.

TO SERVE: Plate the aiguillettes and drizzle with the reduction. Scatter a few blackberries over plus herbs and flowers.

TOP TIP

This dish can be served with a few salad leaves as a starter, or a light main course.

STOCKS AND SAUCES MASTERCLASS

Stocks and sauces are the foundation of a good kitchen and it follows that to make a good sauce you need a good stock. During my years in recipe development, various marketing meetings demonstrated that sales from fish and meat counters were declining whilst sales of 'solutions', i.e meat or fish with a flavoured butter or sauce, were on the increase. But you don't need to buy a readymade sauce. It is actually quite simple to make fresh stocks and sauces at home, with a few simple guidelines.

This isn't to say using stock cubes or stock pot pastes at home is wrong — it isn't. When pressed for time they are very useful, and we sometimes use them at the school. Just bear in mind they can be a little salty though, especially the ambient stock pots.

The sauce recipes below use three key techniques; reducing for flavour, finishing with a little butter for richness and shine (monter au beurre), and thickening towards the end of cooking with a little flour and butter mix called beurre manier.

The sole aim of this particular workshop is to help people who want to buy a piece of fresh fish or meat, cook it properly and make a quick and simple restaurant-style sauce to go with it.

HOW TO MAKE A STOCK

I'm not about to suggest you start making veal or beef stock. This is a 24-hour process that will infuse your kitchen (and the rest of the house too, probably!) with the aroma of simmering bones. Even after 24 hours, the process is not finished as the stock must be reduced to improve viscosity and flavour. But this does give us a clue to the process. Boiling bones until they fall apart will yield all of their gelatinous flavour from between the joints and inside bones. After that there is no point in further cooking. So, for beef it is 24 hours, rabbit it is about 2 hours, chicken bones are about 60 minutes, but for fish it is only about 20 minutes. When using fish bones, do clean them of all blood as blood will discolour the stock.

Firstly, break or chop the bones into smaller pieces then just cover the bones with cold water. Bring to the boil and simmer. Skim every few minutes.

TOP TIP

Breaking bones into smaller pieces will help them to sit low in the pot and you don't need as much water to cover them. Using less water gives a stronger and better flavoured stock.

You may want to add some vegetables for additional flavour (in a kitchen this is called a mire-poix). The type of vegetable to use for stock will vary depending on if you are making a brown or white stock. We don't put carrots in a fish stock because they deepen the colour and may detract from a clean fish flavour. For fish use onion, white of leek, or celery. Fennel trimmings are good in a fish stock too as they add a lovely flavour. The size you chop your vegetables is relative to the length of time the stock will take to cook. For quick stocks, cut your vegetables into smaller pieces. If cooking the stock for a long period, the vegetables can be left larger.

Adding herbs will also give a richer flavour. Don't use soft herbs though, like chives or basil, as cooking these for 20 minutes or longer will extinguish the flavour of these herbs. Save them for garnishing the finished dish or adding in at the last minute. Thyme, bay leaf, parsley stalks (not the leaf) are usual, but it's up to you.

For a brown or roasted chicken stock, roast the vegetables and the bones for additional colour and flavour and if using onion, don't bother peeling it, just chop, or slice it. The skins will give a lovely deep colour to the stock.

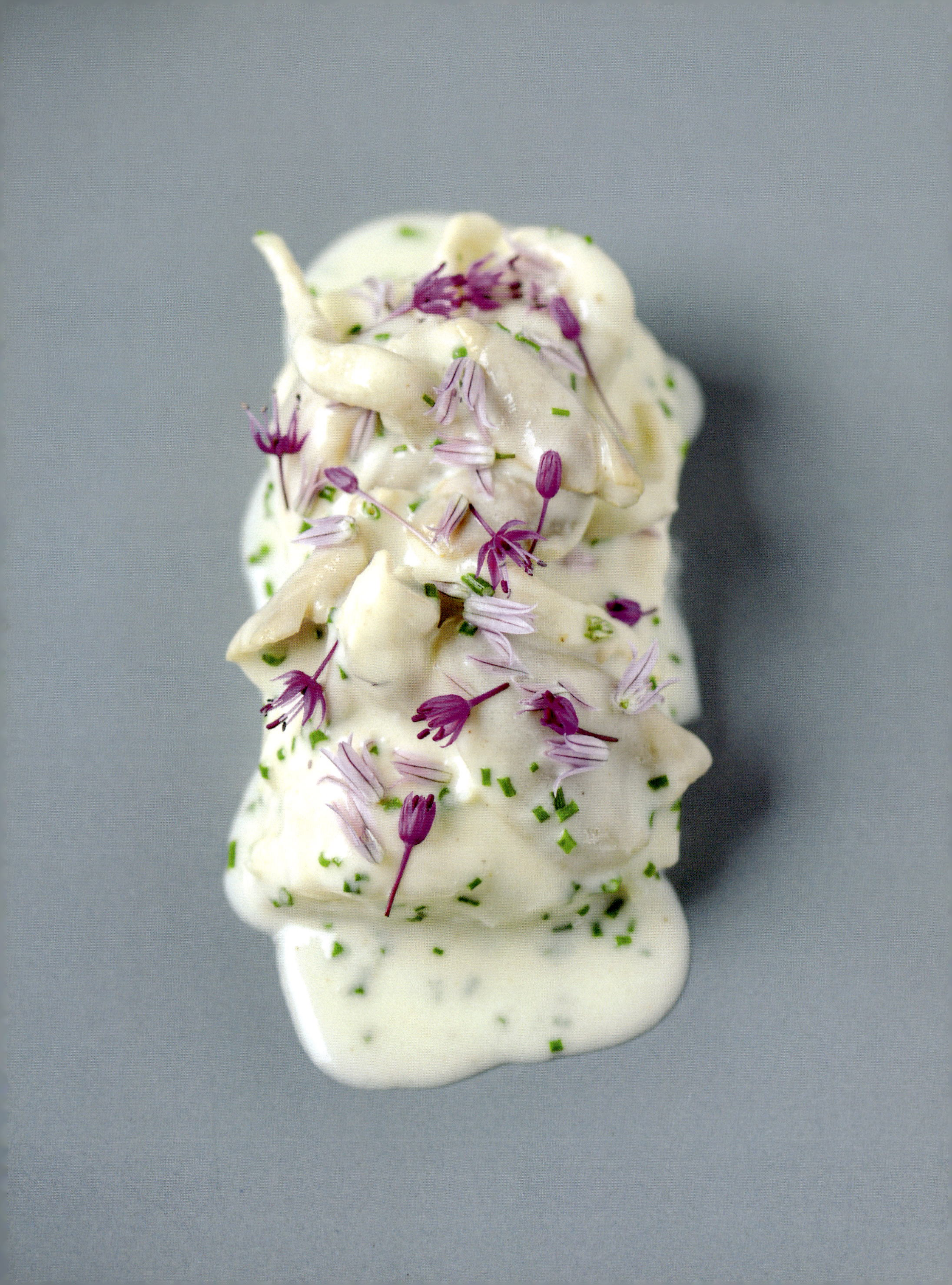

CHIVE VELOUTÉ WITH COD

Serves 1

- 1 loin of cod about 100g
- 75ml milk
- 75ml fish stock (fresh or cube)
- 30g oyster mushrooms
- 12g beurre manier (50 / 50 soft butter and plain flour mixed together)
- Splash of single cream (optional)
- 1 teaspoon chopped chives (or basil, parsley, tarragon)
- Chive flowers for garnish

TO COOK THE FISH: Place the milk and fish stock in a small saucepan. Season the fish and put in the saucepan with the oyster mushrooms. Bring the pan to the boil and the second it boils, turn the heat off, put a lid on the pan and leave it for 5 minutes. After 5 minutes remove the cod and mushrooms from the pan and keep warm.

TO MAKE THE VELOUTÉ: Bring the cooking liquid to the boil and whisk in the beurre manier. Turn the heat down to a simmer and cook gently for 2 minutes. Taste and season, add chopped chives and a splash of cream if using. Return the mushrooms to the sauce and drain any liquid from the cod back into the sauce. Spoon the sauce over the fish and decorate with a few chive flowers if you have them.

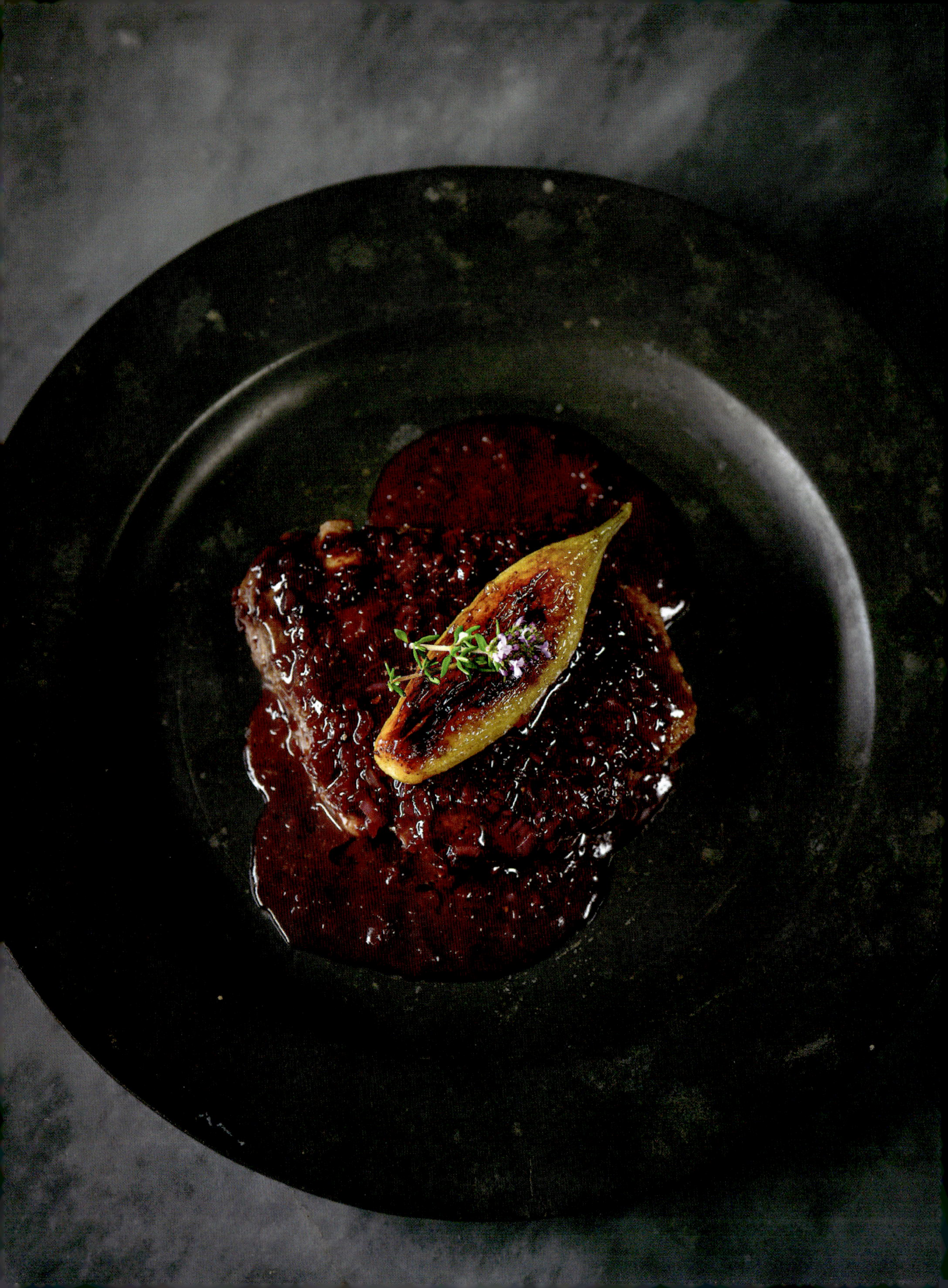

SHALLOT & RED WINE REDUCTION WITH STEAK

Serves 1

1 small steak, about 100g

2 teaspoons finely chopped shallots

50ml red wine

1 bay leaf

1 sprig of fresh thyme

1/4 teaspoon beef stock pot (optional)

20g cold unsalted butter

TO COOK THE STEAK: Pan-fry in a little hot oil and butter to your liking. Remove from the pan and keep warm.

TO MAKE THE REDUCTION: Add the chopped shallots and cook in the remaining fat to soften. Add a touch more butter if the pan is a little dry.

Add the red wine, bay leaf, thyme and boil to reduce, until you have barely 2 tablespoons left. The wine should look syrupy, if not reduce a little more.

Add a touch of beef stock pot, if you want a meatier sauce. Whisk in the cold butter over a high heat so that it emulsifies into the reduction and **remove from the heat** immediately. If you leave sauces like this bubbling away, the butter will separate out and produce a greasy sauce

Remove the bay leaf, taste, season and pour over the steak to serve (don't forget to add the juices from the resting steak).

BBQ MASTERCLASS

The word barbeque conjures many different images depending on what part of the world you are from; the braai of South Africa, the Australian barbie, the asado of South America, Mongolian barbeque, Japanese yakitori — and that's just a few! When the sun comes out, we love to cook outside, and let's be honest, what can beat the smoky aroma of succulent barbecued meat and fish?

Understanding how to cook properly on the barbecue is essential, nobody enjoys something raw on the inside and black on the outside. I am only going to talk about charcoal barbecues here because, to me, that invokes the true spirit of the occasion. Gas might be more convenient, but if I wanted convenience I'd cook in the kitchen and bring it outside. Much easier! So, if you want to get in touch with your inner caveman, charcoal is the way to go.

The best charcoal you can buy is Japanese binchotan or white charcoal. Ogatan charcoal is similar but pressed from wood dust rather than whole pieces of wood. A very pure product with no fillers, binders, or accelerants, it burns for several hours at an even temperature and is nearly as good as binchotan at less than half the cost. A chimney starter is the best way to get this charcoal going (I don't allow firelighters or accelerants anywhere near my food!). Sitting the chimney over a portable gas stove works really well.

Standard charcoal (even lump wood) that you can buy from supermarkets and petrol stations, gets going quickly but also dies down just as rapidly. The biggest problem is the bag contains a mix of big lumps and small pieces right down to dust. This makes controlling the heat much more difficult.

When barbecuing, aim to keep a cool spot so you can move things off the heat if you need to slow things down. A spray bottle filled with water is useful to damp down any unruly flames, and a barbecue with a lid is essential to cook larger pieces of food well. In effect you are creating a nice smoky oven and you will cook far more evenly as a result.

Brining is well worth considering as a method to get and keep flavour and moisture in barbecued food. In theory a marinade will work the same way if it contains salt or sugar (or both) and only a little oil. Oily marinades generally are not such a good idea for barbecues, the food will flare and burn easily. With wet brining, water is forced into spaces between meat cells (osmosis) and this keeps food moist during slow cooking or smoking. It also carries salt evenly through a piece of meat. Over-brining will lead to mushiness though, so don't leave it too long.

Hot smoking is a fantastic way to barbecue and is easily achieved if you have a barbecue with an off-set smoker, or a smoke-box that sits on a hob. Smoke is a complicated substance of over 200 components that inhibit microbe growth and retard the oxidation of fat. Not to mention the wonderful flavour!

I find there is a lot of confusion when it comes to cooking food safely on a barbecue. Cooking food at the right temperature and for the correct length of time is essential to ensure that any harmful bacteria are killed. Bacterial growth slows and dies over 60°C. Therefore, the shorter the cook, the higher the internal temperature of the food needs to be. The Food Standards Agency provides guidelines on combinations of time and temperature for the safe cooking of food (www.food.gov.uk/safety-hygiene/cooking-your-food). They state that an internal temperature of 60°C needs to be held for 45 minutes, a temperature of 65°C needs to be held for 10 minutes and at 70°C it only needs to be held for 2 minutes. Don't forget the temperature is internal, not on the surface, so a probe should be used to be absolutely sure.

So, to use these guideline, if you are cooking a large piece of meat that needs a long, slow cook (e.g a butterfly leg of lamb), an internal temperature of 60°C must be reached and held for at least 45 minutes. If you want to cook something very quickly e.g steak, then the internal temperature needs to reach 70°C for at least 2 minutes for it to be safe. For chicken and anything minced, always make sure the juices run clear.

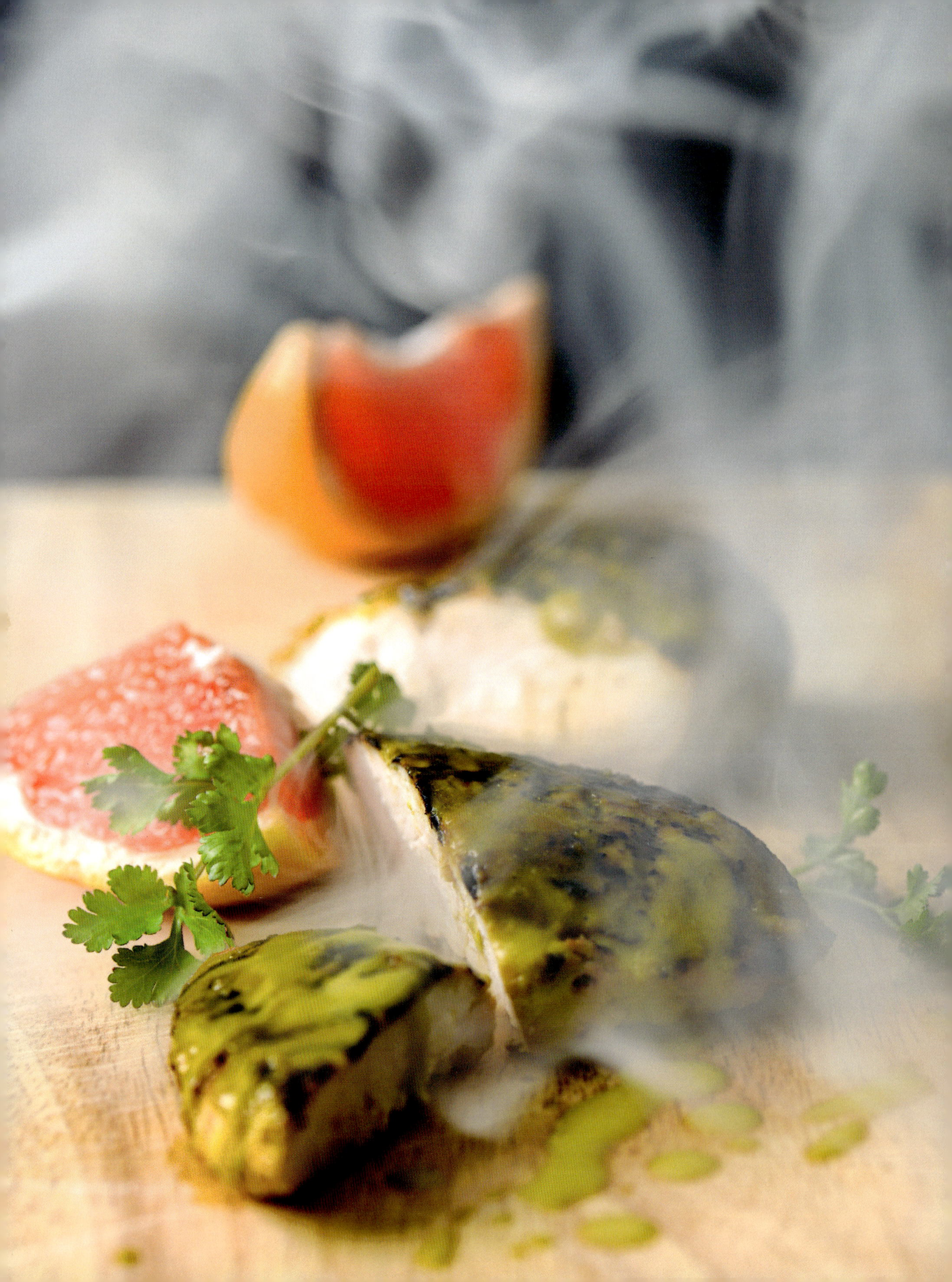

CORIANDER CITRUS CHICKEN

Serves 1

- 1 skinned chicken breast or 2 boneless thighs
- 2 tablespoons honey
- 1 lime or 1/2 grapefruit
- 50ml water
- 1 teaspoon ground coriander
- 1 teaspoon salt
- 1 teaspoon sunflower oil
- 1 fat clove garlic
- 2 tablespoons fresh coriander

Place everything except the chicken into a blender and pulse to a smooth paste. Add the chicken and marinate for 2 hours.

Barbecue using the guidelines above, with a lidded barbecue. Brush with spare marinade as the chicken cooks.

TOP TIP
You can dice and skewer the chicken if you wish.

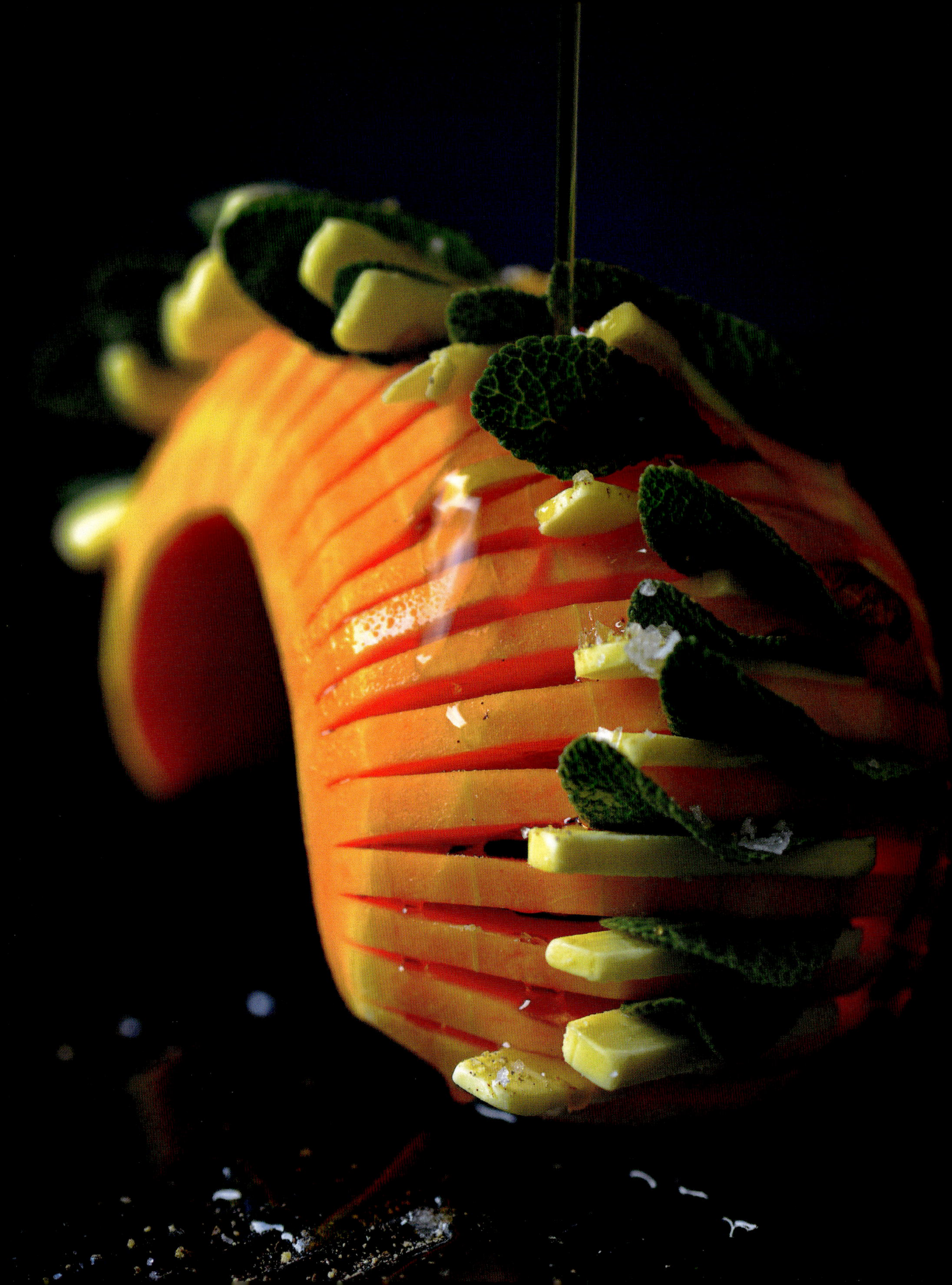

HASSELBACK BARBECUE SQUASH

1 butternut squash

Fresh sage leaves

Butter

Maple syrup

Salt & pepper

It can be a good idea to have a vegetarian option to barbecue and this one can be prepared a day in advance to save time. One squash will serve two people as a main dish.

Peel the squash, cut in half lengthways and remove the seeds.

Place the squash outer side up on a cutting board and place two wooden chopsticks either side.

Using a sharp knife cut slices 5mm apart down to the chopsticks. Carefully open each slit without breaking the squash and add a sliver of butter and a sage leaf. Place each half on a large piece of tin foil and (shortly before cooking) drizzle with maple syrup and season with freshly ground black pepper and sea salt flakes. Fold the tin foil loosely over the top and cook on a cooler part of the barbecue for about 40 minutes, or until tender.

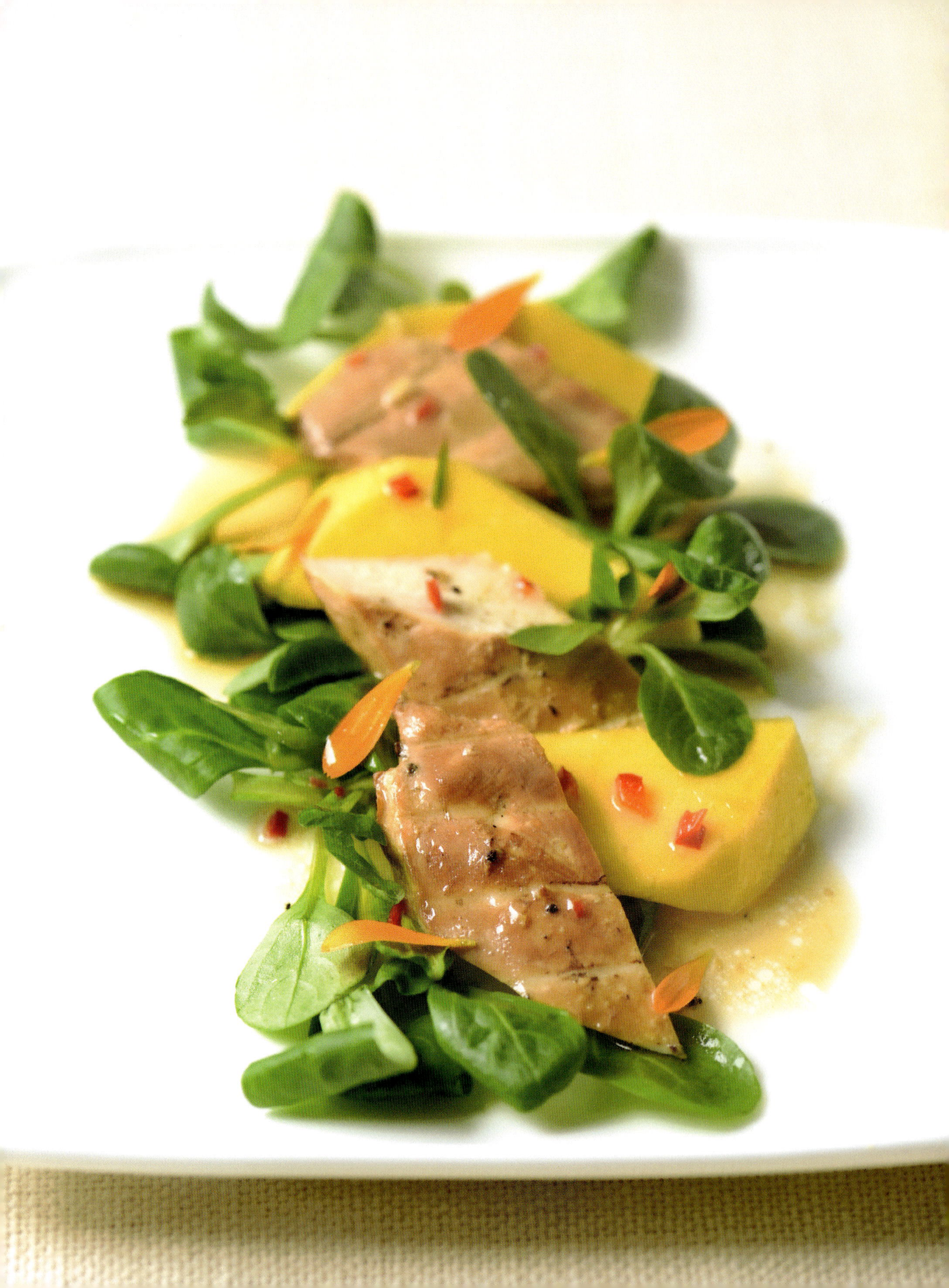

OAK-SMOKED CHICKEN, MANGO, GINGER & SOY

Serves 1

BRINE:

1 tablespoon fine sea salt

1 tablespoon honey

1/2 teaspoon cracked black peppercorns

250ml water

1 breast of skinless chicken

DRESSING:

1/2 tablespoon rice vinegar

Juice of 1/2 a lime

1 tablespoon sunflower oil

Small piece of preserved ginger, finely chopped

1 tablespoon ginger syrup (from jar)

1 small clove of garlic, finely chopped

1/2 fresh red chilli, deseeded, chopped

1/2 teaspoon soy sauce

TO FINISH:

Fresh mango

Few salad leaves

TO BRINE THE CHICKEN: Add the salt, honey and black pepper to the water in a small pan, heat to dissolve the salt and leave to cool. Using a fork, pierce the chicken breast all over, on both sides, all the way through. Place in the brine and chill for 3 hours.

TO MAKE THE DRESSING: Combine all the dressing ingredients and mix well. The easiest way to do this is to use a clean jam jar and shake well.

TO SMOKE THE CHICKEN: Smoke over wood chips (see guidelines above), or simply grill / barbecue the chicken, it will still be delicious!

When the chicken is cooked, allow to cool briefly, slice thickly and serve with slices of mango, a few salad leaves and the dressing

CUISINES

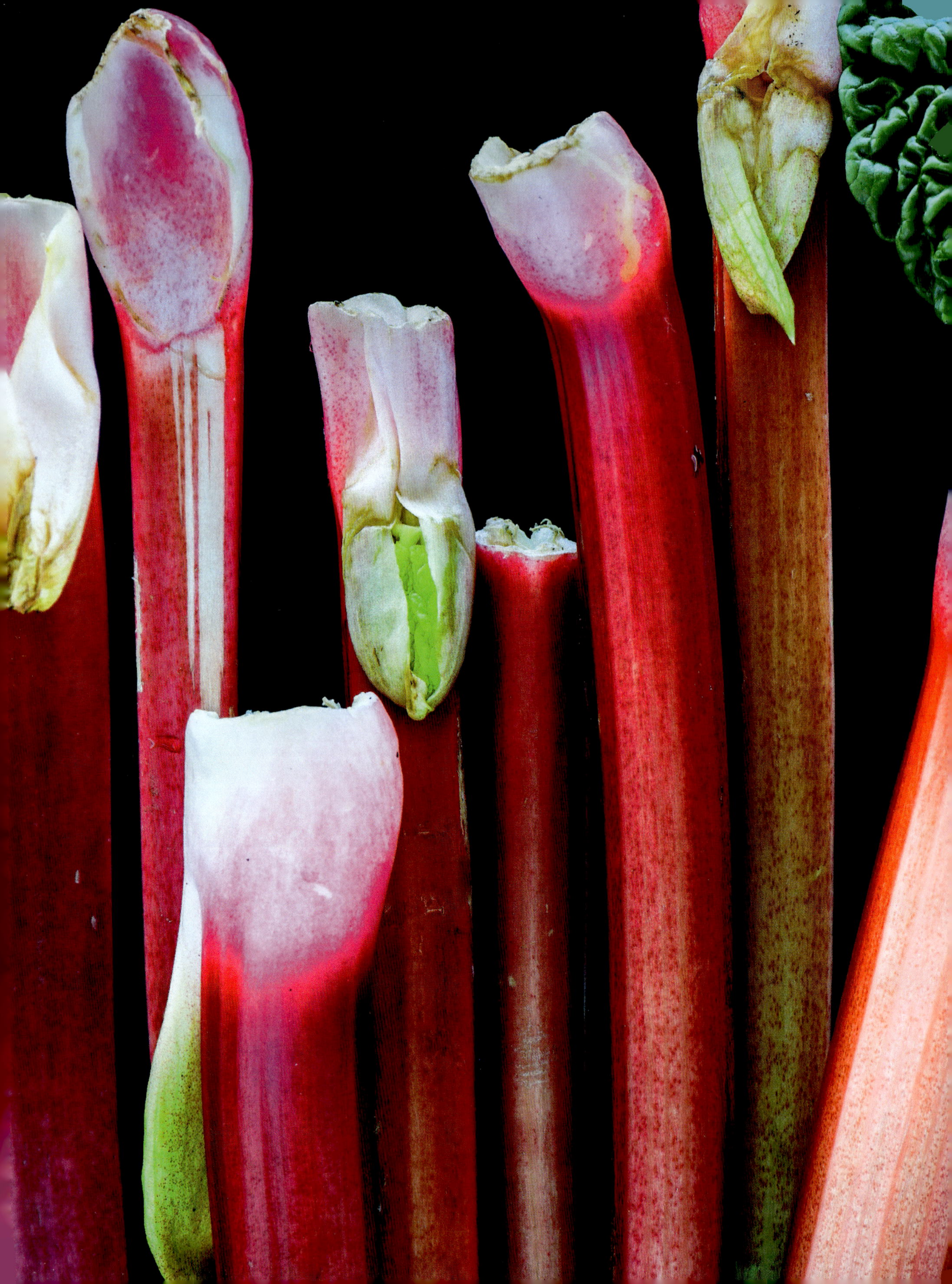

PLANT-BASED COOKING

A plant-based diet has grown steadily in popularity over the last few years and, as we were beginning to receive requests for more recipes suitable for vegans, I decided to create this new course. The term plant-based refers to just diet, i.e. someone has excluded most, or all, animal products from their diet, whereas if someone describes themselves as vegan, they usually have excluded all animal products, not only from their diet but also from their lifestyle, including clothing and household products. I am not vegetarian or vegan but do believe plants should form a large part of our diet.

Once you delve into plant-based cooking, the joy of cooking creatively with vegetables, fruits, seeds, pulses and nuts (all edible parts of plants), may well make you wonder why you ever bothered with meat, fish and dairy in the first place, but to ensure a balanced meal, it helps to think in the same way as you would with a mixed diet; i.e. what is the carbohydrate element (grains, pulses), what is the protein (nuts, seeds, pulses) and then the vegetables (mostly carbohydrate). Choosing a selection of colourful vegetables helps to ensure a good balance of essential vitamins too. The only vitamin that is absent (but essential) from a plant-based diet, is vitamin B-12. To compensate, most plant milks and cereals have this added as a supplement or it is often recommended that you take a B-12 supplement.

Presentation is clearly of the utmost importance as a chef. It is well known that the way the food looks has just as much impact as smell and taste — 'we eat with our eyes'. It is therefore even more important to think about presentation when using just vegetables, but this is not always something that people think about when serving food at home. On all of the workshops, I like to demonstrate how a chef would present a dish and it is very rewarding to see that 'lightbulb moment' when people understand the importance and the simplicity of it.
On the plant-based workshop, I talk about presentation in more detail and show you how to create a colourful, appealing plate of food.

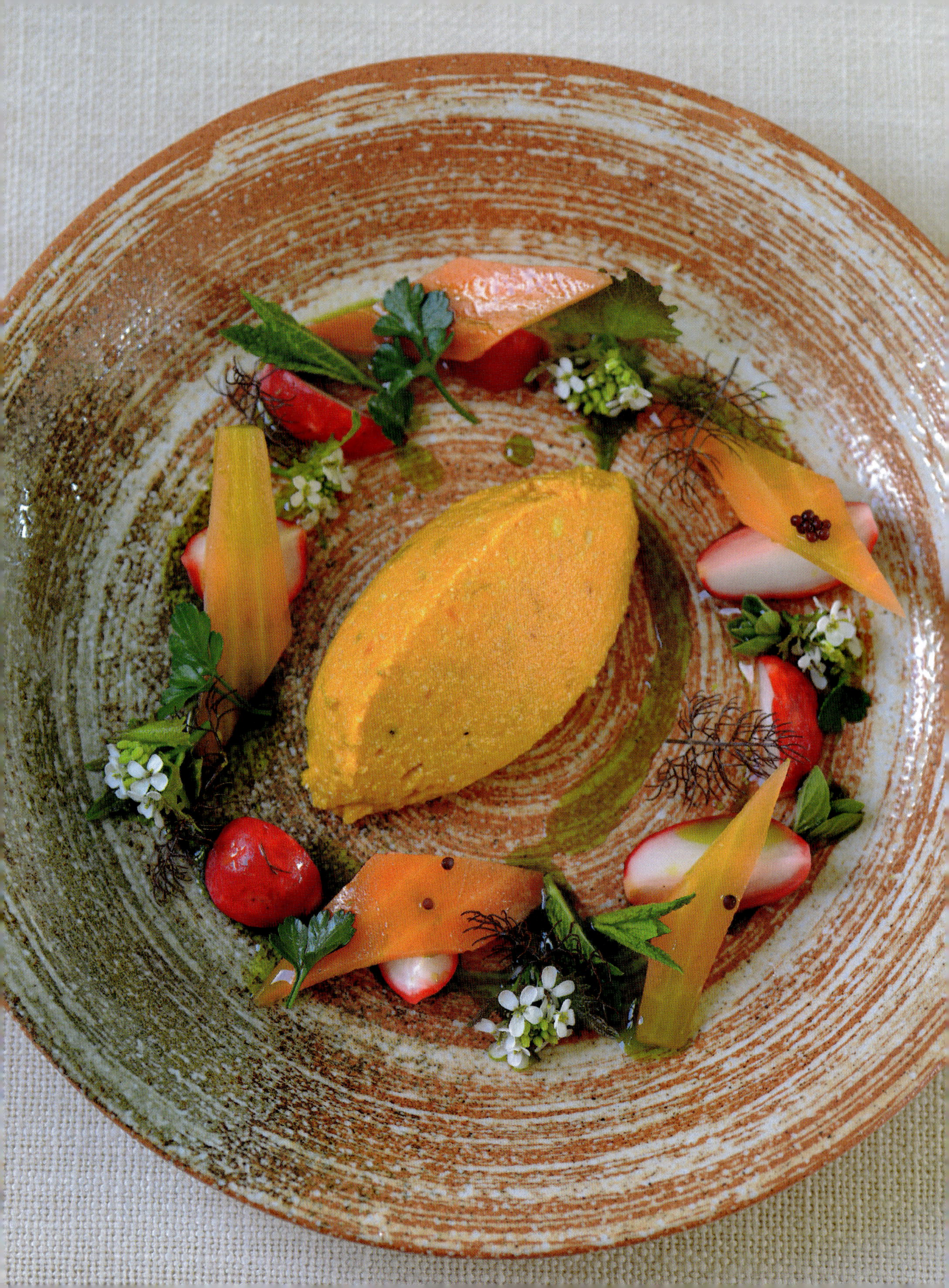

CARROT & CASHEW PÂTÉ, PICKLED RADISHES & CARROT

Serves 4

PÂTÉ

20g sliced ginger

3g coriander seeds

5 star anise

600g trimmed, peeled large carrots

2 tablespoons sunflower oil

4g sea salt

100ml water

2g agar agar

135g cashew nuts

PICKLE

1/2 bunch radishes stem and root ends removed and cut into quarters or halves if small

1 medium carrot cut into matchsticks

50ml white or cider vinegar

50g caster sugar

25g water

1/2 teaspoon salt

1/2 teaspoon mustard seeds

1 bay leaf

TO MAKE THE PÂTÉ: Chop the carrots into large chunks and tumble with the oil, ginger (no need to peel), spices and salt. Take a piece of tin foil, place the carrot mix in the centre and seal into a parcel, making sure you leave plenty of room for the air inside the parcel to steam the carrots. Bake at 160°C (fan) for 45 minutes. Put the water into a small saucepan, sprinkle in the agar and simmer. Reserve for later.

Once cooked, remove the spices from the carrots and blend with cashews and agar water until smooth and silky. Check the seasoning.

TO SERVE: Either serve in individual dishes, or 1 large dish. Scoop into 'quenelles' (domed oval shapes), using two serving spoons. Leave for at least two hours in the fridge to firm up and then decorate with pickled vegetables (see below).

> **TOP TIP**
>
> This dish is ideal as a first course served with Borodinsky (see Breadmaking Masterclass).

TO MAKE THE PICKLE: Place the radishes and carrots into a hot, sterilised jar then bring the vinegar, sugar, water, salt, spices and bay leaf to the boil.

> **TOP TIP**
>
> It's best to use a stainless steel or enamel saucepan for this.

Ladle the hot pickling liquid over the radishes and store in a refrigerator for up to 4 months.

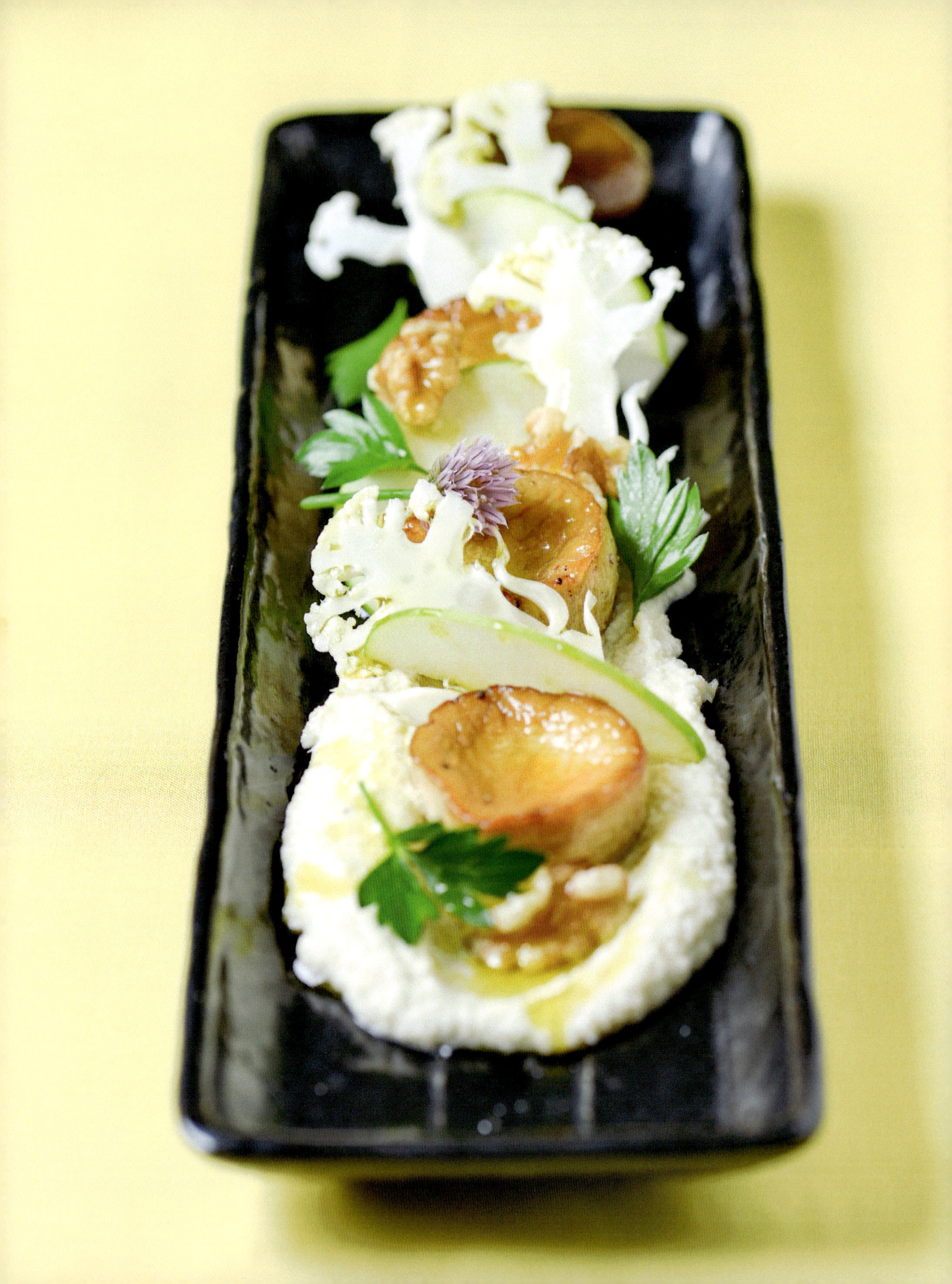

KING OYSTER MUSHROOM, CAULIFLOWER HUMMUS, SHAVED CAULIFLOWER, APPLE & WALNUT

Serves 2

- 1/4 medium cauliflower (135g)
- 1 tablespoon olive oil
- 2 tablespoons tahini
- 20ml water to blend
- Squeeze of lemon juice
- 2 king oyster mushrooms
- 1/4 Granny Smiths apple
- 8 walnut halves
- Little more olive oil and lemon juice to dress
- Fresh parsley and chives to decorate

TO MAKE THE HUMMUS: Cut two thirds of the cauliflower into chunks (reserve the rest) and boil with a splash of lemon juice until just cooked. Drain, and then blend until smooth with the tahini paste, olive oil and lemon juice. Season with sea salt and freshly ground black pepper and keep warm.

TO COOK THE MUSHROOMS: Cut each king oyster mushroom into three pieces. Heat a tablespoon of olive oil in a frying pan, place the mushrooms in the pan and fry gently until lightly golden on both sides. Season lightly, then cover with butter paper, or a piece of tin foil, and cook on a low heat until soft.

Take the remaining cauliflower, slice very thinly and toss in a little olive oil and lemon juice. Do the same with the apple.

TO SERVE: Put some cauliflower hummus on the plate and top with the mushrooms. Garnish with the shaved cauliflower and apple and dot the walnut halves around. Drizzle with a little more olive oil and serve. Scatter with a few herbs to add a little more colour.

TOP TIP

Ideal as a first course or serve with a few new potatoes as a main.

PINE NUT PARFAIT, AQUA FABA MERINGUES, MACERATED RASPBERRIES & BASIL

Serves 4

MERINGUES

50g aquafaba (the liquid from a tin of unsalted chickpeas)

1g sea salt

50g caster sugar

2g thyme leaves

Freshly ground black pepper

PARFAIT

50g pine nuts

75g cashew nuts

1 tablespoon lemon juice

Zest of half a lemon

75g water

120g caster sugar

5 teaspoon glucose syrup

4g sea salt

1g xanthan gum

150g fridge cold coconut cream (use the top of a tin of coconut milk)

TO PREPARE THE NUTS: Place the cashews and pine nuts on a baking sheet and bake until golden — keep a close eye on them, pine nuts burn easily, and I've thrown away far more than I can afford!

TO MAKE THE MERINGUES: Turn the oven down to 100°C (fan). Whisk the aquafaba and salt until it forms stiff peaks (this takes longer than whisking egg whites). Continue whisking and add the sugar gradually. Fold in the thyme leaves and transfer to a piping bag with a 1 cm nozzle.

Line a baking sheet with parchment and pipe small meringues — they will settle a little so don't pipe them too close together. Grind a little black pepper over the tops and bake for 90 minutes until crisp.

TO MAKE THE PARFAIT: Blend the nuts, lemon zest, lemon juice, water, and glucose syrup in a food processor. Blend the xanthan gum with the caster sugar and salt, and then blend with the nuts. When the mix is very smooth transfer to a large bowl and chill in the fridge while you whip the coconut cream.

Whisk the coconut cream to stiff peaks – or as close as you can get to it. It must be thick and airy. Gently fold into the nut mixture keeping it as light as possible. Transfer to little moulds.

TOP TIP

Pastry cutters lined with cling film work well as moulds.

MACERATED RASPBERRIES

100g ripe strawberries

1 tablespoon caster sugar

1 teaspoon lemon juice

1 tablespoon good olive oil

Few basil leaves and pine nuts to decorate.

Preheat the oven 150°C. (fan)

TO MACERATE THE RASPBERRIES: simply combine all the ingredients together 20-30 minutes before use.

TO SERVE: Turn out and serve with the thyme meringues and decorate with raspberries and coulis (optional).

TOP TIP

To make a simple fruit coulis, simply blend fresh berries with a little lemon juice and sugar to taste, then pass through a sieve to remove the seeds.

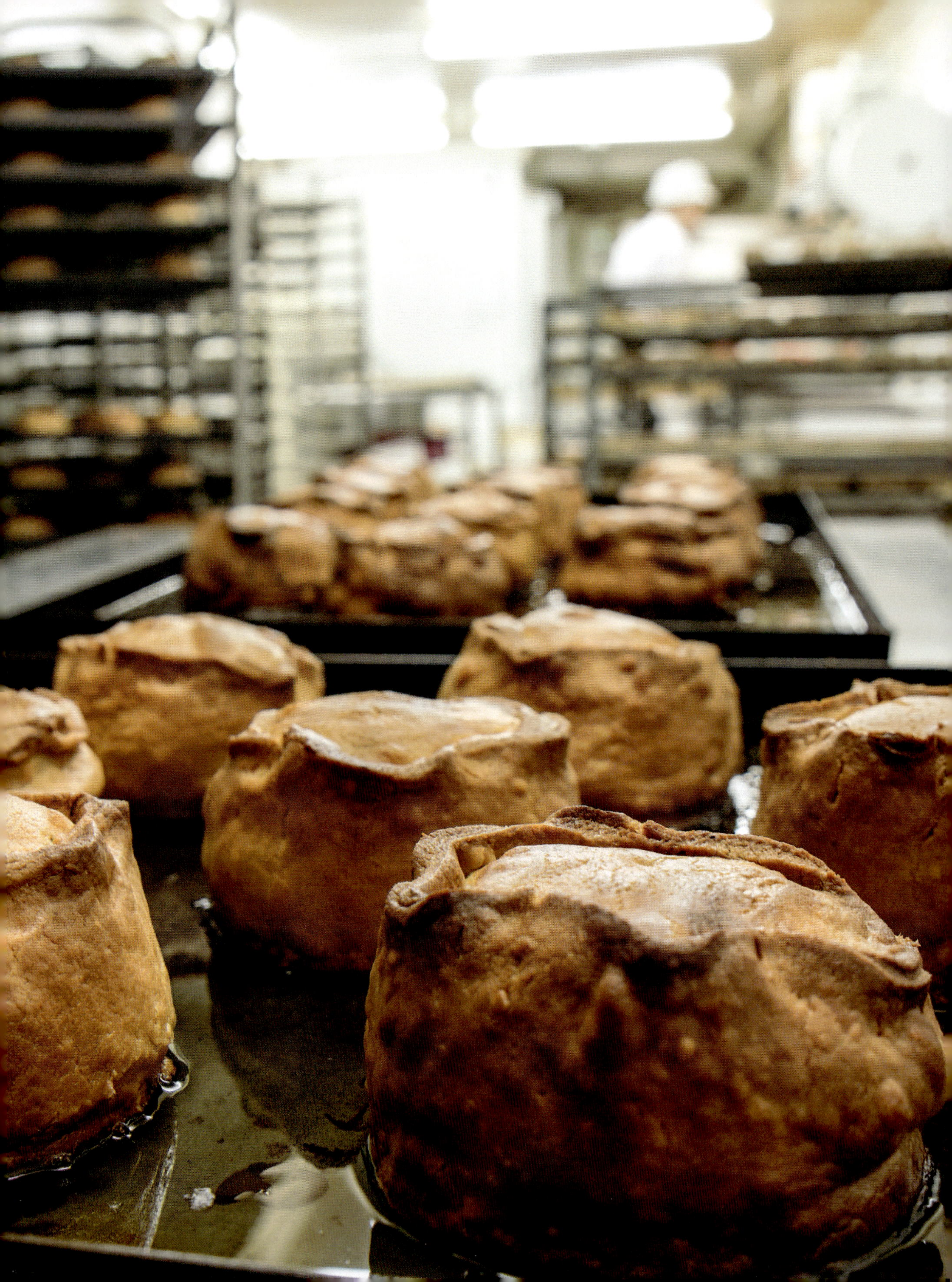

MODERN BRITISH

British food should be the easiest of all introductions, as we have a fantastic repertoire of both ingredients and dishes. But the truth is, over time, we have turned into culinary magpies taking a little of all that glitters from around the world. This should be seen as a positive development though, as nothing stays the same and food continues to develop and evolve.

Historically, of course, Northern Hemisphere countries tend towards warming, hearty dishes — stews, pies, casseroles, that sort of thing, but there's also a history of Indian food in the UK which goes back hundreds of years. Similarly, Chinese and Italian food have been in the UK for many years. Wherever significant numbers of immigrants settle, their own food follows, and the British have a liking for all of these flavours.

The growth in cheap travel and package holidays from the 1970's onwards, further opened our eyes to the tantalising wealth of flavour and ingredients from around the world. Many chefs have embraced these influences with passion and the typical 'British' menu is now a scintillating journey of global ambition.

I was first exposed to this influence when working at the Dorchester Hotel, under a real visionary, Anton Mosimann, an extremely well-travelled Swiss chef, who had spent time working in Japan. His cooking was truly innovative but the dichotomy was the daily offering of traditional British dishes: Irish stew, boiled beef and dumplings, chicken pie, steak, kidney and oyster pudding, braised oxtail, even tripe and onions! It was the same when I worked at the Michelin-starred Connaught Hotel a few years later, there was still a desire for these most traditional (and delicious) British dishes.

I was reminded of this when writing the Modern British workshop. I wanted to incorporate a little of what we do really well, but in a modern, light way. An initial steak and onion pudding has now given way to a pie with Mediterranean influences. Pea velouté is a lighter version of a classic pea soup but enhanced with a poached quail's egg and crispy chorizo oil as well as fresh herbs and flowers. Lemongrass pudding is a simple lightly set custard but infused with lemongrass — the best of Britain and Thailand together!

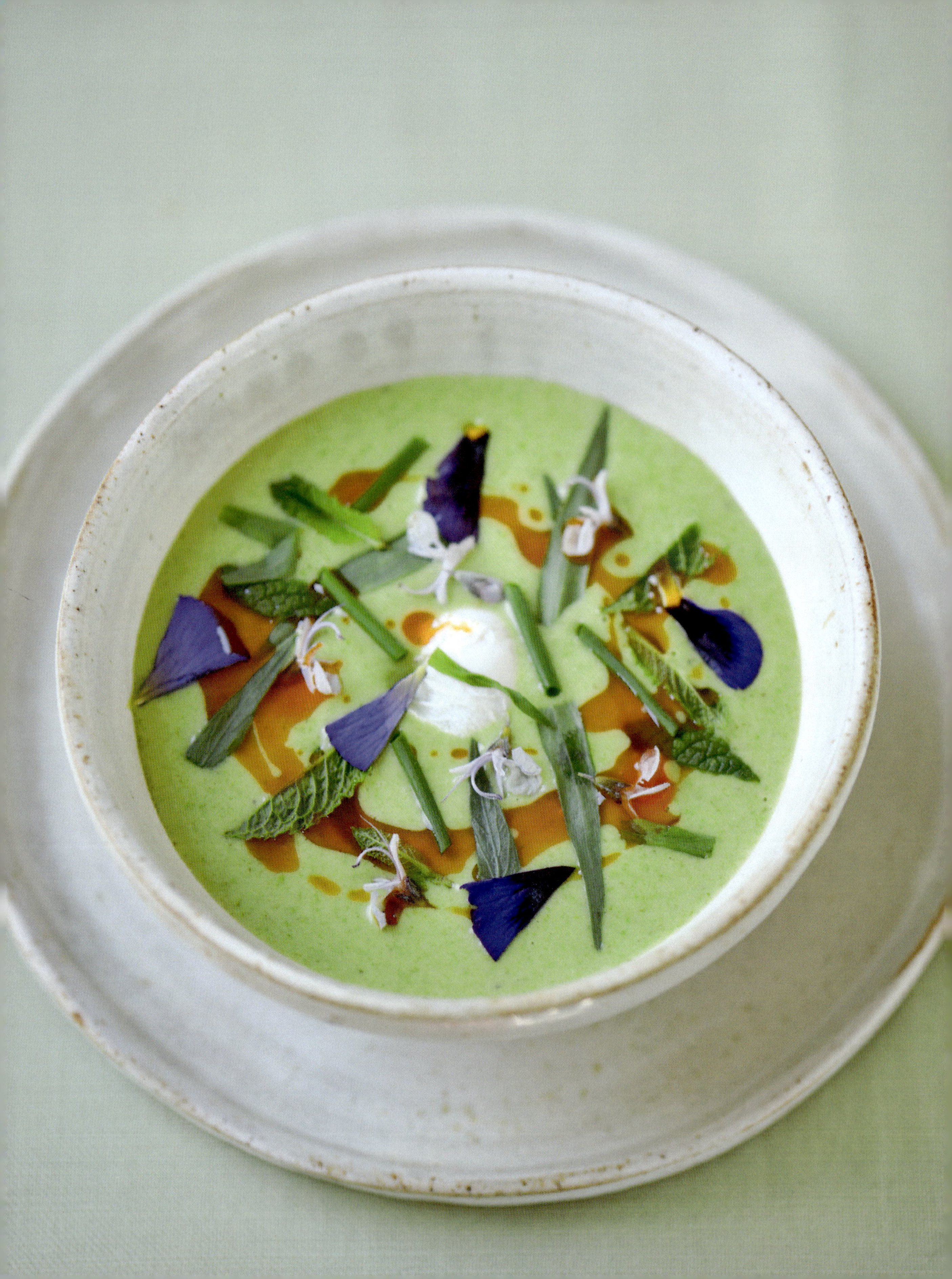

PEA VELOUTÉ WITH QUAILS' EGGS, CHORIZO OIL, SUMMER HERBS & FLOWERS

Serves 2

- 30g chorizo
- 2 tablespoons olive oil
- 2 quails' eggs (optional)
- 60g leek
- 30g butter
- 20g plain flour
- 300ml vegetable stock
- 100g peas
- 1 tablespoon tarragon leaves
- 1 tablespoon chives
- 1 tablespoon mint
- Flowers (herbs, pansy, marigold, nasturtium)

TO MAKE THE CHORIZO OIL: Dice the chorizo into little cubes no bigger than 5mm. Heat the olive oil and fry the chorizo until crispy and the oil has turned a lovely red colour. Reserve the oil.

TO COOK THE QUAILS' EGGS (IF USING): Bring a small pan of water to the boil and add a teaspoon of white wine vinegar. Carefully crack the eggs into a small dish and then slide into the water, swirling the water with a spoon — this helps to wrap the egg white around the yolk. Turn the heat down and simmer for 1 minute. Remove the eggs with a draining spoon and place in a bowl of cold water to stop them overcooking. Reserve.

TO MAKE THE SOUP: Finely slice the leeks and wash well, lift out of the bowl with a draining spoon, leaving any grit and dirt in the bottom. Melt the butter in a small saucepan and add the leeks. Cook gently until soft.

Stir in the flour and cook gently for a minute or two. Add the vegetable stock gradually, stirring well until smooth. Cook gently for 5 minutes, add the peas and cook for a further 2 minutes. Tip the soup into a liquidiser, or use a stick blender, and process until smooth. The soup should be a bright summery green and the consistency of double cream. If it is a little thick, thin it down with a little water or milk. Return to a clean pan and taste for seasoning.

TO SERVE: Place a quail's egg into a warm bowl (if using), carefully re-heat the soup and pour over the egg. Drizzle the chorizo oil around the egg and scatter the herbs over the top. If the leaves are big, chop roughly. Finish by adding a selection of torn flower petals.

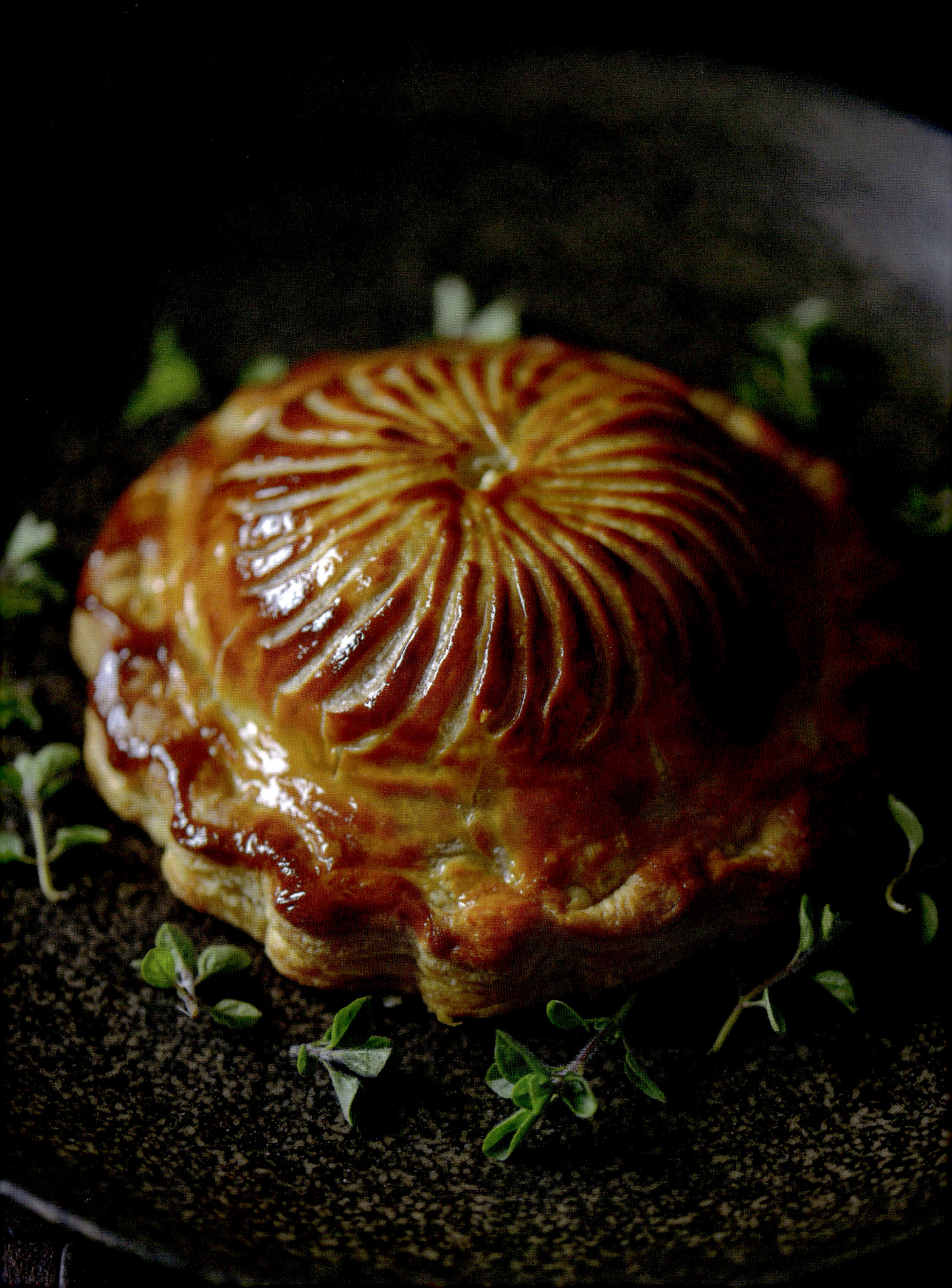

CHICKEN, RED PEPPER, MARJORAM & SAFFRON PIE

Serves 2

- 30g butter
- 2 chicken thighs 80-100g each, boneless, skinned, cut into 2cm dice
- 1/2 red pepper cut into 2cm dice
- 30g flour
- 300ml milk
- 2 teaspoons of fresh marjoram (or oregano) leaves
- Pinch of saffron
- 1 sheet of readymade all butter puff pastry

TO MAKE THE FILLING: Melt the butter in a small pan. Season the chicken and add to the pan along with the red pepper. Cook gently with the lid on (to trap the steam), until the chicken is sealed all over and the peppers are starting to soften.

Add the flour and stir. Add the milk gradually, stirring to avoid lumps until you have a smooth sauce. Finally, add a pinch of saffron and the marjoram leaves. Cook gently, stirring so the base of the pan does not catch, for about 5 minutes— just long enough to barely cook the chicken.

Check the seasoning and reserve half of the sauce to pour over the pie. Line a small teacup with cling film and fill with the chicken filling. Ensure it is packed tightly into the teacup as the mix must be set firm before use. Leave to set.

TO CONSTRUCT THE PIE: Cut a square of puff pastry for the base, about 11cm and a larger square for the top and sides, about 18cm.

Remove the set pie filling from its cling film and place on the smaller square. Allow 2 cm all around the edge and brush this edge with egg yolk. Carefully place the larger piece of pastry over the top, tucking it down the sides and sealing at the base. Using a pizza wheel or knife, carefully cut around the pastry until you have a circle with at least a 1cm edge. Crimp this edge to create a good seal. Pierce a small steam hole in the top and egg wash carefully.

Preheat the oven to 200°C (fan). Bake for 25 - 30 minutes until the pastry is crisp and golden.

Serve the pie with the reserved (warmed) sauce poured around.

TOP TIP

To decorate the pie as in the photograph, take a small knife and using the side of the tip of the blade, score the pastry in a spiral before cooking without cutting into the pastry itself.

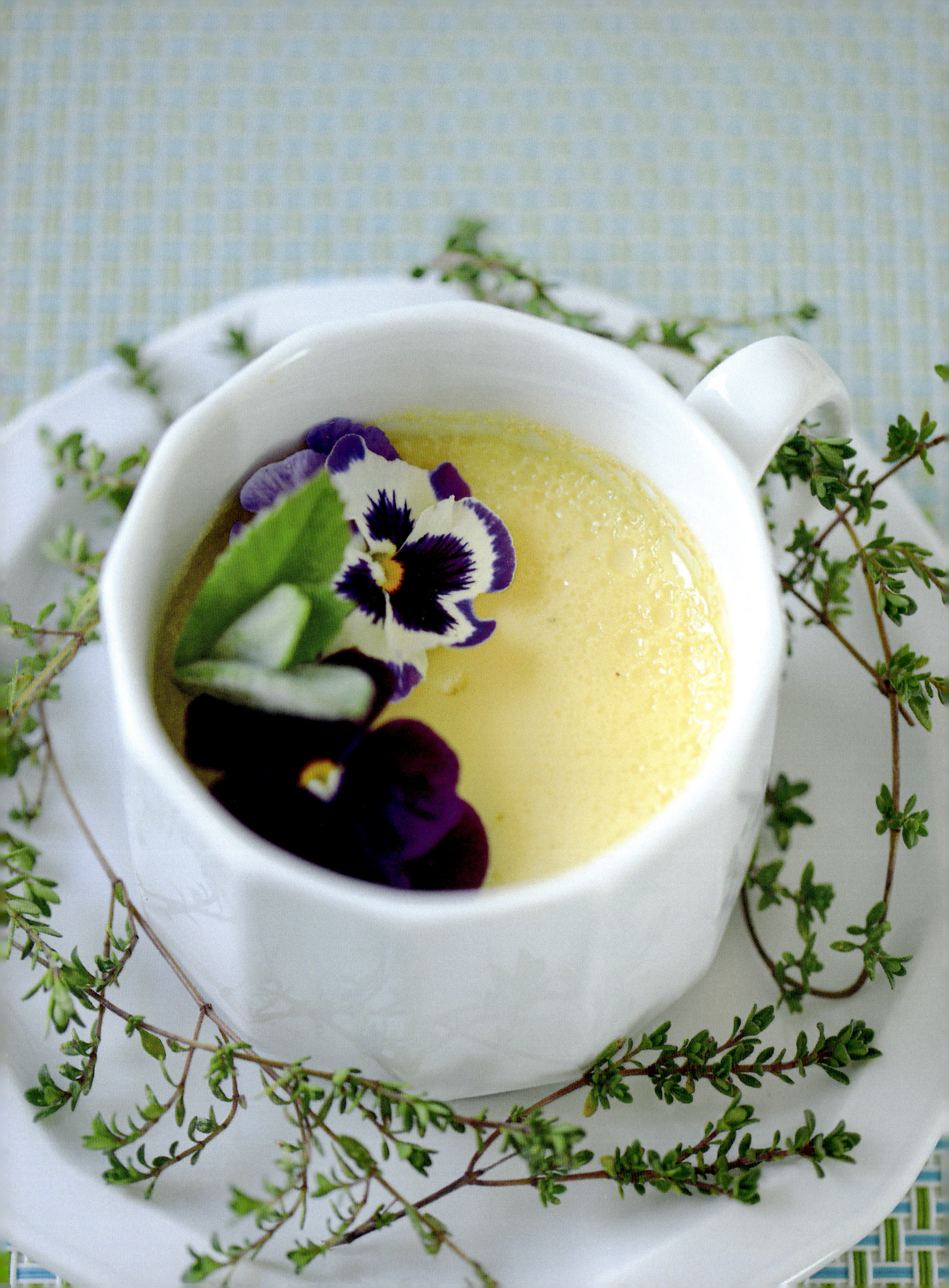

LEMONGRASS & THYME CUSTARD POTS

Serves 2

160ml milk

1 stick of lemongrass

2 big sprigs of thyme

2 egg yolks

42g caster sugar

Chop the lemongrass as finely as possible and place in a small saucepan with the milk and thyme. Bring to just boiling then take off the heat, cover and leave to infuse for about 15 minutes.

Cream the egg yolks and caster sugar together. Strain the infused milk onto the egg yolk / sugar mix and whisk thoroughly.

Preheat the oven to 150°C (fan).

Divide the mix between two ramekins or teacups. Place the ramekins into a small ovenproof dish and pour in enough boiling water to reach halfway up the sides of the ramekins. Place a piece of tin foil over the top of each dish and bake for 30 minutes. The centre should still be wobbly.

Chill in the fridge before serving.

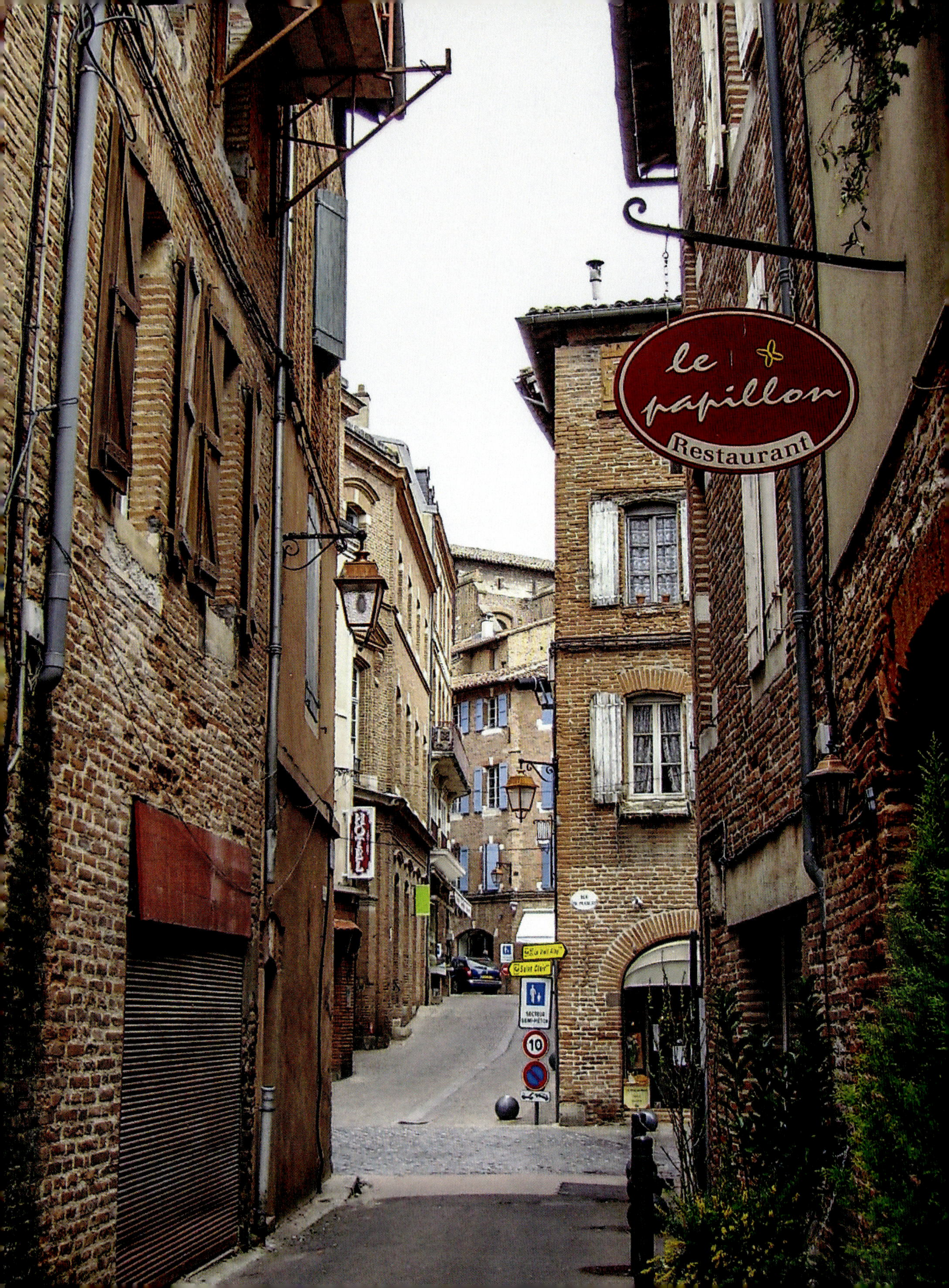
le papillon
Restaurant
HOTEL

FRENCH BISTRO

In the 1970's, despite the prevalence of Indian, Chinese and Italian restaurants in the UK, if you wanted to cook professionally, the training was French. With hindsight it seems odd that those other three cuisines barely got a look in, and if they did, it was from a typically UK perspective: curry sauce with generic curry powder, desiccated coconut and sultanas!

By the time I started cooking in 1974 the traditional, heavy sauces (and many were very heavy and rich) had begun to be replaced with lighter reductions, and crème fraiche was being used in place of double cream. But there were still some exceptions.

At Gleneagles, the French Head Chef Maurice Coty was close to retirement when I worked there, and we worked our way through all the traditional (and heavy) sauces: espagnole, demi-glaze, béchamel and its variations (soubise, mornay), velouté, rich butter hollandaise and its many variations (Maltaise, foyot, bearnaise, choron), cream sauce, thick chaud-froid and aspic to decorate whole and massive turbot, hams and other cold buffet delights. The approach was not dissimilar to recipes detailed by the great food writer M.F.K. Fisher:

'Monsieur Paul threw chopped chives into hot sweet butter and then poured the butter off, …added another nut of butter and a tablespoon of thick cream for each person, stirred the mixture for a few minutes over a slow fire, and then rushed it to the table'.

I'm not sure how we survived with so much fat, an addiction that took years to shrug off and I'm still partial to butter.

The light, modern techniques employed at the Carlton Tower Hotel (where I worked twice) were a revelation. The chef, Bernard Gaume was a young forward-thinking Frenchman who had fully embraced the Nouvelle Cuisine of Fernand Point and his disciples, Paul Bocuse, Michel Guérard, Roger Vergé and the Troisgros brothers. The emphasis on fresher, lighter ingredients and techniques were delightful to cook and we felt that we were at the cutting edge of modern cuisine. The two and a half years I spent at the Dorchester Hotel, latterly as the Chef Saucier under Anton Mosimann, continued this light, thoroughly modern and forward-thinking approach to cooking, that also embraced global influences.

At the two Michelin-starred Connaught Hotel in Mayfair, the Head Chef Michel Bourdin was from Normandy and trained at Maxims in Paris. The quality of cooking was, needless to say, superb and the brigade of chefs tight knit and friendly. Not quite so quiet a demeanour as either Bernard Gaume or Anton Mosimann, Michel Bourdin had a passion that was always bubbling just beneath the surface. My experience in these three great kitchens has left a lasting impression on me and the first cookery book I ever bought was *Great Chefs of France*.

Understandably, when I opened the school, French cuisine was an obvious topic to teach but where to start? How could I distil all those years of experience into a six-hour workshop? Not easily, I have to admit and eventually I settled on 'French Bistro'. French Bistro food is a relaxed way of dining (and cooking) that still incorporates lots of techniques.

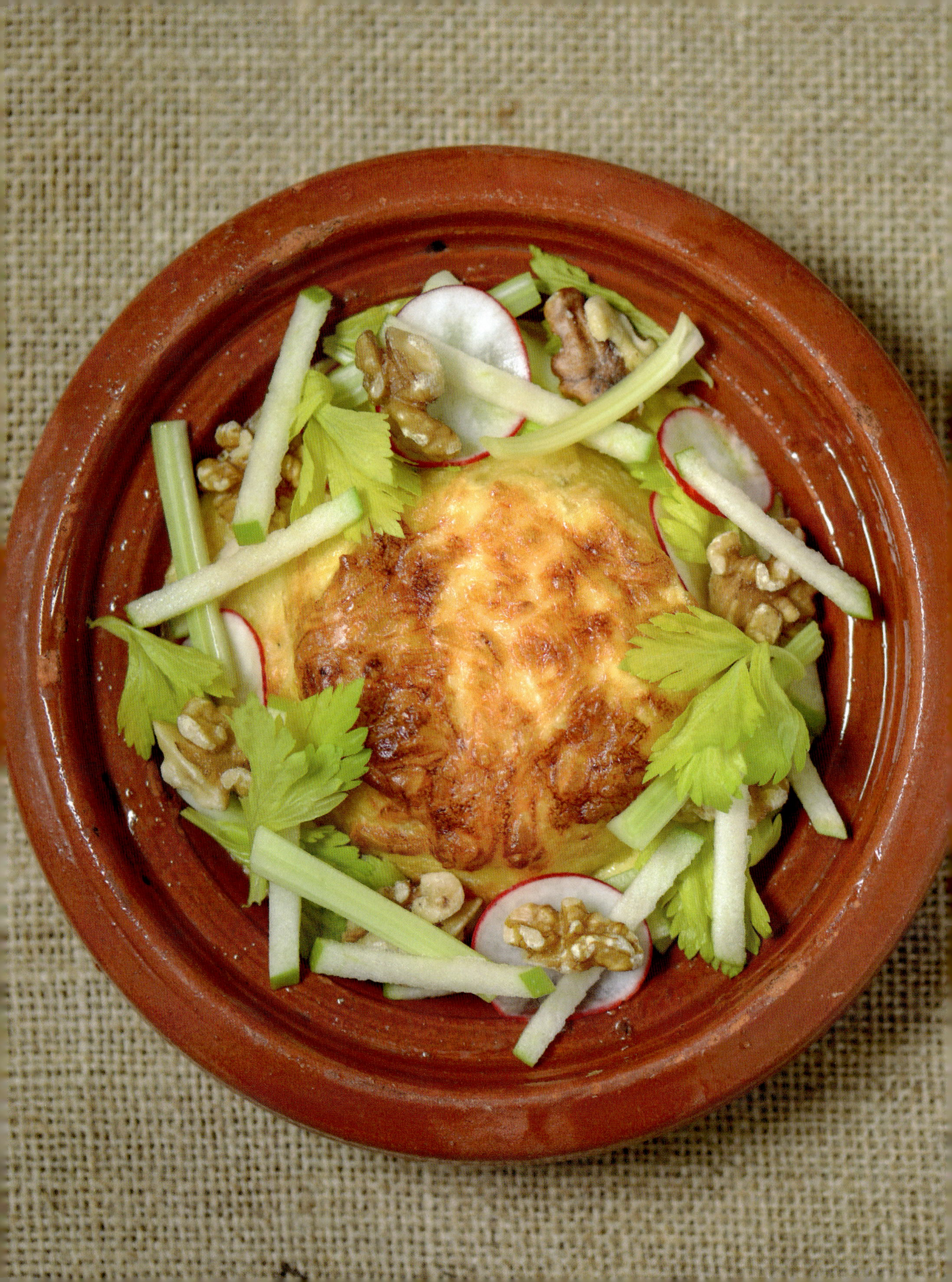

TWICE BAKED CHEESE SOUFFLÉ

Serves 1 as a main dish

SOUFFLÉ

15g butter + extra to butter the ramekin.

15g flour + extra to line the ramekin

100ml milk

1 egg, separated

25g grated cheese Emmental / Cheddar / blue cheese etc.

1 teaspoon Dijon mustard

Salt, pepper, nutmeg

GLAZE

50ml double cream

1 egg yolk

25g grated Parmesan

TO MAKE THE SOUFFLÉ: Butter a ramekin thoroughly with softened butter, using upward brush strokes. (This helps the soufflé to rise evenly.) Put in the fridge for a few minutes, to set the butter, and then repeat with another layer of butter. Whilst the butter is still soft, add a large spoonful of plain flour and tip around the base and sides of the ramekin. Tip out all the excess flour and tap the base to ensure you are left with just a fine dusting. Return the ramekin to the fridge.

Melt the butter in a small saucepan and stir in the flour. Keep stirring the flour for a few minutes (this cooks the starch in the flour) and then gradually add the milk, stirring all the time, to make a smooth sauce. Season and stir in the mustard, followed by the cheese and egg yolk.

Whisk the egg white to a stiff peak and fold into the sauce. Just stir in 1/4 of the egg white to start with, to loosen the mix, and then carefully fold in the rest.

Place the mix carefully into the ramekin and smooth the top. Bake in a preheated oven at 200°C for 11 minutes.

When the soufflé is cooked, remove from the oven and allow to cool before turning out of its ramekin.

> **TOP TIP**
> The soufflé can be left at this stage for up to 24 hours.

TO GLAZE: Stir all the glaze ingredients together, put the soufflé in an ovenproof dish, and spoon over the glaze. Bake for 10 minutes (225°C preheated oven) until golden and puffy

> **TOP TIP**
> This souffle is delicious served with a simple watercress, apple, celery and walnut salad.

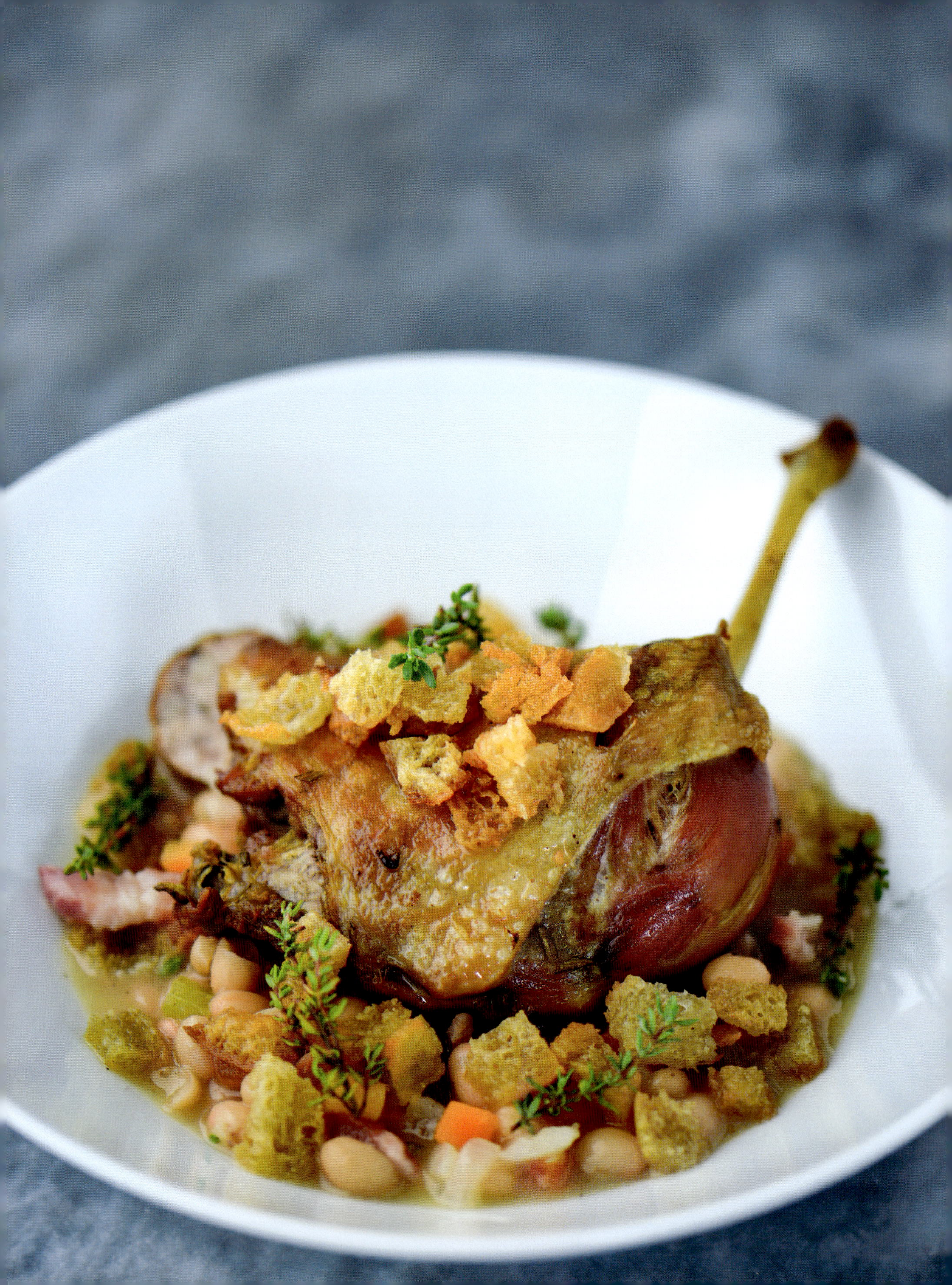

DUCK CASSOULET

Serves 1

CONFIT DUCK

1 duck leg

3 teaspoons fine sea salt

1 clove finely chopped garlic

1 teaspoon finely chopped thyme or rosemary

Enough duck or goose fat to cover the leg in a small saucepan

CASSOULET

1 tablespoon smoked bacon lardons

1 tablespoon 5mm diced carrot

1 tablespoon 5mm diced onion

1 tablespoon 5mm diced celery

1 fat clove of garlic, chopped

1 fresh tomato, peeled, seeded chopped

60g cooked haricot beans (tinned are fine)

2 tablespoons white wine

1 sprig thyme or rosemary,

1 bay leaf

Garlicky sausage, cooked and sliced 10mm thick

2 tablespoons coarse breadcrumbs

1 tablespoon olive oil

TO CONFIT THE DUCK: Rub the salt, garlic and thyme over the duck leg, wrap in cling film and chill for 1 hour minimum, 24 hours maximum.

Warm the duck fat (enough to just cover the duck) in a small casserole, or saucepan. Rinse the duck leg in plenty of water to remove the salt and pat dry with kitchen paper. Place in the fat. Cover and simmer gently for two hours or until the duck is very well cooked and tender – it should just hold on the bone.

> **TOP TIP**
>
> At this stage the duck can be cooled in the fat and kept for up to 3 weeks in the fridge – provided the meat is completely covered by fat.

MAKE THE CASSOULET: Take a tablespoon of duck fat and gently cook the lardons, carrot, onion, celery and garlic until just softened. Add the haricot beans, chopped tomato, thyme, bay leaf, white wine and just enough water to cover. Simmer for 30 minutes, adding a little more water if the mix dries out. It should be soupy when cooked. Season with plenty of freshly ground black pepper and add the garlic sausage.

Remove the duck leg from its fat, place on a foil-lined baking sheet and bake in a hot oven (200°C fan) for about 20 minutes, or until golden and crisp.

Heat the tablespoon of olive oil in a small frying pan and cook the breadcrumbs until golden and crisp.

Serve the duck on top of the beans and scatter the breadcrumbs over the top.

> **TOP TIP**
>
> A crisp green salad is all you need to eat with this.

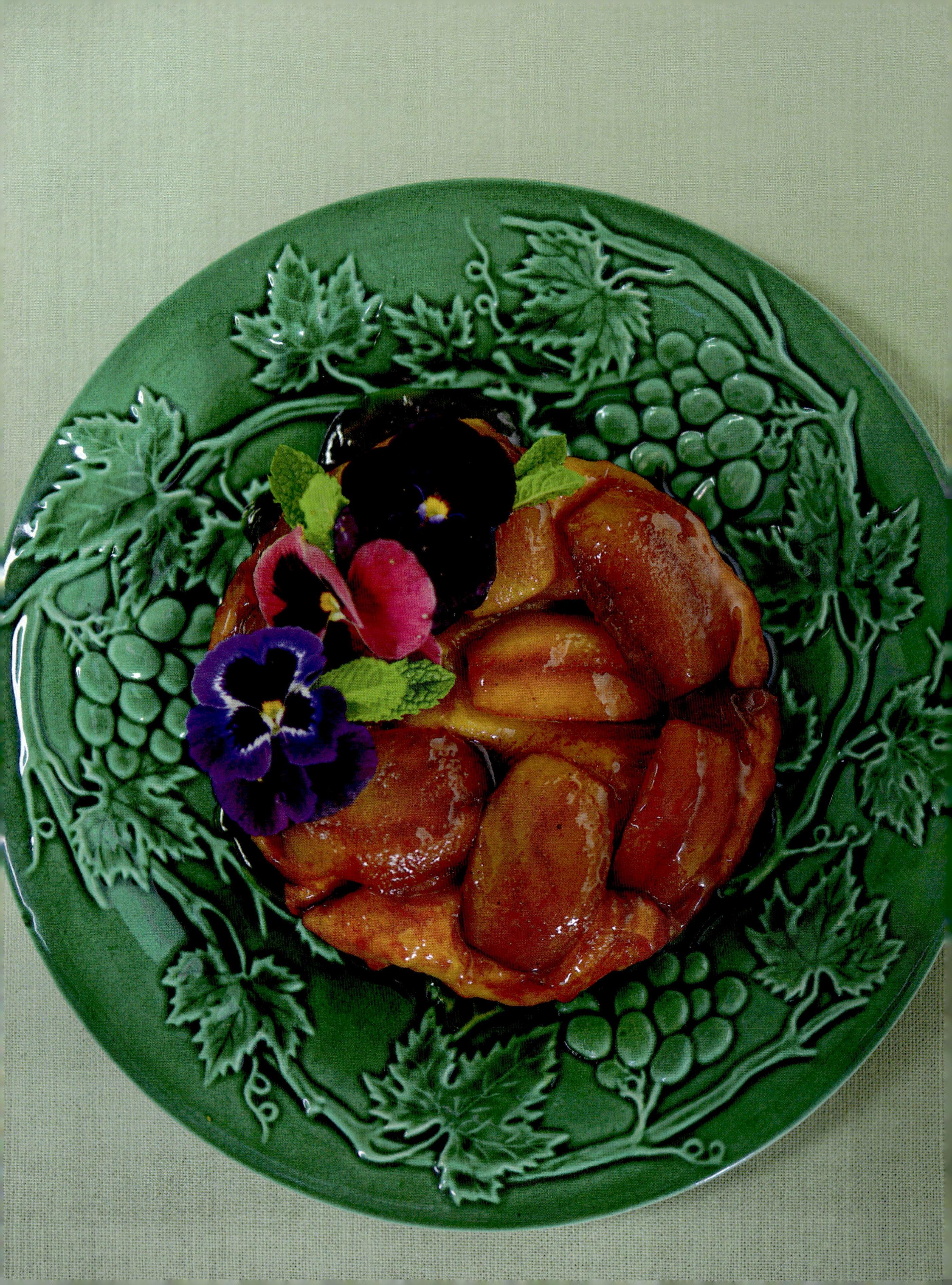

TARTE TATIN

Serves 1, generously.

1 sharp apple, Granny Smiths are ideal

20g caster sugar

16g cold butter

1 pack all butter puff pastry

NOTE: To cook the tarte tatin, you will need a small ovenproof dish/pan about 10cm round. If you have a small frying pan that is ovenproof, that is perfect, as you can make the caramel and the tarte tatin in the same pan. If not, use a normal frying pan to make the caramel and transfer to an ovenproof flan tin or dish when making the tarte tatin.

TO MAKE THE CARAMEL: Put the sugar in a small frying pan and heat gently until it melts. Don't stir it, just gently tip the pan from side to side to help the sugar melt evenly. When the sugar has melted, turn the heat up and keep gently tipping the pan until the syrup turns a deep golden colour. Take the pan off the heat and add the butter. Swirl the pan to melt the butter fully into the caramel. If this pan is not going in the oven, tip the caramel into your ovenproof dish.

TO CONSTRUCT THE TART: Peel, core and quarter the apple. Cut each quarter into half lengthways. Arrange the apple pieces on top of the caramel. Take a sheet of puff pastry and cut a piece to fit your dish/pan allowing 2cm extra all the way round. Place the puff pastry on top of the apples, tucking the sides down the insides of the pan, and around the fruit. Poke a couple of holes in the top to allow steam to escape. Bake in a preheated oven at 200°C for 20 minutes.

Leave for a few minutes before carefully inverting over a warm plate. Don't worry if it doesn't drop out immediately, just leave it to drop in its own time.

Serve with cream / custard / ice cream / crème fraiche.

TOP TIP

If you need to reheat the tarte tatin, put in a medium oven to warm through. DO NOT use a microwave as the pastry will go chewy and hard.

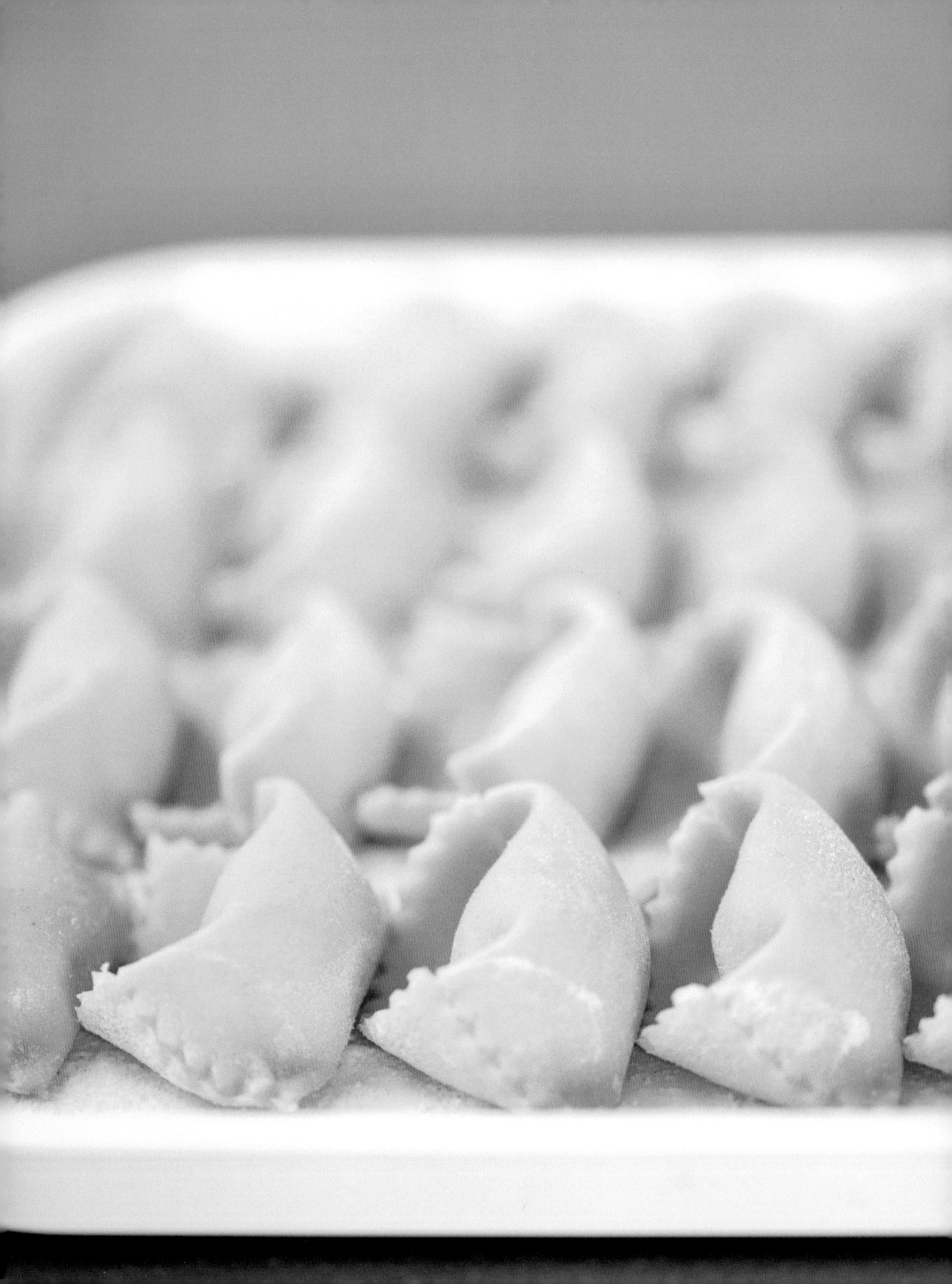

TASTE OF ITALY

I have long been an admirer of all things Italian, from the beautifully preserved walled towns and villages, to the effortless style and design, automotive in particular. This love affair led to the ownership of three Moto Guzzi motorbikes and a tour around Tuscany on one of these bikes with my wife, Karen.

Many years before that, I was the head chef for the flagship Corney and Barrow restaurant in the City of London. After a few years, the company sent me on a sabbatical, and I chose Italy. I started in Florence, because I had a wine connection there, at Villa Antinori. The Antinori family have been making wine since 1385 and continue to do so, twenty-six generations later! Palazzo Antinori is their head office and one of their restaurants is there too, Cantinetta Antinori (little wine cellar). The chef Franco was very helpful and also very proud of Tuscan cuisine. At the end of my visit he agreed to come to London and cook with me for a week in my kitchen. One of the dishes we put on the menu when he came was risotto ortolana, a simple spring vegetable risotto to which I have added roast saddle of rabbit.

Pasta is obviously a well-known staple dish of Italy. When I worked in Switzerland, the staff cook was a lovely Italian 'grandmother' and she made the best rustic and wholesome brown pasta I had ever tasted, using strong wholemeal flour! You don't have to use pasta flour or extra fine 00 flour to make pasta.

At Rutland Cookery School, we run a half day pasta workshop that focuses just on how to make different types of fresh pasta and how to cook it properly. So many people come to the school and tell me they have an unused pasta machine at the back of the cupboard! The Taste of Italy course has a much greater variety of dishes, with just one pasta dish.

There is no great secret to making pasta. Many chefs develop quite complex recipes but all you really need is 100g of flour to 1 egg. We use Italian 00 flour which is easily available, bread flour can be used if not, and wholemeal bread flour works well too.

AGNOLOTTI, SWEET POTATO, BACON, SAGE, BROWN BUTTER

Makes 24

PASTA

200g 00 flour

2 medium size free-range eggs

Generous pinch of fine sea salt

FILLING

1 large sweet potato

4 rashers of dry-cured, smoked streaky bacon

1 teaspoon soft butter

BROWN BUTTER

6-7 fresh sage leaves per person

1 tablespoon unsalted butter per person

Squeeze of lemon juice

Maldon sea salt flakes

Note: you will need a pasta making machine to roll the pasta.

TO MAKE THE PASTA: (Note: you will need to make this at least 30 mins before you need it or even the night before)

Tip the flour out onto the table, add the salt and mix together. Make a well in the centre of the mix and crack in the eggs. Using the fingers of one hand start to draw the flour in from the edge of the well until the dough starts to come together.

Knead the dough (you can use both hands now) and really work at kneading the dough until you have a stiff, smooth ball — this should take a good 10 minutes. Occasionally the dough may be a little too dry or too wet, egg sizes vary. If you feel it is too dry, then add a little egg yolk only. If too wet, add a little flour. But be careful, pasta dough needs to be stiff or you will have problems rolling it, and filled pasta that is too soft breaks down quite easily. Wrap in cling film and rest in a cool place for at least 30 minutes, or overnight.

TO MAKE THE FILLING: Bake the sweet potato in a hot oven (180°C), in its skin, until it is soft all the way through, about 30 minutes.

Line a baking sheet with a piece of greaseproof paper, place the rashers of bacon on it and bake until very crispy. This will take about 10 minutes — you need to be able to crumble the bacon into tiny pieces.

To finish the filling, scrape the flesh from the sweet potato, discarding the skin, mash until it is completely smooth, then finely chop the crispy bacon and mix into the sweet potato mixture. Add about a teaspoon of soft butter, season with freshly milled black pepper and fine sea salt, mix well and reserve whilst you roll the pasta.

TO ROLL THE PASTA: Starting with the rollers on the widest setting, take half the pasta dough and roll through once then fold in half and roll through again on the same setting. Repeat five more times, folding the dough in half each time. You are aiming for a nice rectangle about half the width of the rollers. Repeat with the other half of the dough.

> **TOP TIP**
>
> Rolling just half the dough at a time is much easier than trying to roll all of it.

Now you should have 2 pieces of really smooth, elastic dough. Close the rollers by one notch and roll each piece of dough through again. Repeat, closing the rollers by one notch each time. Stop on the penultimate setting (some machines roll very thinly, and this can make the pasta difficult to fill). If you are not used to your machine, experiment.

> **TOP TIP**
>
> Do not add flour at any stage except the last roll through, unless the dough is sticking. Adding flour as you roll may make the dough too stiff and dry.

TO CONSTRUCT THE AGNOLOTTI: Dot several small teaspoons of filling 3-4 cm apart, just off the centre line of your sheet of pasta. Wet the top edge of the dough with a little water and fold the pasta over the filling.

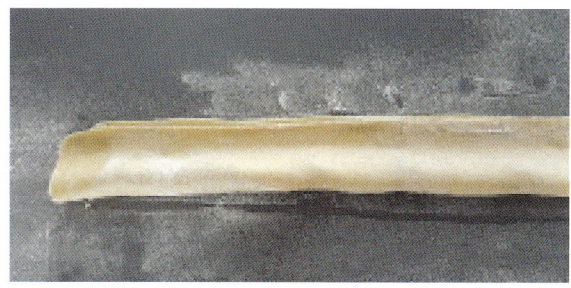

Next, using both thumbs and forefingers, pinch the pasta together between the filling and then run a fluted pasta wheel along the long top edge to trim. Finally, run the fluted pasta wheel between each portion of filling. This helps to shape and seal the pasta.

TO COOK THE PASTA: Bring a pan of water to a simmer and add the agnolotti. Remember they will swell to twice their original size! Poach gently for 10 minutes, then drain carefully and place on warm plates.

BROWN BUTTER TO SERVE: In a small frying pan add one tablespoon of unsalted butter per person and 6-7 sage leaves per person. Cook until the butter turns nut-brown and then add a squeeze of lemon juice. Be careful, the pan will splutter at this stage. Quickly spoon over the pasta, sprinkle with Maldon sea salt flakes, and serve.

TOMATO & COURGETTE RISOTTO, ROAST SADDLE OF RABBIT, CHIVE OIL

Serves 1

1 small saddle of rabbit

RISOTTO

2 medium size tomatoes

1/2 a medium size courgette

1 banana shallot

1 fat clove of garlic

Pinch of saffron

1/2 tablespoon tomato paste

1 tablespoon olive oil

60g risotto rice

25ml dry white wine

300ml vegetable, chicken, or rabbit stock

15g unsalted butter

15g Pecorino, Grana Padano or Parmesan, grated

Few chopped chives to finish

CHIVE OIL (optional)

1 bunch of chives

4 tablespoons extra-virgin olive oil

TO COOK THE RABBIT: Preheat the oven to 200°C (fan). Heat an ovenproof pan, add a splash of olive oil and a knob of butter. Season the rabbit and add to the pan. Seal all over in the oil and butter until nicely browned. Cover with foil and roast in the oven for 8 minutes. Remove from the oven and leave to rest.

TO MAKE THE CHIVE OIL: Bring a small pan of water to the boil, plunge in the chives, and remove immediately to a bowl of iced water. Drain well and blend until smooth with the olive oil. Season with salt and let the oil drip through a tea strainer or piece of muslin. This creates a chive oil which will keep in the fridge for up to 1 month. Reserve until needed.

TO MAKE THE RISOTTO: Blanch the tomatoes. Start by boiling a small pan of water. Score the tomatoes lightly across the top, plunge them into the boiling water for a few seconds, just enough to loosen the skins and then plunge them into very cold water. Peel, quarter, remove the seeds and dice into 5mm cubes.

Finely chop the shallot followed by the courgette and garlic.

Heat the olive oil in a small saucepan. Add the shallot, stir until softened, then add the garlic and cook for 2 more minutes. Add the tomato paste and saffron, cook for 2 minutes then add the rice. Stir well to combine all the ingredients. Add the wine, boil to reduce stirring all the time, then add a ladle of stock (it does not matter if it is hot or cold). As the stock is absorbed into the rice, add another ladle and so on until half the stock has been absorbed by the rice, stirring gently, but continuously. This stirring breaks down the starchy outer layer of the rice, and creates a creamy risotto.

When half the stock has been added, add the blanched, chopped tomatoes, and carry on adding more stock. Before you add the last of the stock add the courgettes, the aim is to keep them just cooked but not mushy.

Take the risotto off the heat, add the butter and pecorino, stir through, season to taste, and keep warm.

TO SERVE: Carefully remove the fillets from the rabbit and slice. Plate a portion of risotto (which should still be a little 'sloppy'), arrange the rabbit slices on top and drizzle with the chive oil and chopped chives.

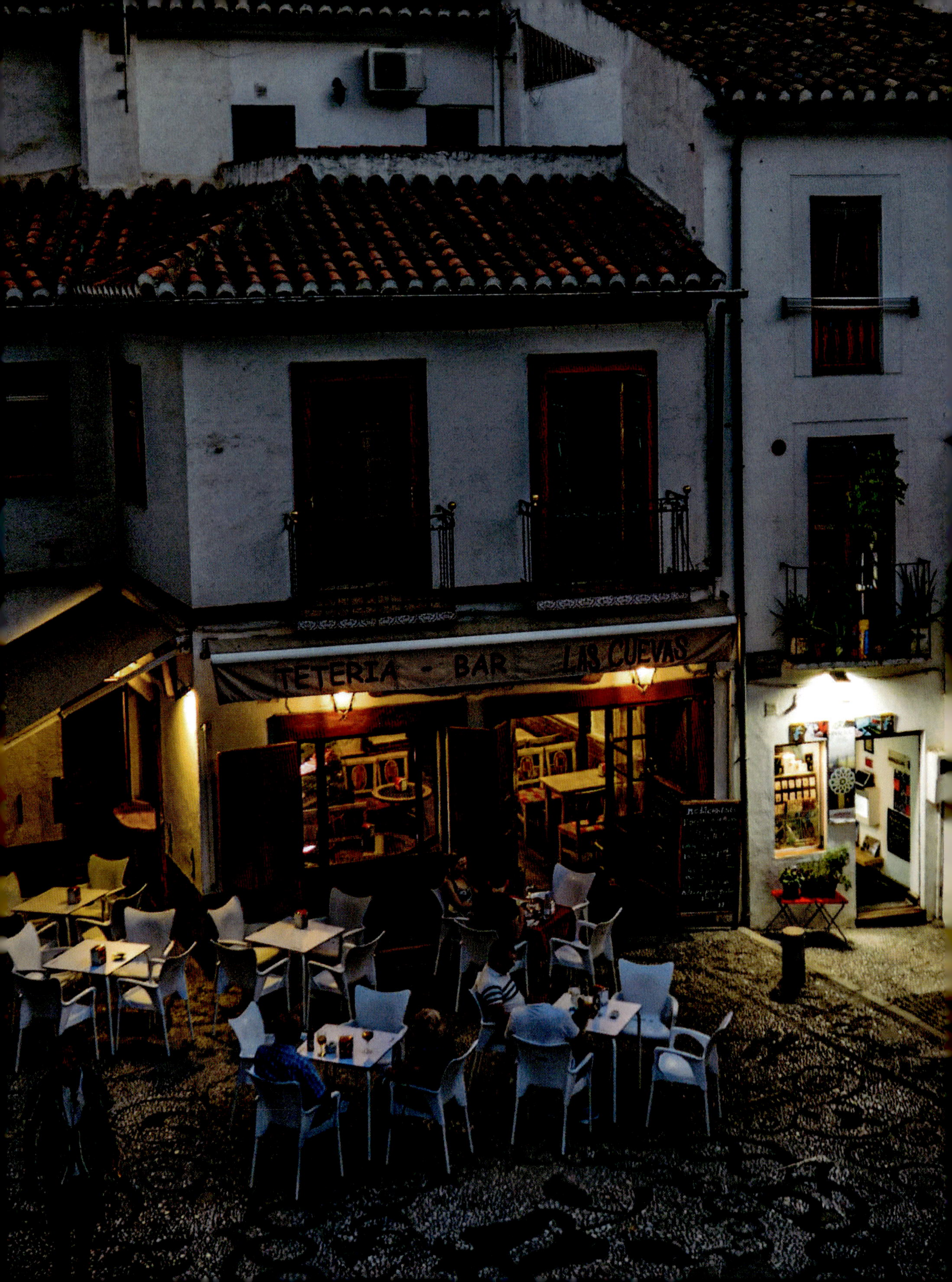
TETERIA - BAR
LAS CUEVAS

SPANISH CAFÉ

My travels took me to the beautiful city of Granada, in the region of Andalusia, in September 2018 specifically to research the cafés and bodegas (cellars) for which the city is well known.

Many people think of tapas when they think of Spanish Food and Granada is arguably the home of tapas. The word 'tapas' is derived from the Spanish verb 'tapar', (to cover), a cognate of the English top. Traditionally it was a piece of bread forming a useful lid to keep the flies out of the sherry. Later, other ingredients were added on top of the bread. Adding a slice of salty ham encouraged customers to keep drinking!

Granada has a tradition of offering a complimentary tapa with each drink. Since I had travelled there specifically to research the food in café culture, this pairing of a tapa with each drink became quite hard work…! Staying in the old quarter meant a steep walk back home and, after all this research, it just kept getting steeper and steeper!

Seafood is plentiful in Granada and mostly deep fried until crisp. Delicious with a cold beer! One dish that took a little research to understand properly though, was migas. A simple shepherd's dish, originally of breadcrumbs fried in olive oil, that is elevated by serving with chilled melon in good cafés. Sounds bizarre I know, but it was delicious! At the school we cook this dish first. We use peppers, garlic and chorizo in olive oil, then add breadcrumbs topped with a fried quail's egg and iced grapes. It's a bit like a mini breakfast.

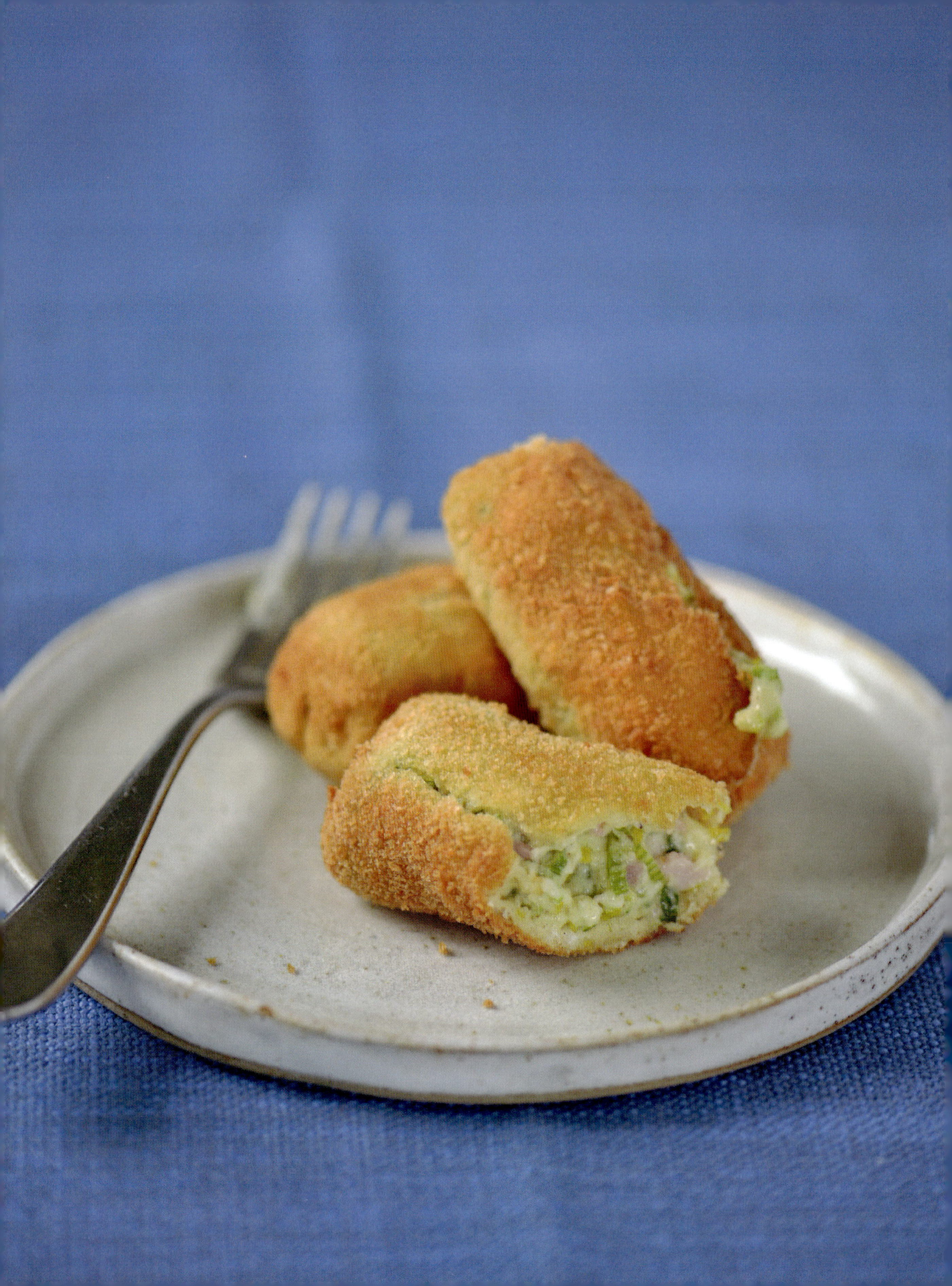

CROQUETAS DE JAMÓN

Makes 4

- 2 teaspoons olive oil
- 20g unsalted butter
- 1/4 small leek, finely sliced & washed (40g)
- 30g dry cured ham, chopped
- 20g plain flour
- 133ml milk
- Nutmeg, to grate
- 1 free-range egg, beaten
- Handful of breadcrumbs
- Handful of plain flour
- Oil, to fry

Croquetas de Jamón are a popular bar snack and customers to the school are always keen to learn how to make them properly.

TO MAKE THE FILLING: Heat the oil and butter in a small, heavy-bottomed saucepan over a medium heat and, when the butter melts, add the leek and fry gently for a minute. Turn the heat down, gradually stir in the flour and cook gently, stirring regularly, until it loses its raw flavour. This should take about 3-4 minutes.

Gradually stir in the milk, beating it in well, until you have a smooth paste. Cook for another 10 minutes until it is thick and smooth. Stir in the chopped ham and season to taste with a grating of nutmeg and some black pepper and sea salt.

Put the sauce in a bowl pressing a piece of cling film on to the surface of the sauce to prevent a skin from forming, and allow to cool, then refrigerate for at least 2 hours.

TO MAKE THE CROQUETAS: Once chilled, put the beaten egg into one bowl and the breadcrumbs and flour into 2 other separate bowls. With floured hands, roll spoonsful of the ham and leek mixture into cylinders and dip these into the flour, then egg, then roll in the breadcrumbs until well coated.

Repeat this process — a double coating is essential to stop the croquetas from bursting when fried.

Heat the oil in a large pan to 180°C, or until it begins to shimmer. Prepare a plate lined with kitchen roll. Fry the croquetas in batches for a couple of minutes until golden all over, then lift out with a slotted spoon and serve at once.

> **TOP TIP**
>
> The croquetas freeze well and can be re-heated in the oven.

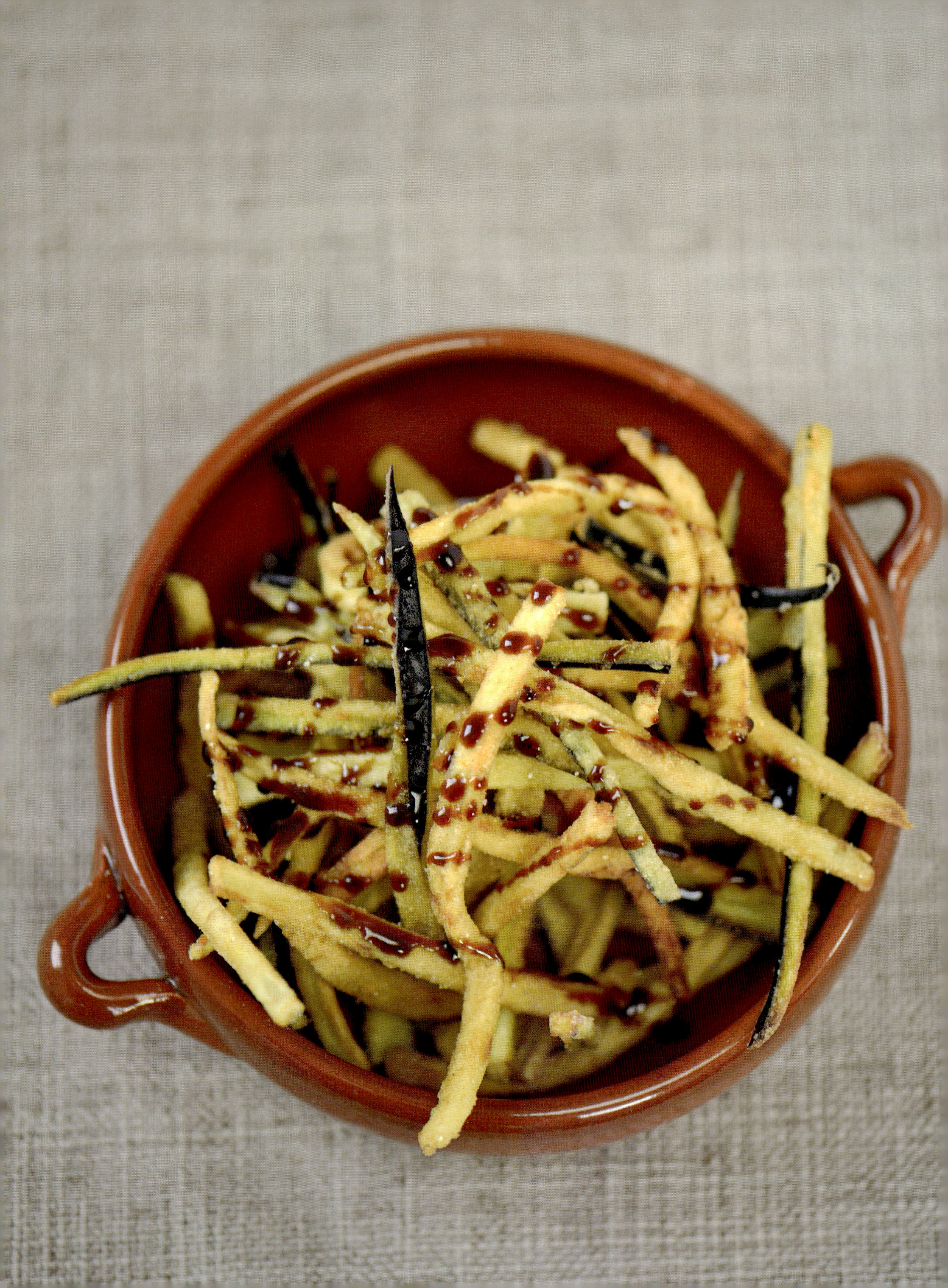

BERENJENAS CON MIEL

Serves 2

- 1/2 an aubergine
- Milk to cover the aubergine
- 2 tablespoons black treacle
- 100g fine semolina
- 100g wheat flour
- 25g polenta
- Pinch of sea salt

Berenjenas con miel or crisp, deep-fried aubergine with honey is another popular snack, although the name is a little misleading. Crispy aubergine is drizzled with cane 'honey', but this is not honey from bees. Miel de caña or cane honey is actually black treacle — although clear honey works well too. The flour, polenta and semolina used to coat the aubergine before frying is sold in Spain as a 'berenjenas flour'. The ratios in the recipe correspond to the pack I brought home with me and give a lovely crisp texture.

Cut the aubergine into long, thin matchsticks. Season lightly with salt and mix well. Cover with milk and set aside for 20 minutes.

Mix together the semolina, flour, polenta, and sea salt.

Drain the aubergine, squeezing out excess liquid, and coat thoroughly with the flour mix. Deep-fry in small batches until golden and crisp. Drain on kitchen paper, season with fine sea salt and drizzle with black treacle.

TOP TIP

When deep-frying at home use a large saucepan, fill no more than halfway with oil (vegetable, rape, sunflower or frying oil) and use a temperature probe. You need a temperature of 190°C. Fry in small batches (it really depends on the size of your pan), do not overcrowd. The oil will rise in the pan when you add the aubergines so you must allow for this. Have ready a tight-fitting lid, just in case it rises too much.

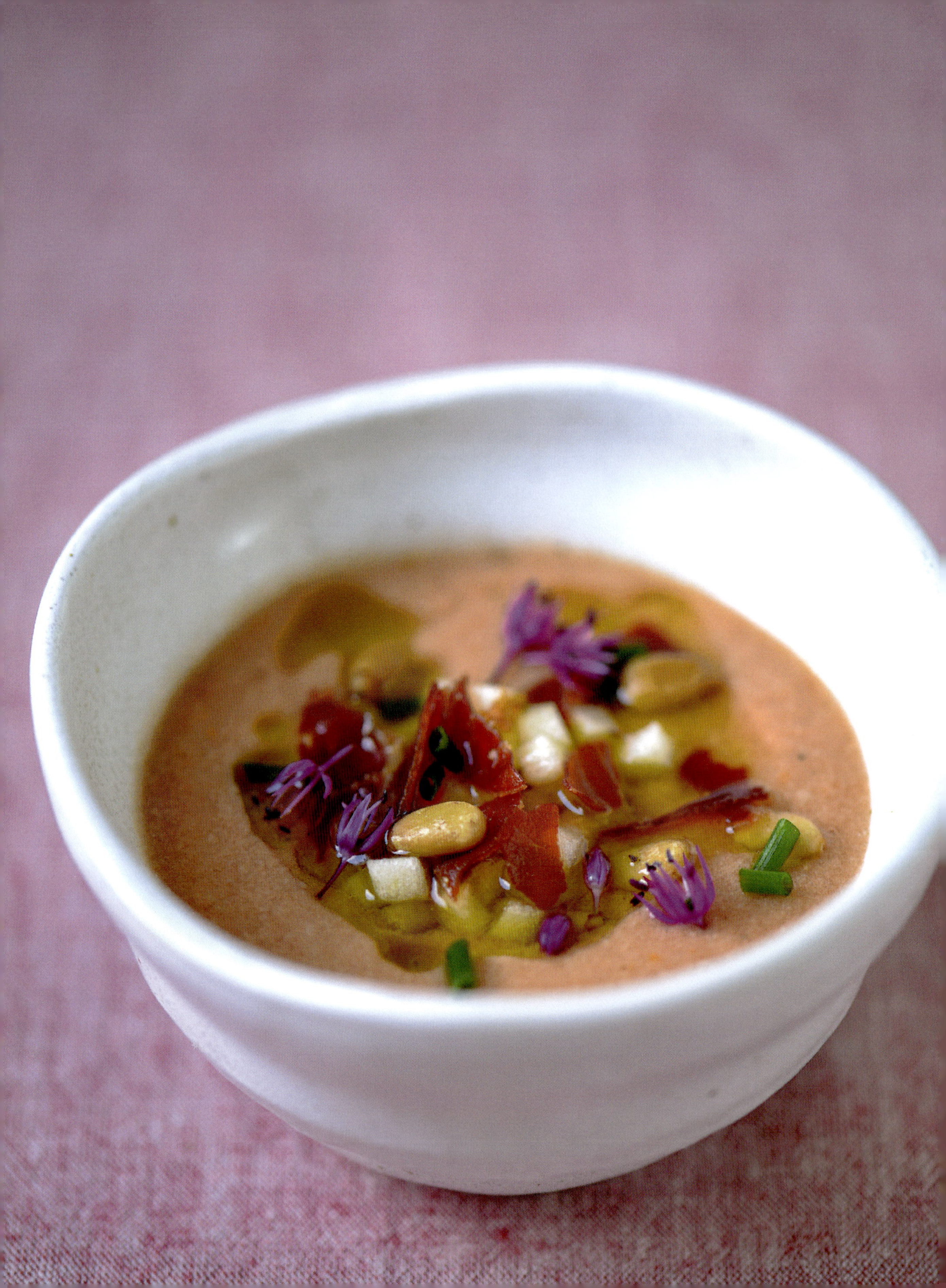

SALMOREJO

Serves 2 as a tapa

SOUP

1 slice stale bread, crust removed

1 large vine-ripened tomato (120g)

1 small clove peeled garlic (3g)

5g sugar

50ml water

2 teaspoons sherry vinegar

1 tablespoon olive oil

Sea salt and black pepper

TO GARNISH

1 teaspoon toasted pine nuts

1/4 apple finely diced (keep it in a little lemon juice so it doesn't brown)

1 slice of serrano ham

Olive oil to drizzle

Considering how open we are in the UK to food from around the world, we seem to have a block when it comes to 'cold' soup, which is a shame. In context, on a lovely summer's day, a chilled soup is bright and refreshing. In hot countries, hot soup would generally be unwelcome! Salmorejo is similar to a gazpacho but without the bother of neatly diced vegetables and can be made in just a few minutes.

TO MAKE THE SOUP: Liquidise everything together, except the garnish, until completely smooth. Adjust the consistency with water if required, the consistency should be similar to double cream. Season to taste and adjust the vinegar / sugar to achieve a very mild sweet / sour flavour (this will vary depending on the sweetness / acidity of your tomatoes). Chill for several hours — the soup must be served very cold.

The slice of serrano ham can be cooked gently in a frying pan until crisp (better still in the oven if it is on). When the ham is cold, crumble into pieces.

TO SERVE: Serve the soup in little bowls or glasses scattered with the pine nuts, apple, and serrano ham. Drizzle with a little good quality olive oil.

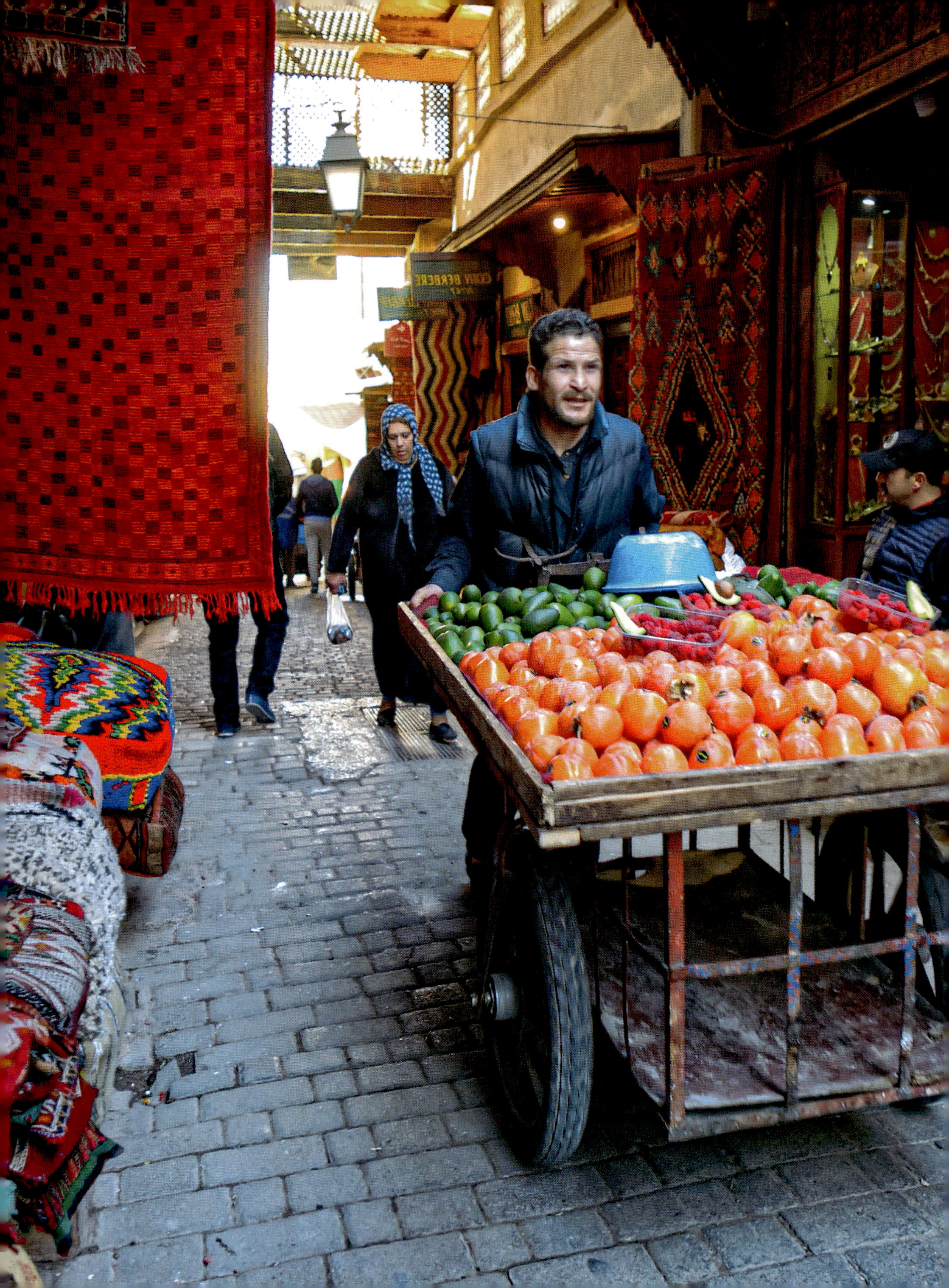
BERBERE

TASTE OF MOROCCO

Moroccan cuisine is influenced by their interactions with other cultures and nations over the centuries. It is typically a mix of Berber, Arabic, Andalusian and Mediterranean cuisines with a slight European and Sub-Saharan influence.

Some years ago, I visited Marrakech. Arabic markets can be quite intimidating, and I quickly learnt not to linger if I wasn't interested in buying. 'Window shopping' is an alien concept in Morocco! When I revisited last year, I stayed in Fez. The old part, or the Medina, is medieval and because traffic is banned (the lanes are only passable on mopeds anyway) it is the quietest city I have ever visited. Even the modern part wasn't noisy!

I do find food variable when I travel, it's not always as fantastic as the travel supplements would have you believe and the first tagine and pastilla I had in Fez were bitter disappointments. Both places had been recommended on a well-known review site too! But it did get better and I was delighted to see little clay tagines lined up at roadside cafés when I travelled into the Atlas Mountains. The unique shape of a tagine is designed to be used in the embers of the campfire. The conical lid traps moisture, which runs back into the dish to keep the meat moist. I was determined to take 10 back with me to use at the school and in Meknes I was in luck. Exactly the right size and the equivalent of £1.80 each — bargain! At least that is what I thought until I got to the airport and was charged £40 excess baggage!

Apart from tagine, pastilla is another typical Moroccan dish. The pastry for this is 'warqa', an elastic, glutinous pancake-type mix that is spread by hand over a heated copper hob. It is very delicate and very difficult to make at home, so when we make pastilla at the school, we use filo pastry instead. Whilst in Fez, I videoed some warqa being made in the souk, so anyone who attends the Moroccan workshop at the school can view how this classic pastry is traditionally made.

The house I stayed in had a very good cook and she kindly showed me how to make pastilla properly with pigeon, which is the most traditional recipe. The addition of a little sugar in the filling and then icing sugar on top sometimes surprises people, but this combination of sweet and savoury is both delicious and essential.

Little pastries are ubiquitous in Morocco and kaab el gharzal, or gazelle horns, are the most popular. This pastry is very simple to make, as is the filling, and they eat very nicely with mint tea as a snack or as a simple dessert.

A meal in Morocco would not be complete without bread or khobz. This is a simple bread baked in a disc, in the numerous communal wood-fired ovens dotted throughout the Medina. Salads too are an essential part of a meal and usually comprise a variety of vegetables in the form of dips and these are eaten at the start of a meal.

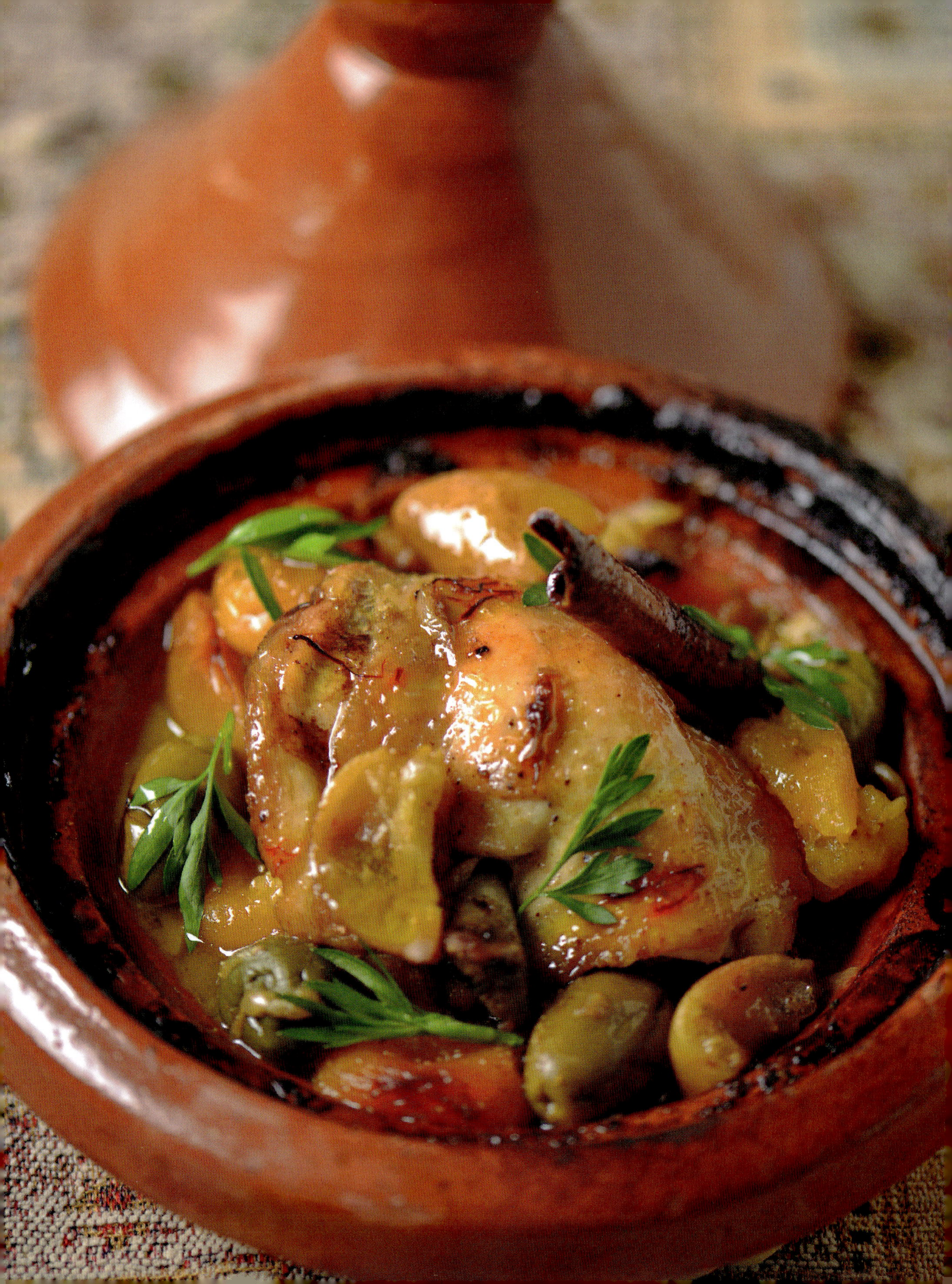

CHICKEN TAGINE

Serves 1

1 leg of chicken, cut in half to provide 1 drumstick and 1 thigh (on the bone)

1 tablespoon olive oil

1/2 an onion, peeled and sliced

1/2 a cinnamon stick

Pinch of saffron

1/2 teaspoon ground ginger

1/2 teaspoon ground cumin

2 cloves peeled garlic

4 dried apricots

Salt and pepper

Water, to barely fill base of tagine

Good olives - Green

1/2 salted lemon cut into strips (buy, or make your own using the recipe below)

Preheat the oven to 180°C

Season and brown the chicken in the olive oil, remove and add the onions. Cook to soften a little, before adding the garlic, spices, olives and apricots. Add about 100g water to the pan and tip everything into the tagine (or use a small casserole dish). Place the chicken on top and the salted lemon on top of the chicken. Put the lid on and bake for 1 - 1 1/2 hours. The meat should be very tender and falling away from the bone and the liquid should have reduced leaving just 2 - 3 tablespoons.

Scatter some chopped parsley on top and serve with bread.

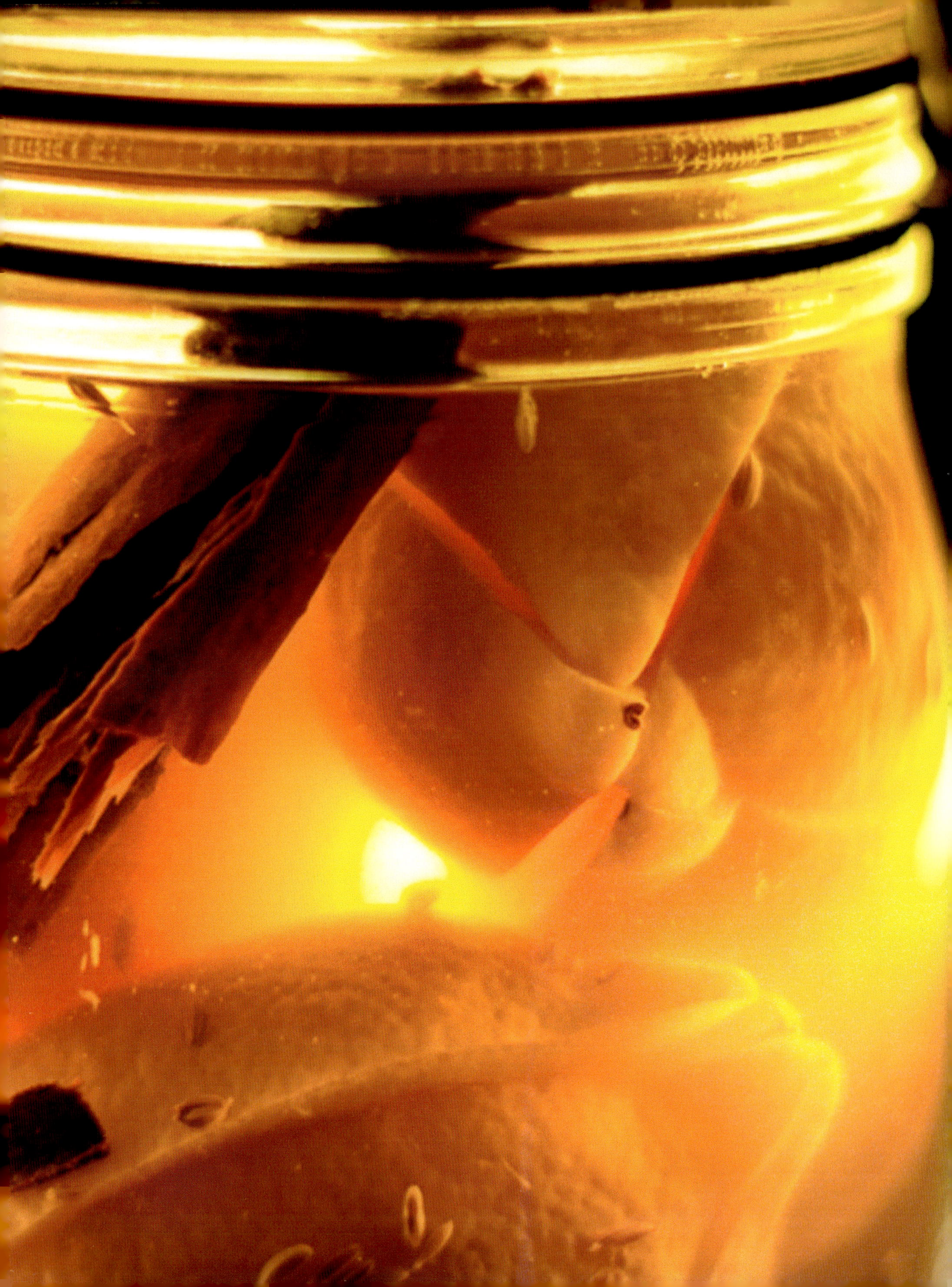

SALTED LEMONS

Makes 1 jar

- 1 lemon, unwaxed
- 1 tablespoon salt
- 1 teaspoon honey
- 2cm stick cinnamon
- 1 bay leaf

Cut the lemon lengthways into quarters but leave attached at the base. Wrap in cling film and freeze overnight (this speeds up the maturation process).

Allow the lemon to defrost and then pack the salt inside it. Place into a clean jar with the honey, cinnamon, and bay leaf. Fill the jar with boiling water and seal tightly.

The lemon will be ready to use in one month but will keep un-opened for 2-3 years. Once opened keep in the fridge.

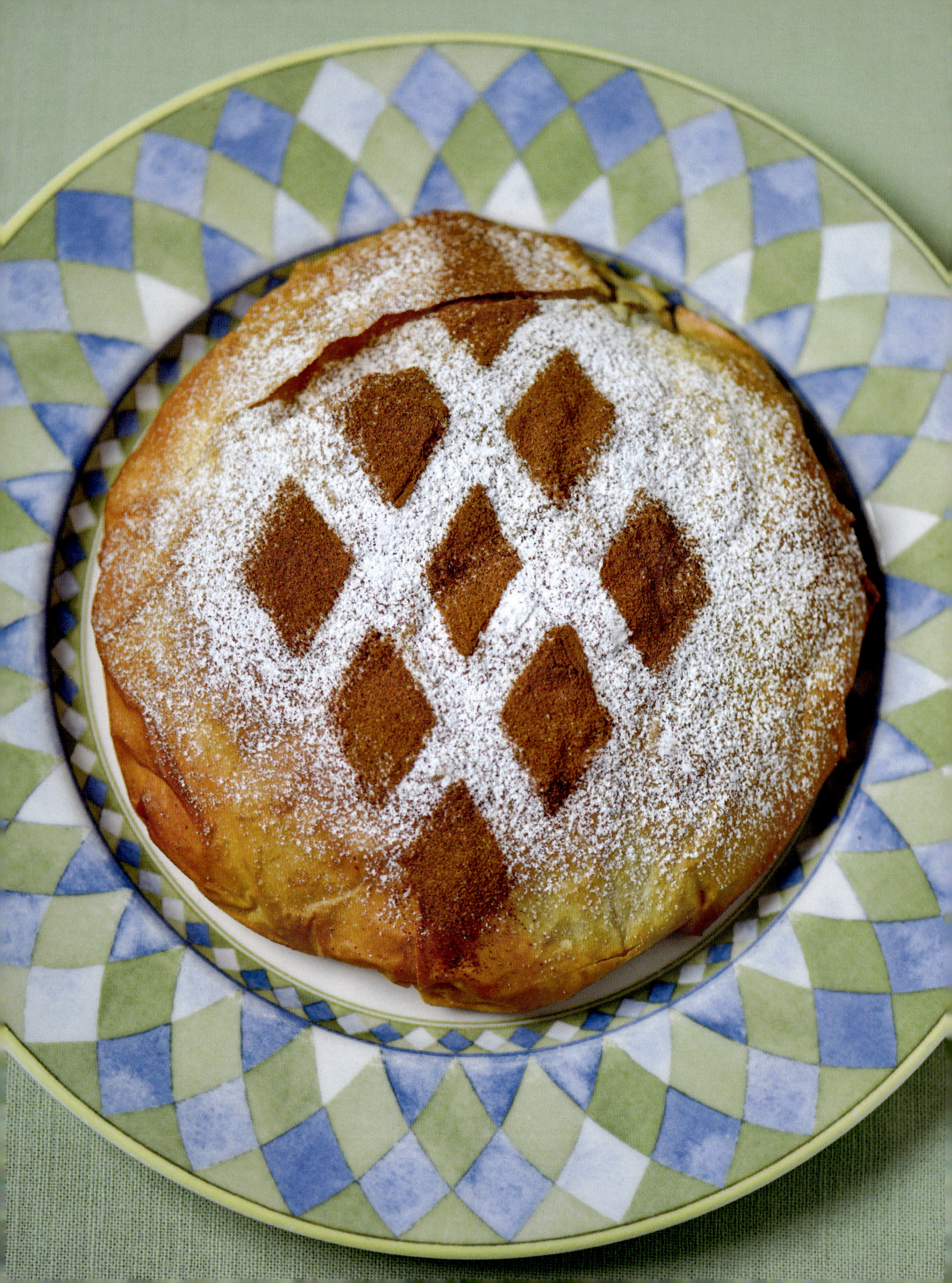

PASTILLA

Serves 2-3

- 3 sheets filo pastry plus melted butter
- 2 chicken thighs, with bone and skin (or duck, pigeon, pheasant, partridge)
- 1 tablespoon olive oil
- 15g butter
- 1 small onion, chopped
- 1 teaspoon ground ginger
- 1/2 teaspoon ground cinnamon
- Pinch of saffron
- 1 teaspoon caster sugar
- Water
- 1 large egg
- 1 tablespoon orange flower water
- 25g flaked, toasted almonds
- Icing sugar and ground cinnamon to decorate

TO MAKE THE FILLING: Heat the oil and butter in a pan and lightly brown the onions. Add the chicken, spices and sugar and cook for a couple of minutes. Add enough water to barely cover the chicken, put a lid on the pan and cook gently until the meat falls off the bone.

When cool enough to handle, remove the chicken and shred. Discard the skin and bone. You need about 2-3 tablespoons of liquid remaining. If you have more, boil to reduce it. Add the shredded chicken back into the pan. Crack the egg into the pan too and scramble. Add the orange flower water and almonds and check the seasoning.

TO ASSEMBLE: Ensure the filling is cool before assembling.

Brush a sheet of filo pastry with butter and then lay another sheet on top. Repeat twice.

Place the chicken mix in the centre and wrap to form a disc. Brush the top with melted butter.

Bake in a preheated oven at 200°C for about 20 minutes.

> **TOP TIP**
>
> To prevent filo pastry from drying out, keep it covered with a slightly damp tea towel.

TO SERVE: Decorate with icing sugar and cinnamon.

> **TOP TIP**
>
> You can create a pattern with the cinnamon by cutting a template out of card or using a paper doily.

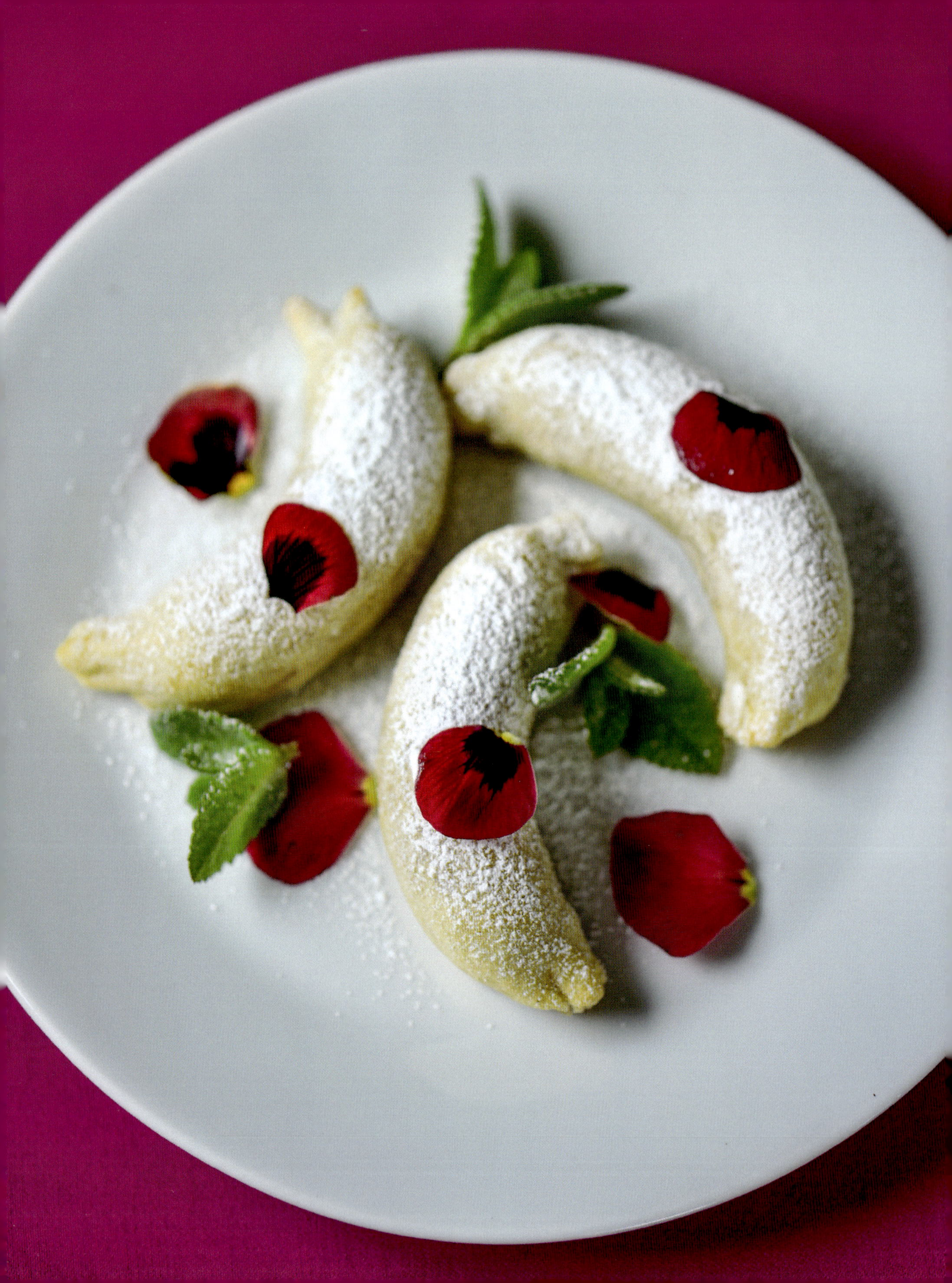

GAZELLE HORNS

Makes 6

FILLING

62g ground almonds

35g caster sugar

1 tablespoon orange flower water

15g butter (unsalted, melted)

1/8 teaspoon ground cinnamon

PASTRY

94g plain flour

1/8 teaspoon salt

1/2 egg, beaten

42g butter (unsalted, melted)

1 tablespoon orange flower water

TO MAKE THE FILLING: Mix the ground almonds with the sugar, butter, cinnamon and orange flower water into a smooth, moist paste. Divide this mix into six and shape into sausage-like sticks about the size of your small finger. Cover, and set aside.

> **TOP TIP**
>
> This prepared almond paste can be refrigerated at this stage for several days.

TO MAKE THE PASTRY: Mix all ingredients together to form a soft dough and knead by hand for 10 minutes, or longer, until the dough is very smooth and elastic. Wrap in clingfilm and rest for 15 minutes.

TO ASSEMBLE: Lightly dust a work surface with flour. Roll the pastry out evenly until it is no thicker than 2mm. Use flour as you roll, to ensure the dough doesn't stick to the table. It is quite easy to roll because of the high fat content.

Ideally use a large round pastry cutter and cut 6 circles. Roll these out a little more. Lay a piece of almond paste on one end and roll, pinching the ends together into little points. Carefully mould the pastries into the traditional horn shape. Repeat until all 6 have been assembled.

> **TOP TIP**
>
> An optional egg wash mixed with a little orange flower water may be used to glaze.

Transfer to a greaseproof lined baking sheet. Bake for 10 minutes, in a preheated oven at 180° C until barely golden. Cool for a couple of minutes and then sprinkle with icing sugar.

> **TOP TIP**
>
> Do not overbake, as this will toughen the pastry and almond filling will burst out.

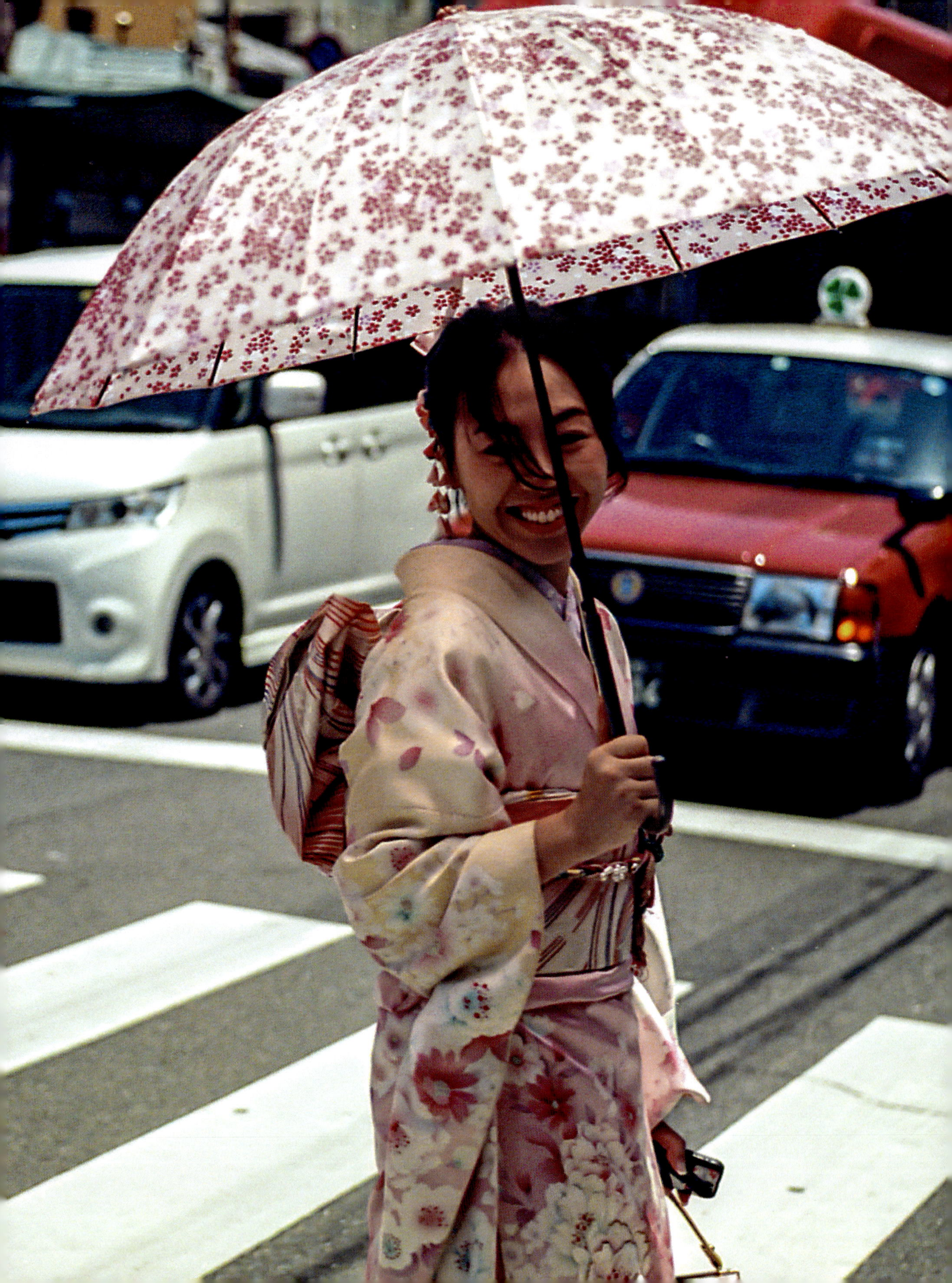

KYOTO – A TASTE OF JAPAN

I used chop sticks for the first time when I was 16, working on the Queen Elizabeth II. The ship docked at both Kobe and Yokohama and I got the train into Tokyo. This was very exciting, as I had never been abroad before! Ordering food was also a whole new experience. Restaurants in Japan in those days, commissioned wax mock-ups of the food they had on offer on the menu. This is called sampuro and is considered an art form, with each item made by hand. These were displayed in the window; very handy for me as I could just point and hope! I can still remember sitting at the counter watching intently how the chap next to me held his chopsticks.

I returned to Japan in 2019 and to say I was excited to be going back was an understatement! My wife Karen and I managed to combine the trip as our honeymoon too. I was under strict instructions to not spend all my time researching food, but what can I say? We had to eat! We did not go to Tokyo at all, although we had planned to. The beauty and calm serenity of Kyoto held us spellbound and there we stayed. I discovered sampuro is still in use today, although the models are now made of plastic - but incredibly lifelike! At least ordering in modern day Japan is a little easier.

What stands out for me about Japanese food is the portion sizes of proteins. Big bowls of noodles are of course popular (and filling), but fish and meat are expensive and as such, are treated with respect and served in small, perfectly cooked, portions. It seems to me that this approach is much more sustainable than the western approach to protein!

Kyoto is renowned for its refined cuisine, especially tofu and kaiseki, where a 'no choice' selection of dishes is presented by the chefs cooking directly in front of customers. This style of cuisine had its origins in the tea ceremony before evolving into an elaborate dining style popular in aristocratic circles. It can be expensive but is not to be missed!

We discovered a rice cake shop in the Nishiki market, and I was fascinated to watch the traditional process of making Mochi. Cooked rice was pounded with a huge mallet (traditionally a role for the male head of the household) into a paste to be stuffed with anko; sweet red bean paste. There are many different types of Mochi, all delicious and you find them throughout Kyoto as sweet snacks. I knew that I would need to simplify the process for us to be able to make them at the school though. Glutinous rice flour works very well as a substitute (and despite the name, is in fact gluten free).

Nishin soba is also a speciality of Kyoto and traditionally made with herring. When I ate this, I instantly knew it was a dish I wanted to bring back — It was so delicious! It has to be prepared with the utmost care though, to ensure even the tiniest bones are removed. Salmon makes a good and easier substitute. The broth is made with dashi, a stock that is at the heart of so many Japanese dishes. I've added the recipe for dashi below but you could bypass this step if you are struggling to get all of the ingredients and use a fish stock cube or two instead. The soba noodles are made from 100% buckwheat and take years of practice to master. Adding wheat makes the dough easier to work with but I wanted to keep them gluten free. The answer? 100g of buckwheat flour to 1 egg and treat like pasta. Simple!

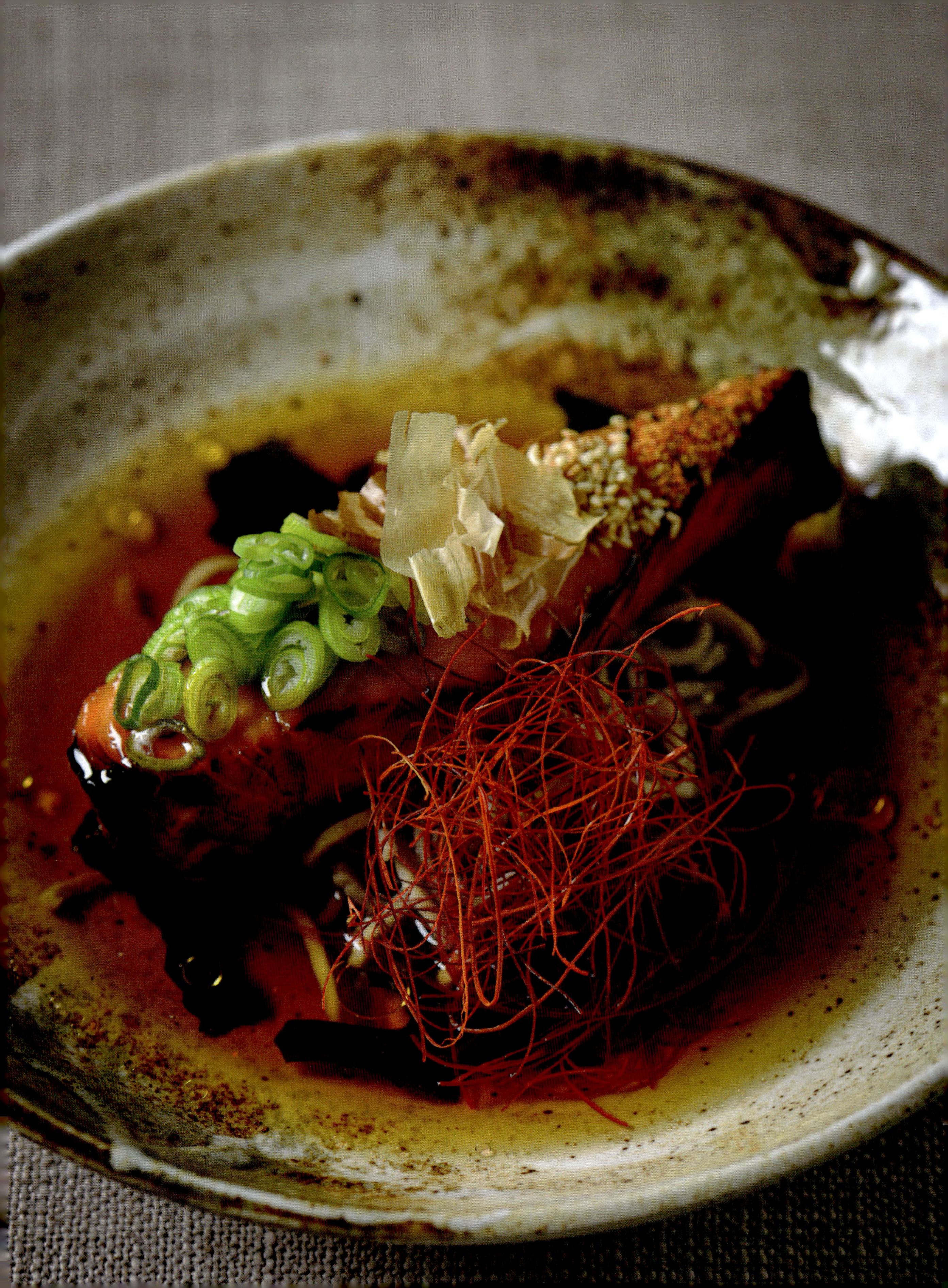

NISHIN SOBA

Serves 2

2 pieces of salmon, about 100g each, skin removed

MARINADE:

2 teaspoons dark brown muscovado sugar

1/2 teaspoon mirin (sweet rice wine)

1/2 teaspoon sake

2 teaspoons soy sauce

DASHI (BROTH)

300ml water

5g dried shiitake

1g kombu (kelp)

2g green seaweed

1 tablespoon katsuobushi (dried tuna flakes)

SOBA NOODLES

100g buckwheat flour

1 egg

TO SERVE

3 teaspoons soy sauce

1 teaspoon dark brown muscovado sugar

2 teaspoons mirin

2 spring onions finely sliced

1 teaspoon sesame oil

TO MAKE THE MARINADE: Combine all of the ingredients together, add the salmon and pop in the fridge for 30 minutes minimum — overnight is even better.

TO MAKE THE DASHI: In a saucepan combine the ingredients for the dashi. Bring to a simmer, turn off the heat, cover and leave for at least 30 minutes.

TO MAKE THE NOODLES: Combine the buckwheat flour with the egg and knead to a smooth dough. It will feel dry to start with but persevere! When ready, wrap in cling film and leave to rest for 15 minutes.

Once rested roll the noodles. Lightly dust your table with buckwheat flour and roll the dough out as thinly as possible, it should be no more than 2mm thick (you can use a pasta machine if you have one, but it is easy to roll by hand). When you have a thin sheet of dough, flour generously and fold in half and then in half again. Using a sharp knife, cut the dough into 2mm strips, and then shake to separate the noodles. Put to one side.

TO COOK THE FISH: Preheat your grill, line a baking sheet with tin foil, remove the salmon from the marinade and place on the foil. Grill under a medium heat for about 6-8 minutes. Every 2 minutes, brush the salmon with the remaining marinade to produce a good glaze. When the salmon is cooked, keep warm while you cook the noodles.

TO COOK THE NOODLES: Bring a large pan of water to a simmer, plunge in the noodles and simmer for 3-4 minutes. Watch carefully, soba noodles boil over very easily so you may need to turn the heat down. Drain and divide between warm pasta plates (or similar).

TO SERVE: Strain the dashi into a clean pan and add the soy sauce, sugar and mirin. Add salt to taste. The noodles will absorb flavour from the broth, so it needs to be well seasoned.

Place the salmon on top of the noodles, bring the broth back to the boil and pour over the noodles. Finish by piling the spring onions on top and drizzle over the sesame oil.

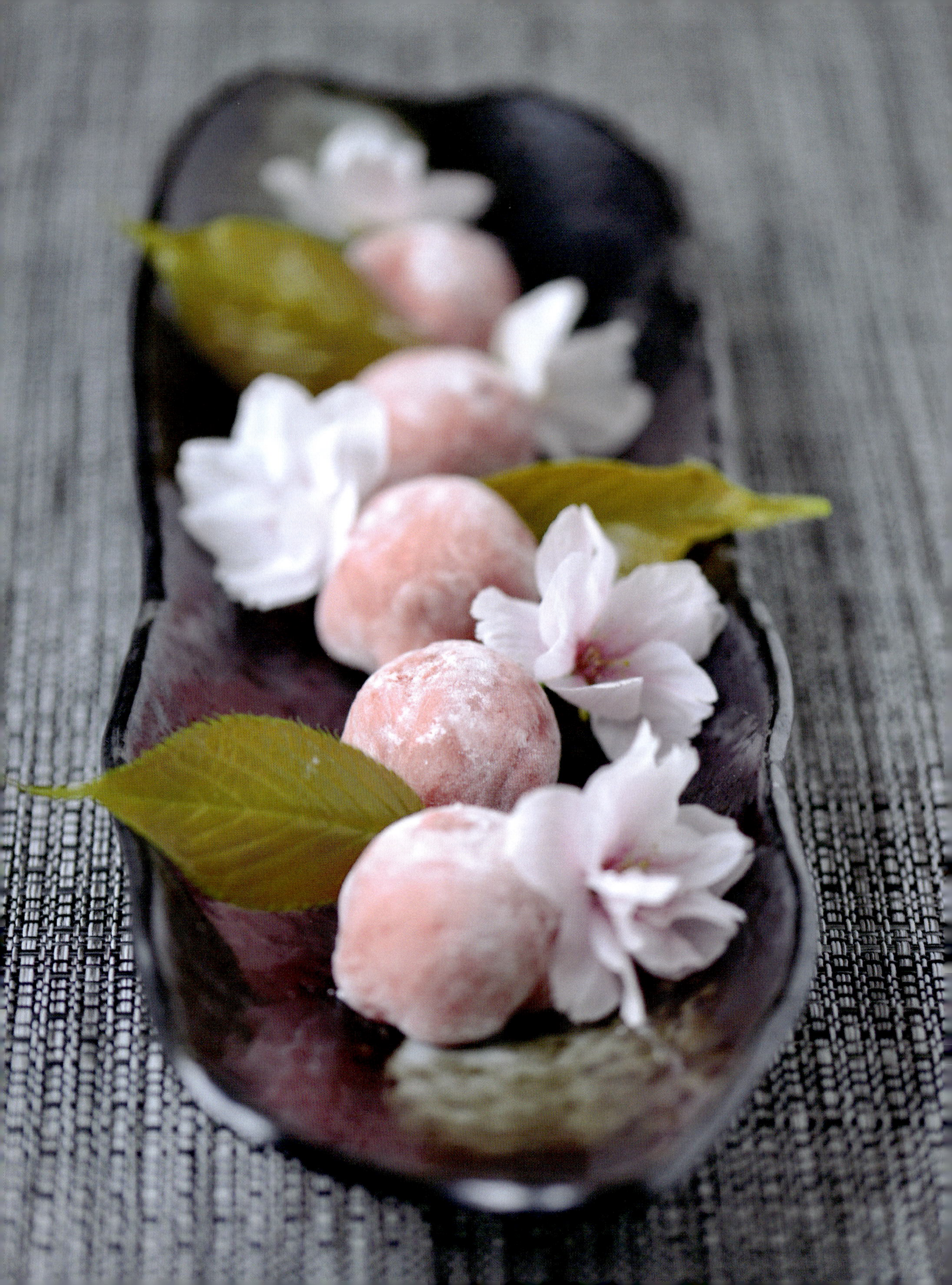

SAKURA MOCHI

Makes 6

50g glutinous rice flour

100ml water

50g caster sugar

1/4 teaspoon matcha tea powder or red colour (optional)

Cornflour

Measure the water into a small saucepan, bring to the boil and whisk in the rice flour and sugar. As the mixture thickens swap the whisk for a wooden spoon and beat well over a medium heat — it must be smooth and thick. This takes about 4 minutes, any less and it will not work.

Lightly cover a plate with cornflour, pour the mix onto the plate and leave to cool. Sprinkle the surface with cornflour too. When cold, cut discs using a 6cm cutter.

Place a teaspoonful of anko (sweet red bean paste – see below) in the centre of each disc and carefully gather up the sides, pinching at the top to seal. Turn over so that the seal is on the bottom. Decorate with flowers and serve.

ANKO

(Sweet Red bean paste)

150g cooked & drained azuki beans

115g caster sugar

Add the sugar to the cooked beans and stir over a gentle heat until the sugar has dissolved. Blend until smooth — a food processor works best for this.

TOP TIP

If the mix is a little wet (when cold it must be the texture of dry mashed potato) line a baking sheet with parchment paper, spread the mix out and dry in a low oven (100 - 125°C) until it is the correct texture.

Chill before use.

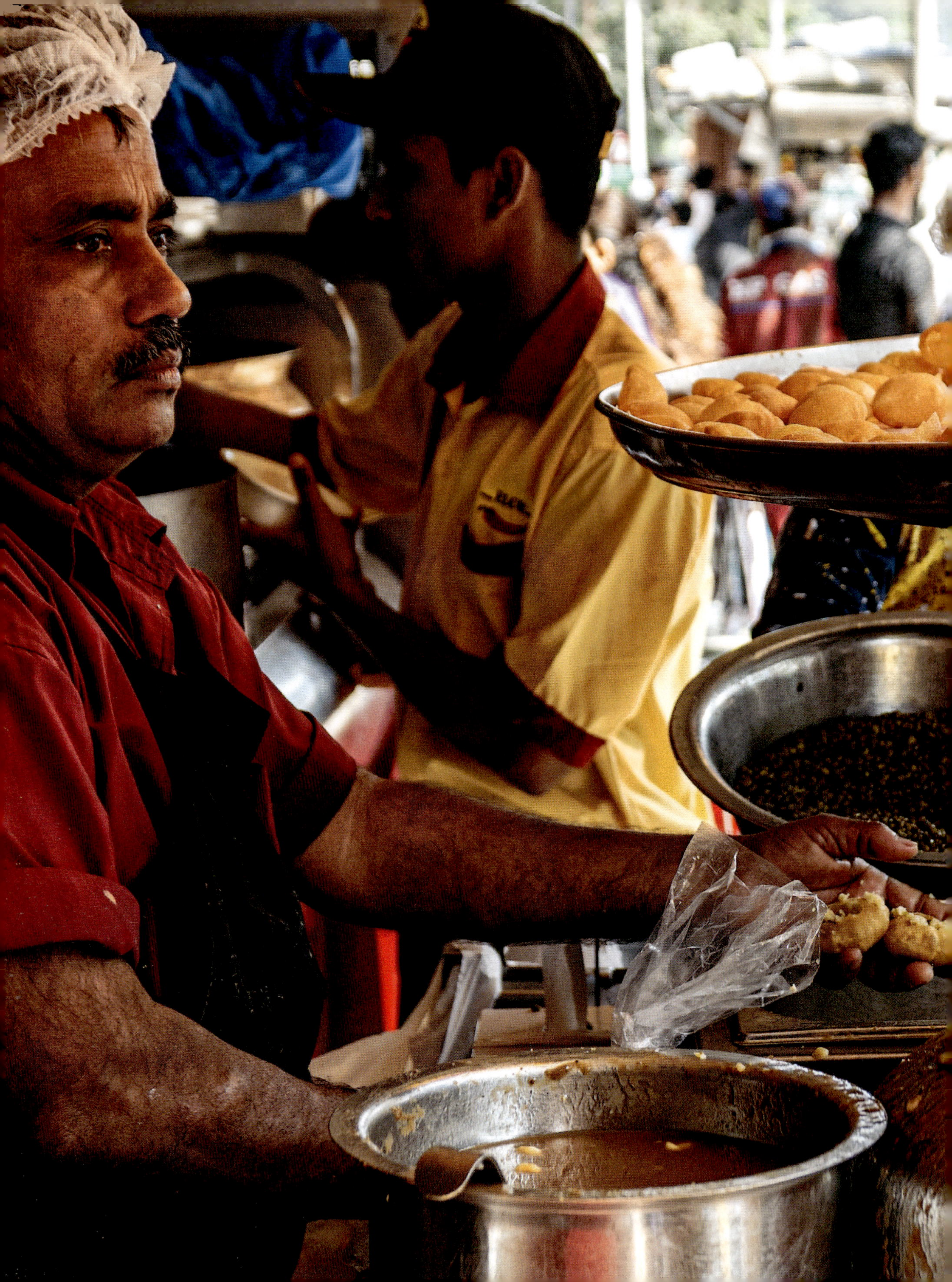

INDIAN CURRIES AND INDIAN STREET FOOD

I visited Mumbai in January 2017 and loved it! Mumbai is chaotic, noisy, hot and home to some fantastic street food. The markets are not picture-postcard friendly but a thriving hub of activity involving humans, dogs, cats and other small critters that would lead to instant closure in Europe. The people are extremely friendly, hospitable, and also love to have their picture taken.

One street butcher I ended up chatting to (I don't know how; I don't speak Hindi and he didn't speak English!) sent a boy off to get a little bag of masala chai and we sat and chatted whilst he smoked a cigarette. I love masala chai, tiny glasses of hot, milky, spiced and sweetened tea, and if you want it to takeaway, it goes into a little plastic bag with an elastic band around the top.

Whilst there, I was on the lookout for an old masala dabba or spice box. Modern ones are stainless steel, functional but lacking the charm of old ones. In the Chor market (Chor is Hindi for thief!) I found a beautiful old wooden one which takes pride of place at the school during the two Indian workshops: Indian Street Food and Indian Curries.

Indian Street Food (as you would expect) teaches you how to make the various snacks found on the plentiful street stalls. One of these is Pani Puri. Pani Puri are little crisp puffs made with flour and water, a very popular street snack in Mumbai. Small groups congregate around the seller as puri (puff balls) are filled with a few spiced chickpeas and dunked in the pani, (spiced water). A generous seasoning of chaat masala lends a tang of sour mango and eggy Himalayan salt. We have a lot of fun making these on the street food workshop. It's wonderful to see the looks of surprise and joy as the little rounds of dough split and puff up like ping-pong balls in the hot oil.

Another popular street snack that we make is dosa. Dosa is a fermented rice and dal pancake. Before we make dosa on the Indian Street Food workshop, I like to play a short video I recorded at 10pm in Mumbai. The dosa stall is in full swing with a vast throng of people waiting to be served. It creates a real sense of the noise and heat that you experience, even at that time of night and makes cooking the dosa so much more fun!

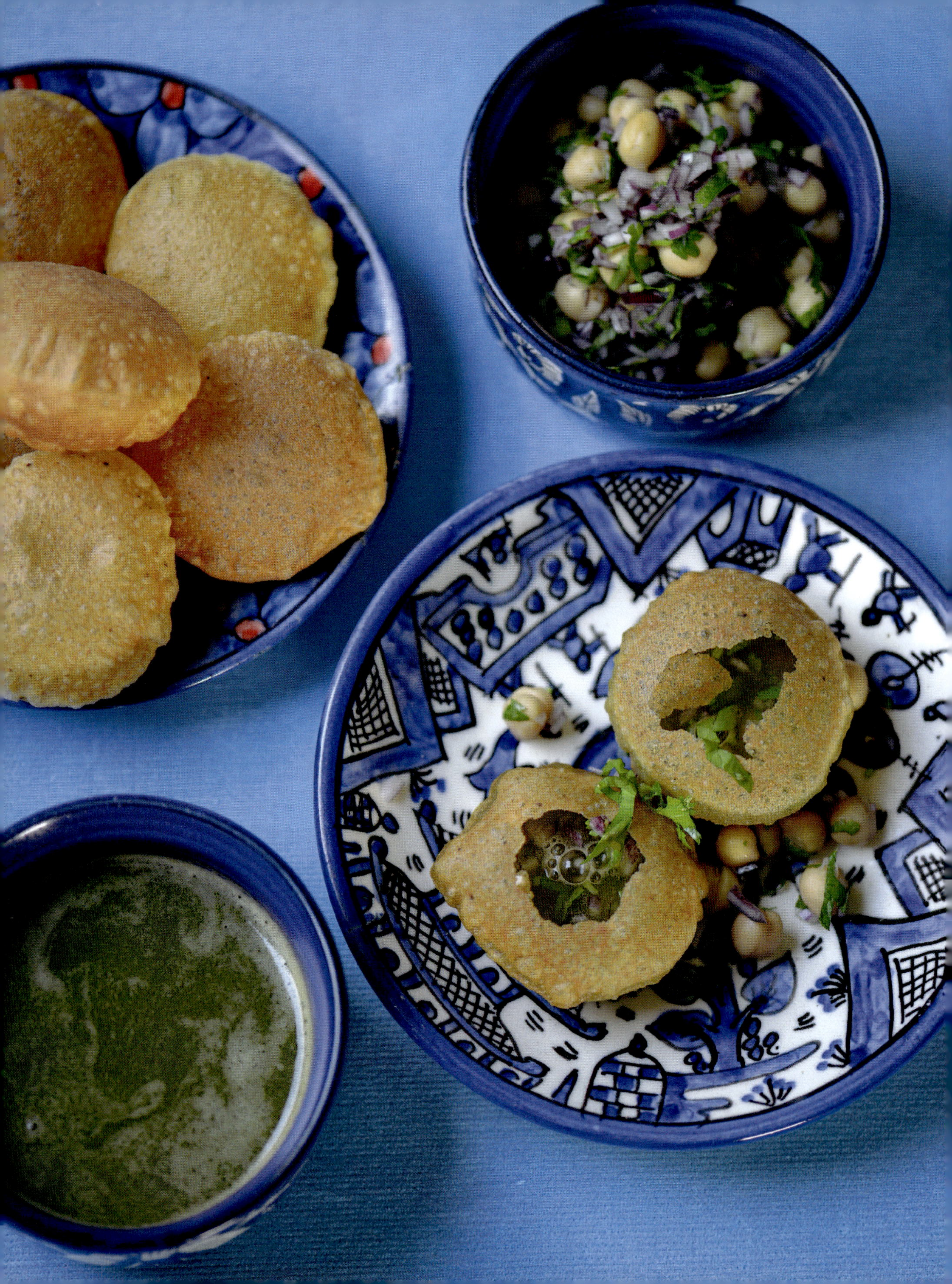

PANI PURI

Serves 2 as a snack

FILLING
1 medium potato (175g) peeled & diced 5mm
75g Cooked chickpeas
1/2 small onion, finely chopped
10g chopped coriander
1 teaspoon roasted cumin powder
1 teaspoon chaat masala powder (you can buy or make your own, recipe below)
1/4 teaspoon red chilli powder
Black salt

PANI (SPICED WATER)
1 tomato
8g mint leaves
12g coriander leaves
2cm ginger
10g green chillies, seeded
20g tamarind pulp
22g powdered jaggery
1 teaspoon roasted cumin powder
1 teaspoon chaat masala powder
75ml water for grinding
About 250ml of water to be added later to get right consistency

PURI DOUGH (12-15 pieces)
50g fine semolina
10g plain flour
Freshly ground black pepper and sea salt
32ml water
Oil for deep frying (heated to 180-190°C)

TO MAKE THE FILLING: Boil the potatoes, add the rest of the ingredients, mix and reserve.

TO MAKE THE PANI: Blend all the ingredients in a liquidiser, thinning with the additional water at the end, strain through a tea strainer and reserve.

TO MAKE THE DOUGH (PURI): Combine the semolina and flour, add a generous grinding of black pepper and season well with sea salt. Add water and knead well to make a smooth, soft and elastic dough. Wrap in clingfilm and rest for 30 minutes.

Once rested, roll out thinly (about 2mm thick) and cut with a small round cutter. Keep the discs covered with a damp cloth whilst rolling the rest of the dough. Deep fry the puri in small batches and drain well.

TO SERVE: Push a hole into the top of each puri with your thumb and place a little of the chickpea mix inside – make sure it is no more than half full. Pour in the spiced water to fill and eat. Just fill and eat one at a time. They go soggy quickly and the pani will leak out.

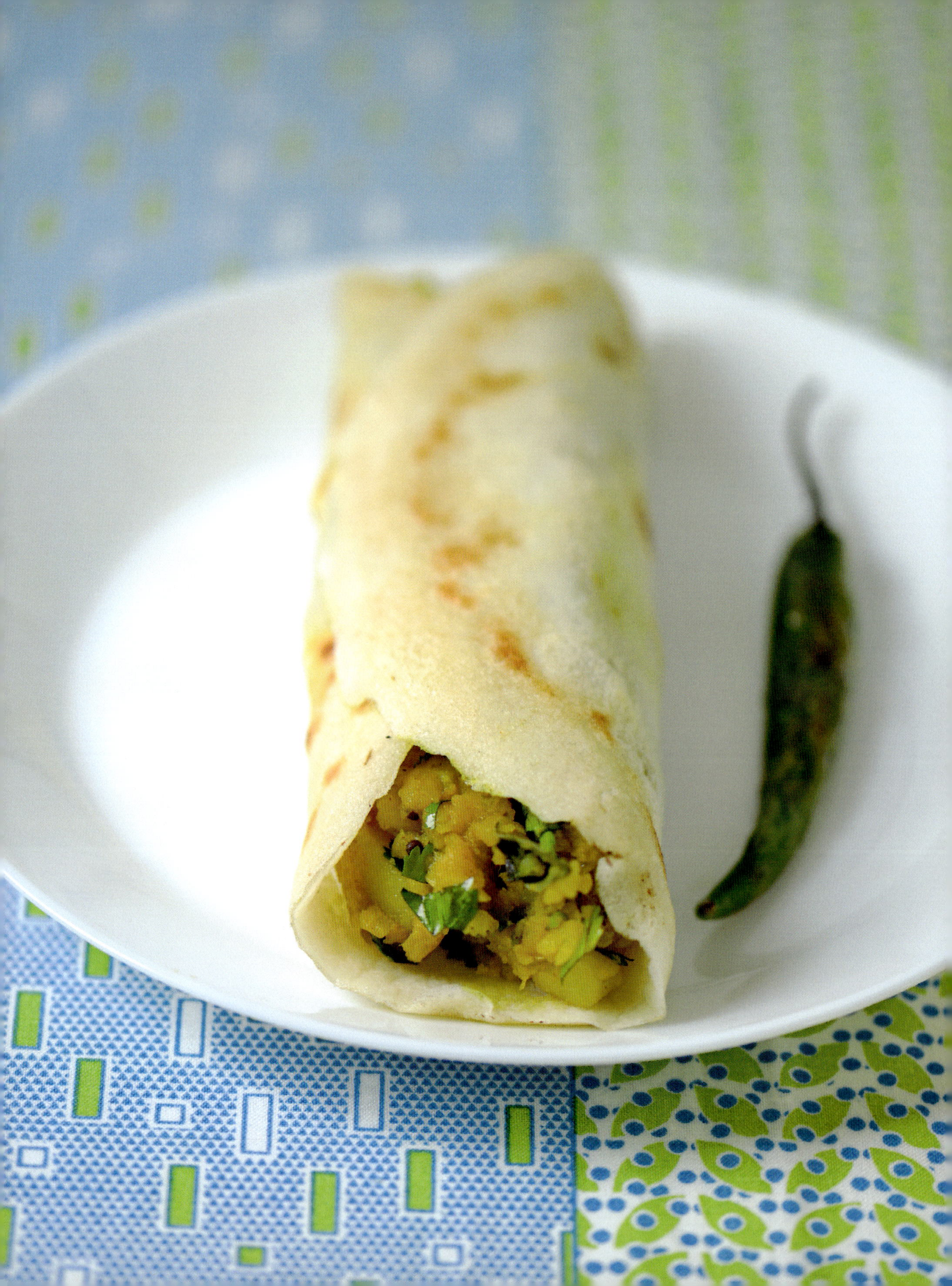

MASALA DOSA

Makes 2 with some leftover batter

45g urad dal

9g chana dal

120g basmati rice

> **TOP TIP**
>
> Wash the rice and dal until the water runs clear and soak overnight in plenty of water.

FILLING:

6g Salt

1 jacket potato

1 onion

2-3 tablespoons vegetable oil

2cm ginger

2 cloves garlic

1/2 teaspoon mustard seeds

1/2 teaspoon ground cumin

1/4 teaspoon asafoetida

10 curry leaves

Green chilli

1/2 teaspoon turmeric

1 small bunch of coriander

The dosa batter is traditionally fermented, but I find this makes little difference to the end result. I do use urad and chana dal, but it is not a problem to substitute dried yellow split peas and red lentils. Do use enough oil to cook your onions. A common mistake is to be careful with the oil. I understand this caution, but it is not how Indians cook and you won't get that authentic flavour without it.

TO MAKE THE DOSA BATTER: Drain the dal and rice and keep the water. Blend in a liquidiser with salt and about 100ml retained water — just enough to make a thick, but pourable frothy batter.

TO MAKE THE FILLING: Peel, dice and boil the potato until cooked, then drain. Peel and chop the onion. Heat the oil and cook the onion until soft and golden, add more oil if required. Peel and chop the ginger and garlic, add to the onion, and cook for a few minutes. Add all of the spices and cook for a couple of minutes, then add the drained and cooked potato and mash roughly into the onion mix. Chop the coriander and add to the mix. Taste for salt.

TO COOK THE DOSA: Heat a non-stick frying pan and add a smear of oil. Wipe out with a piece of kitchen paper. For one dosa pour a generous tablespoon of batter into the pan and quickly, using the back of a spoon work the batter in a circular motion from the centre of the pan outwards. As soon as it starts to set and come away from the edges, add a generous couple of tablespoons of filling and gently press over the surface of the dosa. Cook for a few minutes and then carefully lift one side with a spatula and roll the dosa.

Transfer to a plate and serve.

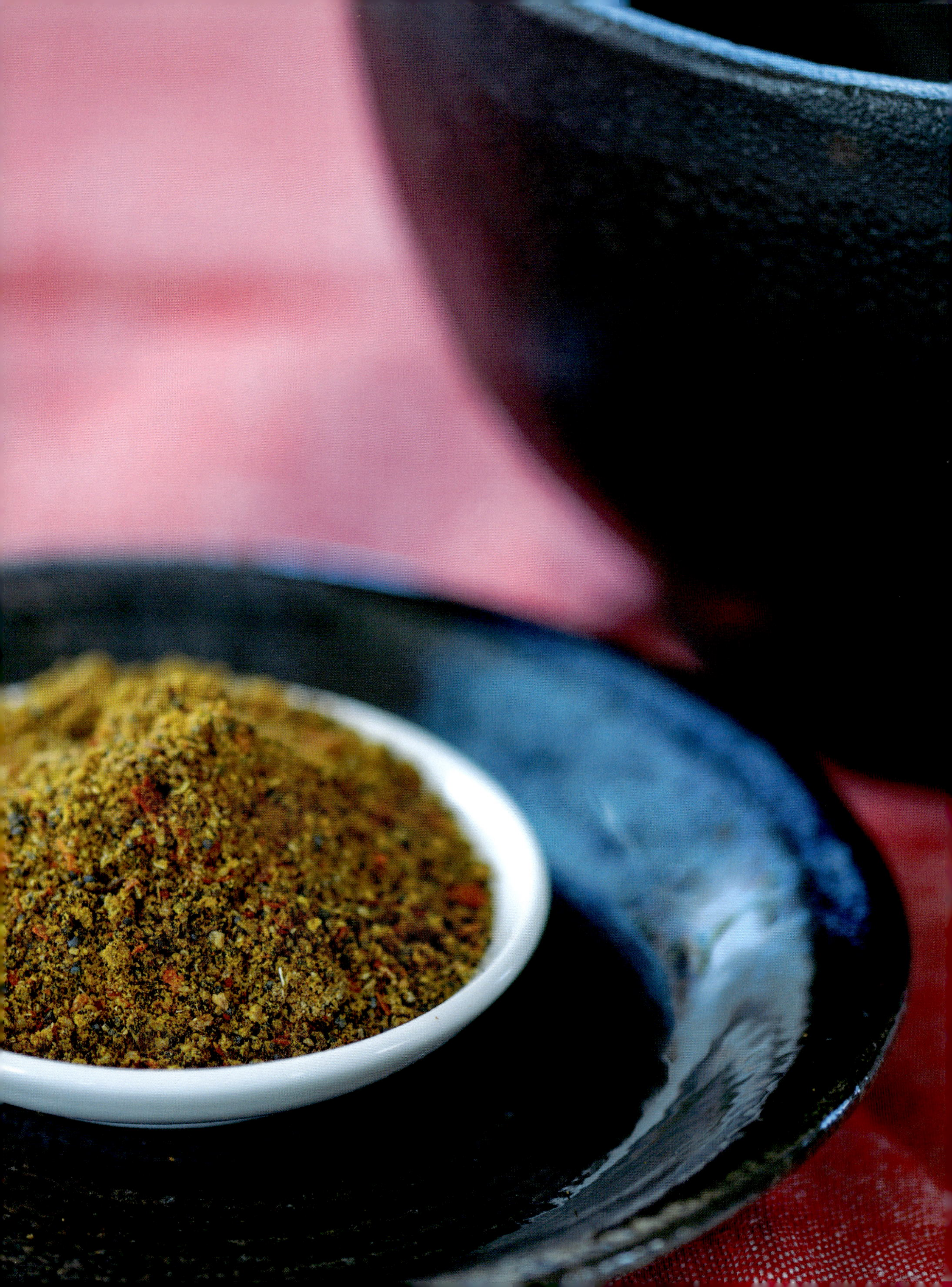

GARAM MASALA

3g black cardamom seeds (6 pods)

1.5g cloves

1/2cm piece of cinnamon stick

2g cumin seeds

2g black peppercorns

1 blade mace

Pinch of grated nutmeg

Garam masala is a simple Indian spice mixture that is usually added towards the end of the cooking just before serving.

Briefly roast all the ingredients, except the nutmeg, in a dry frying pan until they become aromatic. Leave to cool, then grind to a fine powder in a pestle and mortar, spice grinder or coffee grinder and add the nutmeg.

Store the garam masala in an airtight container; it should keep for months.

CHAAT MASALA

2 teaspoons cumin seeds

1 teaspoon coriander seeds

1/4 teaspoon fennel seeds

1/4 teaspoon caraway seeds

1 tablespoon raw mango/amchur powder

2 teaspoons powdered black salt

1/4 teaspoon black pepper (freshly ground)

Pinch of asafoetida powder

1/4 teaspoon ginger powder

1/4 teaspoon dried, powdered mint

Briefly roast the *whole* seeds in a dry frying pan until they become aromatic. Leave to cool, and then grind to a fine powder in a pestle and mortar, spice grinder or coffee grinder. Add the ground spices and mix well.

Store the chaat masala in an airtight container; it should keep for months.

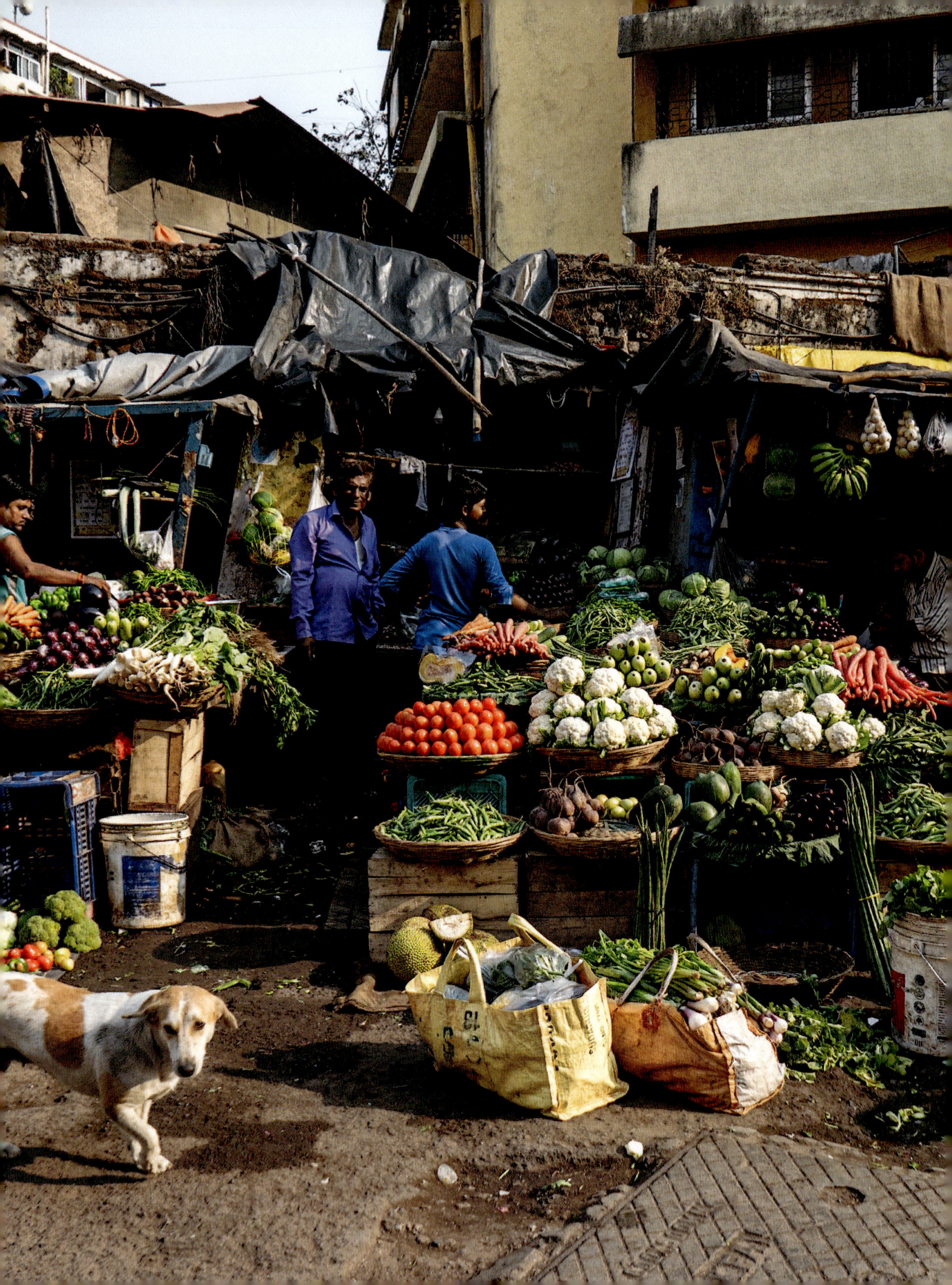

INDIAN CURRIES

The Indian Curries course looks at how to create and blend your own spice mixes and then use these in some fantastic curries. Below is a selection of the recipes we use. Keema pav is a popular breakfast curry of minced mutton served at the Olympia Coffee House in Mumbai. They've been serving it there for over 100 years! It is delicious scooped up with soft white bread, or pav. On the Indian Curries course, we make soft and fluffy naan bread instead, so simple and easy to cook in a dry frying pan.

The prawn curry is a favourite and uses that wonderful ingredient tamarind. It is best to buy a block of semi-dried pulp in an Indian or Asian store and make your own. To do this, simply break off a lump and work it in your fingers with enough hot water to make a paste or liquid – depending on the recipe requirements. Push / pour through a sieve to remove the seeds. Excess can be frozen, and the block keeps well in the store cupboard for a year or more.

If, like me, your taste buds are not attuned/bludgeoned by regular chilli intake you can add whole or halved chillies, rather than chopped, so that you can fish them out when the required heat (for you) is reached. If you add chopped chillies, there's no going back, you're committed. Remember, the heat is in the membrane on the inside of the chilli, not the seeds.

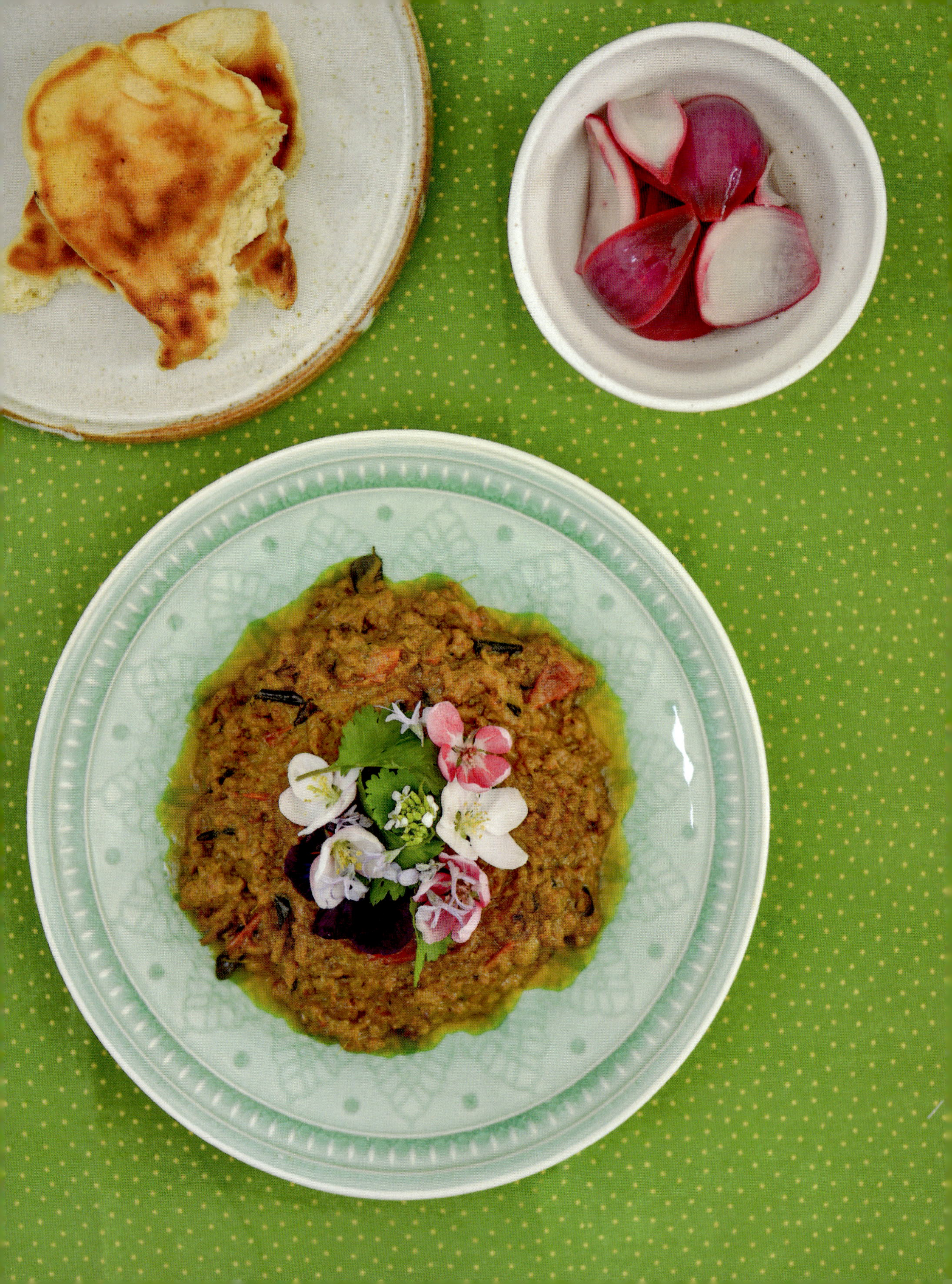

KEEMA PAV

Serves 1

150g minced lamb

1 clove of garlic

1/4 piece ginger

1/2 tablespoon vegetable oil

2 curry leaves

1 small white onion finely chopped

1 small tomato finely chopped

1 green chilli finely chopped

1/2 star anise

1/4 heaped teaspoon chilli powder

1/4 teaspoon turmeric powder

1/4 teaspoon ground coriander

45ml coconut milk

1/4 teaspoon dark brown sugar

1/2 tablespoon white vinegar

Salt to taste

Fresh coriander chopped for garnish

1 tablespoon lemon juice

1/4-1/2 tsp garam masala (buy or make your own. Recipe above).

Blend the ginger and garlic to a fine paste, mix it with the minced lamb and set aside to marinate while you get started on the curry.

Heat the oil in a heavy-bottomed saucepan. Add the curry leaves and let them sizzle for a few seconds. Add the onions and fry for 5-7 minutes until soft and light brown. Now add the chopped tomatoes and fry over a medium heat, cooking until they can be mashed slightly with the back of your spoon (approx. 5 minutes). At this stage add the green chillies, chilli powder, star anise, coriander & turmeric powder.

Stir well to cook the spices for a couple of minutes and then add the minced marinated lamb. Keep stirring on a medium heat and break down the lamb to make sure there are no lumps and all the spices are well mixed in. Cook for 5 minutes and then add 150g of water. Bring to a boil and simmer on a low heat, with the lid half covering the pan. You want to cook the lamb for 20 minutes or so until it has almost absorbed all the water.

Now add the coconut milk and the garam masala, and simmer for a further 5-7 minutes. Lastly add the sugar, vinegar & salt. Stir well and cook for a further 5 minutes. Turn the heat off and garnish with coriander and lemon juice.

Serve warm with pav/ soft bread and butter and some fresh salad.

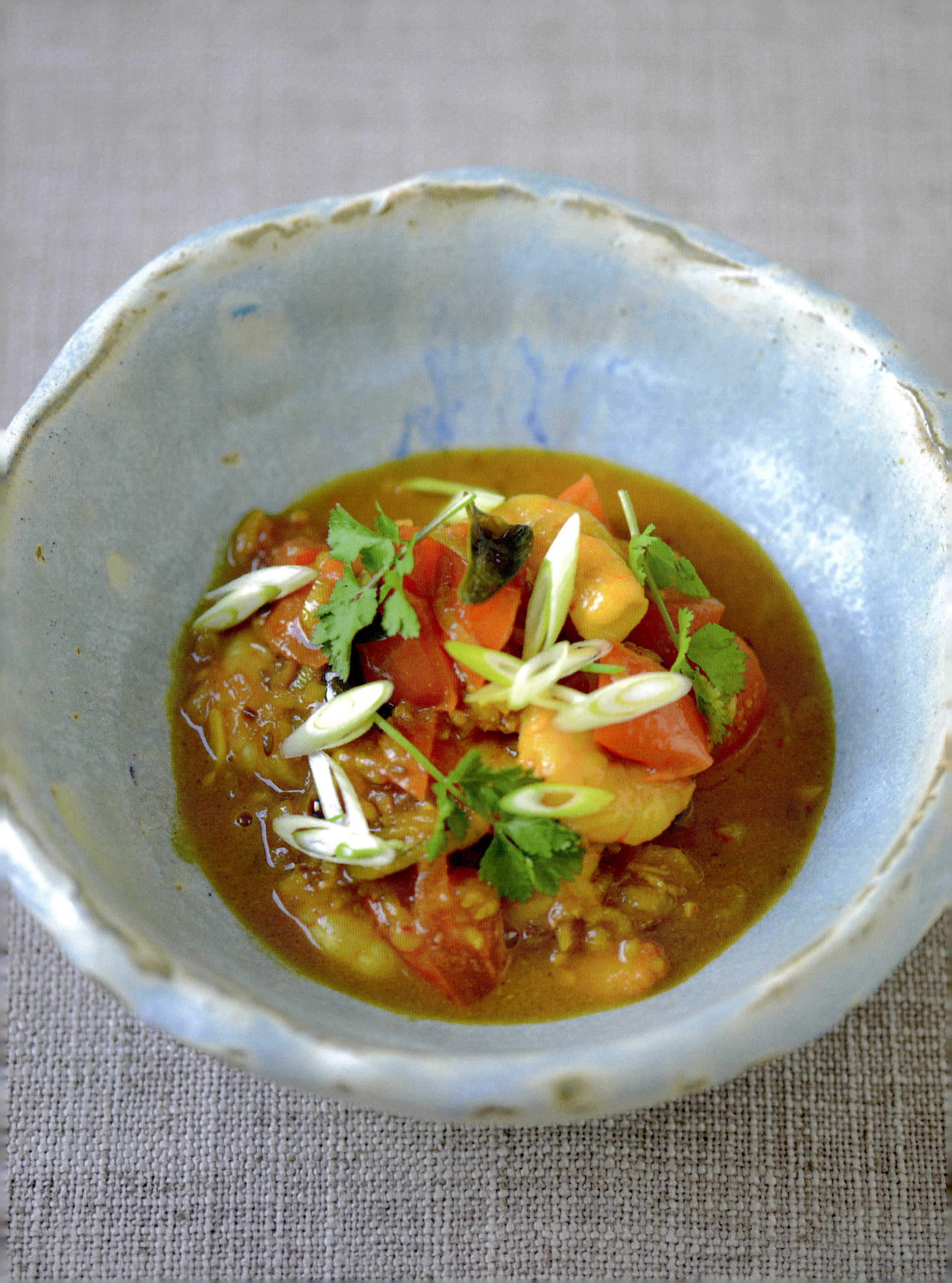

HOT & SWEET PRAWN CURRY

Serves 2

- 2 tablespoons vegetable oil
- 1 large onion, finely sliced
- 2 large cloves of chopped garlic
- 1 green chilli, chopped
- 1/2 teaspoon cumin seeds
- 1/2 teaspoon ground cumin
- 1/2 teaspoon ground coriander
- 1/2 teaspoon red chilli powder
- 1/2 teaspoon Garam Masala
- Pinch of ground turmeric
- 2 tomatoes, chopped
- 2 tablespoons tamarind water
- 1/2 teaspoon jaggery (or light brown muscovado sugar)
- 8 curry leaves
- 2 tablespoons coriander leaves, chopped
- 150g raw prawns
- 3 spring onions, chopped

Heat the oil in a pan and sauté the onions until very soft and light brown in colour. Add the garlic, chilli and cumin seeds and sauté for 2-3 minutes over a medium heat, then add the ground cumin, coriander, red chilli, garam masala and turmeric. Stir well for a minute, then add the chopped tomato, tamarind water, sugar, curry leaves, and salt to taste. Adjust the sweet and sour flavours and add the prawns. Cook for 3 - 4 minutes. Add the spring onions and chopped coriander leaves to the prawns.

Stir well and serve with rice.

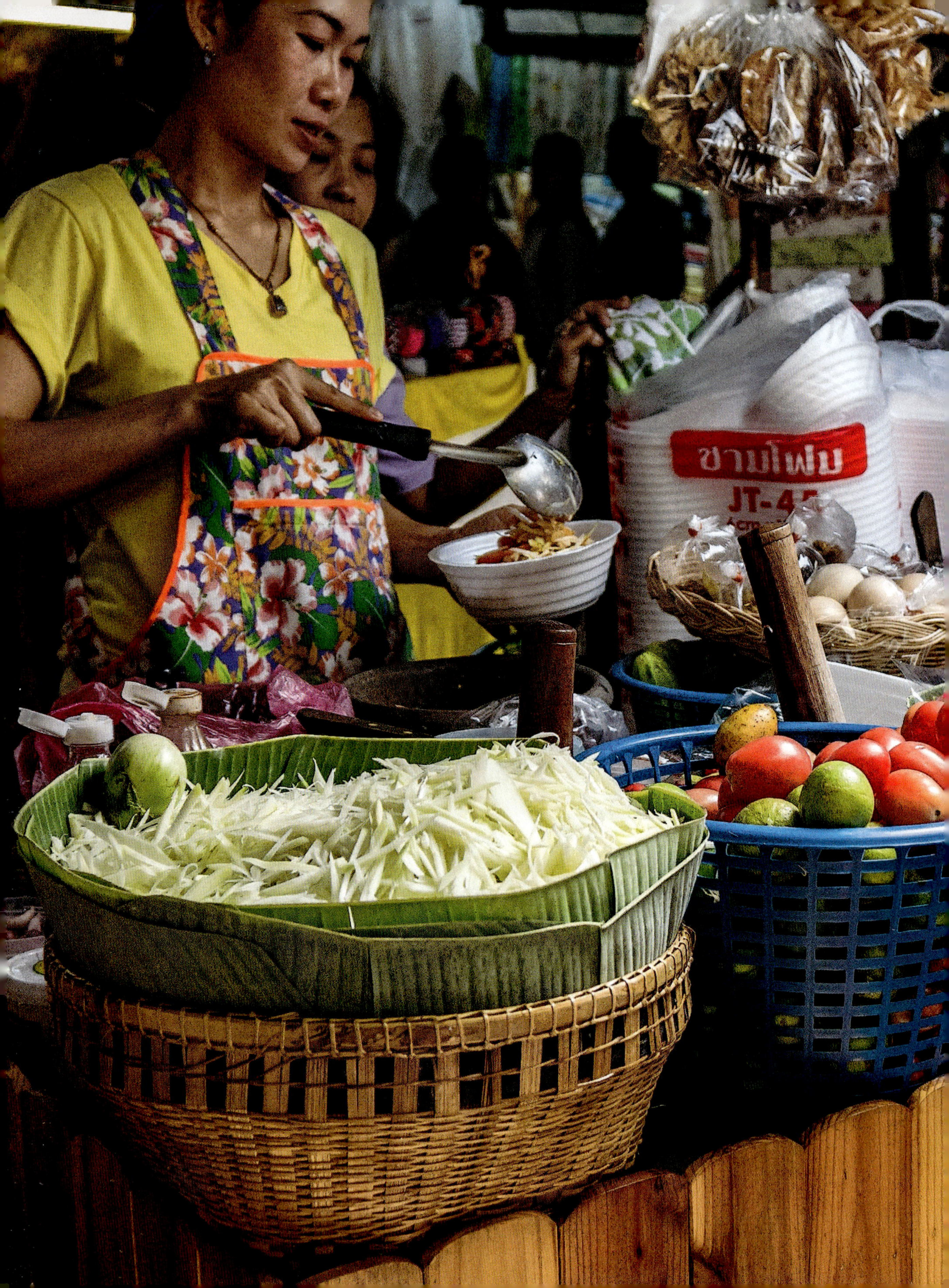
ชามโฟม
JT-45

TASTE OF THAILAND AND THAI STREET FOOD

Thailand is highly regarded, not just for its friendly people and warm welcome but also for its fantastic, flavoursome food. The characteristic flavours of hot, sour, salty and sweet are more pronounced here than across the rest of South East Asia. Vietnamese food has strong Chinese and French influence and Laos and Cambodia have distinct outside influences as well.

Bangkok is renowned for its street food, which literally never stops. It would be impossible to go hungry in this teeming city at any time of the day or night! Street food does however come under closer hygiene regulations than it used to, with many street cooks now working from small cafés instead. There is a multitude of choice — including insects! — some of which are distinctly tastier than others, so pull up one of the tiny, ubiquitous plastic chairs and enjoy.

Chang Mai in the north likes to do things at a slightly less frenetic pace than the southern capital city. A cooler temperature, the laid-back vibe, and stunning temples around every corner, make this a great city to relax in. A favourite dish of mine is coconut rice with mango. Personally, I find the salty / sweet coconut rice addictive, when coupled with juicy, ripe, cold mango. Thailanders like to colour half the rice blue — an odd colour for food — and use a dye made from a pea-like flower to do this.

At the cookery school, I generally try to use ingredients that are easily available, but to cook Thai food well necessitates a visit to your nearest Asian store. Below are some typical ingredients that you will need to use to cook Thai food and some suggestions for alternatives if you have trouble sourcing them.

Chillies are not indigenous to Thailand, as you may think, but were introduced from South America by the Portuguese. Many Thai recipes will use white pepper for heat. Not everything has to contain chilli. Fresh chilly can be substituted for dry, but dried chillies give a deeper colour and consistent heat level in curry pastes. Adjust the recipes in the book to your own heat tolerance but, if making a paste, you must use all the chillies, or the balance and colour of the paste will be wrong. Just use less of it in the dish and freeze the rest. Remove the seeds for appearance only. The heat (capsaicin) is in the membrane on the inside of the chilli, not the seeds.

Tamarind is the seed pod of the tamarind tree, a beautiful plant that grows around the equator. The pods contain a fruity / sour pulp containing rock-hard seeds. You can buy liquid tamarind in most supermarkets, but it is preferable to buy a block in an Asian store and make your own. To do this, break off a lump about the size of a small box of matches and soak in plenty of hot water for 10 minutes. Then massage the pulp with your hands to separate out the seeds. Finally push through a sieve. If the recipe calls for tamarind paste, don't add too much water. If tamarind water is required, just add more water. If you make too much it freezes indefinitely and the opened tamarind block also keeps indefinitely, wrapped in clingfilm in the store cupboard.

Palm sugar is available from Asian stores and has a unique flavour, but if you can't source it, substitute with light brown muscovado sugar.

Peanuts. These are peeled peanuts, not roasted or salted, and are also available from Asian stores. Simply dry roast in a medium-hot oven until golden.

Thai sticky or glutinous rice. Despite the name there is no gluten in this rice. It is a long grain rice that is naturally sticky because of the ratio of the two starches it contains: amylose and amylopectin. The ratio of these two starches affects the stickiness of the rice. Do not try and boil this rice or a gloopy mess will result! Soak in cold water overnight and then drain and steam in a bamboo (or similar) steamer basket.

Galangal. This is a hot and fibrous member of the ginger family with a unique flavour quite different to ginger. If not available fresh, you can usually buy sliced and frozen in tom yum packs.

Finger root. Another ginger relative, nicely perfumed. Substitute ginger if not available.

Pestle and mortar. Absolutely essential to making a good curry paste. It is simply not possible to achieve the same result in a blender. The ingredients are too tough, often fibrous and you will find yourself desperately adding liquid of some sort to blend them, which will ruin the paste. You need a big granite job that will take a pounding. Make lots in one go and freeze for future ease. Yes, you can buy curry paste, but fresh is so much better!

At the school we offer 2 Thai courses: Thai Street Food and Taste of Thailand. Thai Street Food is, as you would guess, food found on the street stalls/small cafés of Thailand, whereas Taste of Thailand is more about the food found in a typical Thai restaurant.

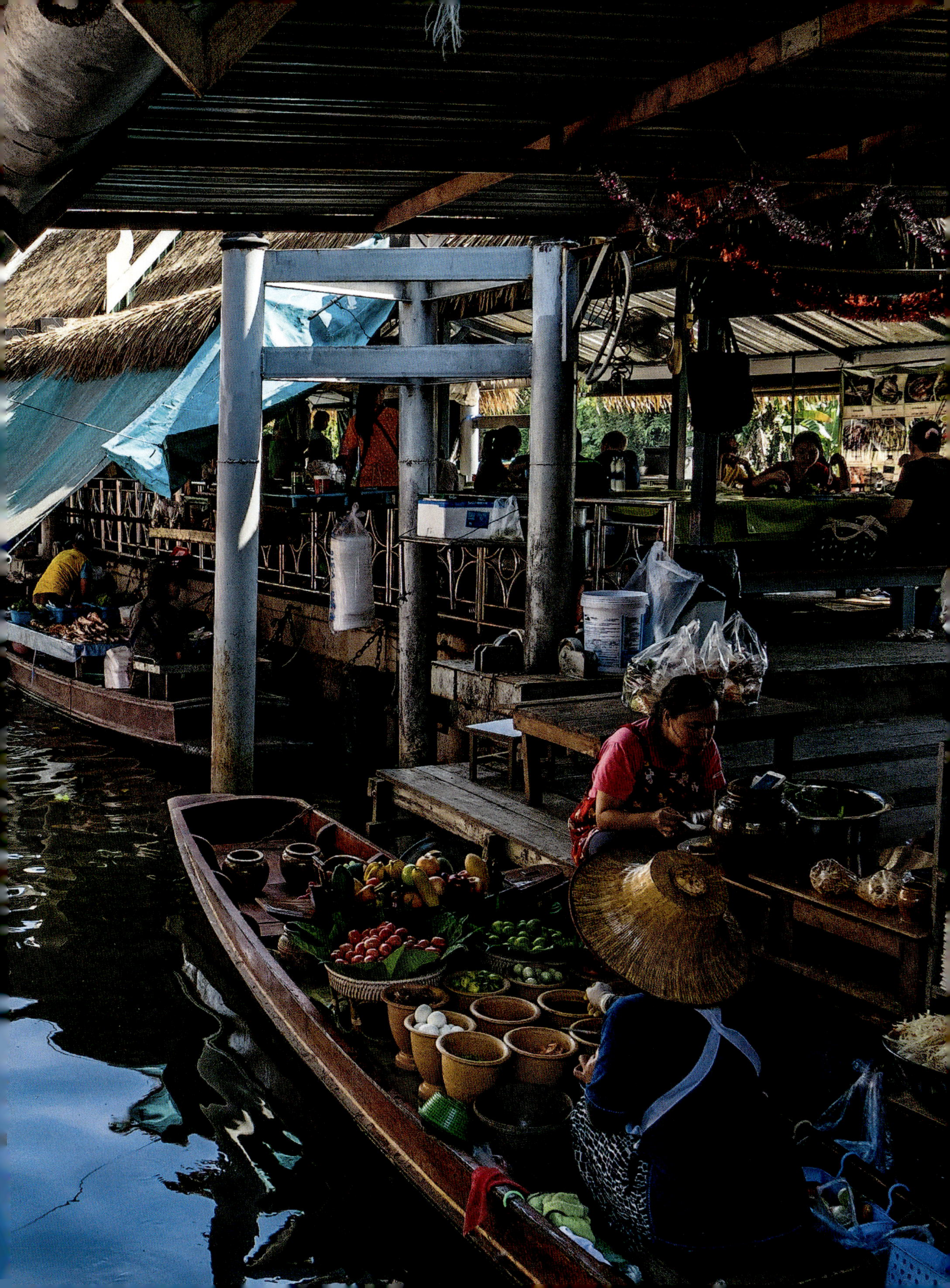

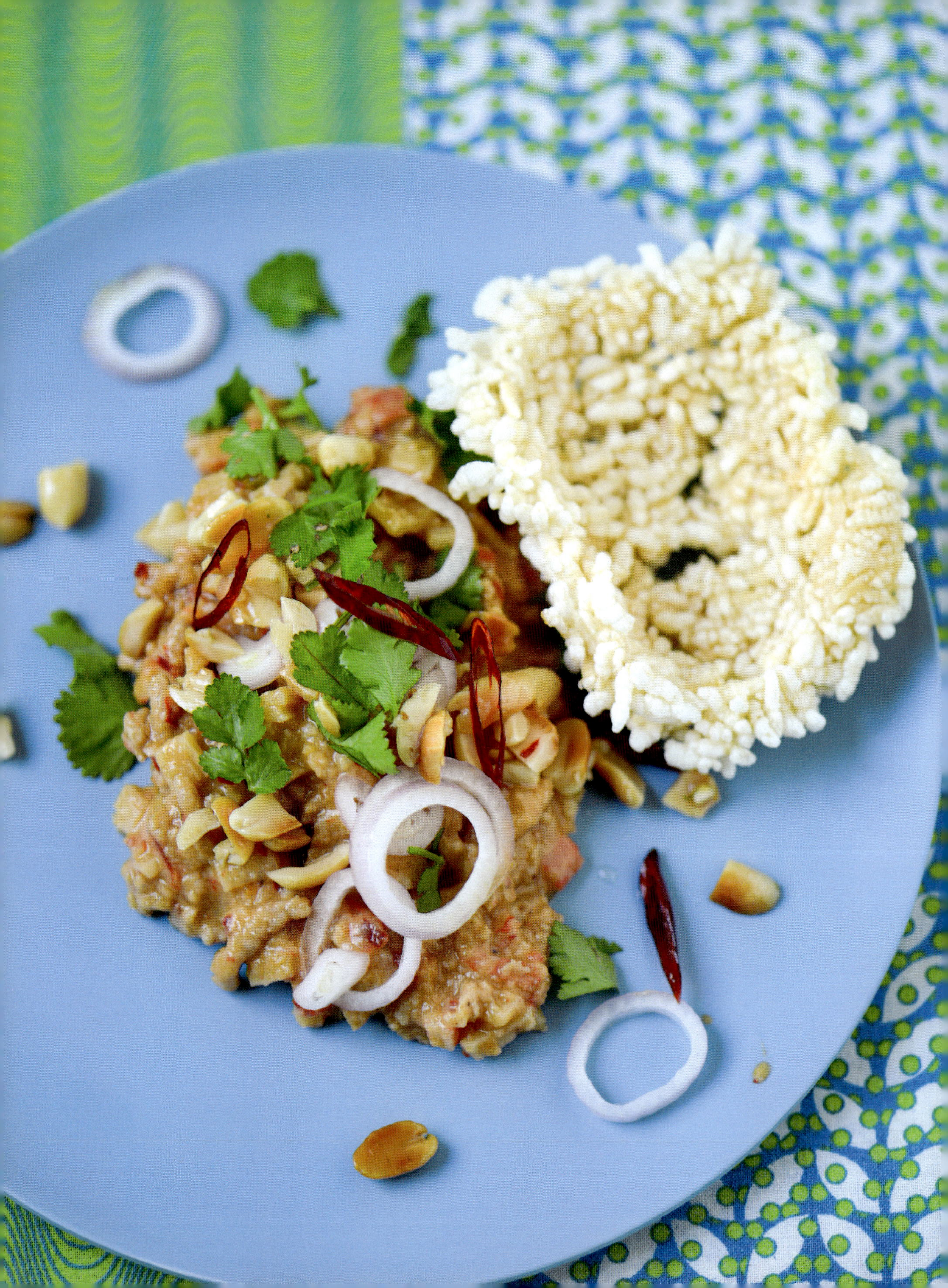

RICE CAKES WITH CHILLI, PRAWN AND PORK SAUCE

Serves 1-2

100g Thai sticky rice

4 dried red chillies, soaked in hot water for 10 minutes, then split and seeds discarded

1/4 teaspoon salt

1 tablespoon chopped shallot

1 tablespoon chopped garlic

5 white peppercorns

75ml coconut milk

1 tablespoon palm sugar

1 tablespoon fish sauce

2 tablespoons tamarind paste

30g minced raw prawns

15g minced raw pork

1 red shallot, sliced

1/2 tablespoon ground roasted peanuts (unsalted)

1/2 tablespoon coriander leaves

TO MAKE THE RICE CAKES: Soak about 100g Thai sticky (glutinous) rice in cold water overnight. The following day drain the rice and steam in a bamboo steamer basket for 25-30 minutes until well cooked.

With wet fingers, press a small ball of sticky warm rice into a rough flat circle about 6cm by 1/2cm high. Let the rice circles dry for about 2-3 hours to let them firm up a bit, then tip them onto a rack so they will dry faster and let them dry completely. I prefer to leave them uncovered, in the fridge for several days and pop them into a low oven (50°C) for about an hour to finish drying them. You can check whether they have dried completely by trying to bend the rice crackers—they should not bend at all. You can store the dry rice crackers in an airtight container indefinitely.

When ready to serve, fry the rice crackers in 190°C oil until they puff and bloom open (this takes seconds!).

TO MAKE THE SAUCE: Blend the chillies, salt, shallot, garlic and peppercorns in a pestle and mortar to make a paste.

Simmer a tablespoon of coconut milk until it separates or 'cracks', then add the paste and fry over a medium heat until fragrant. Season with palm sugar and continue to simmer for a few minutes.

Add fish sauce, tamarind, minced prawns and pork, stirring to prevent it sticking together in clumps. Moisten with coconut milk and simmer for another minute or so. Check the seasoning – it should be salty and sweet. Finally, stir in shallots, peanuts and coriander.

Serve with the cooked rice crackers.

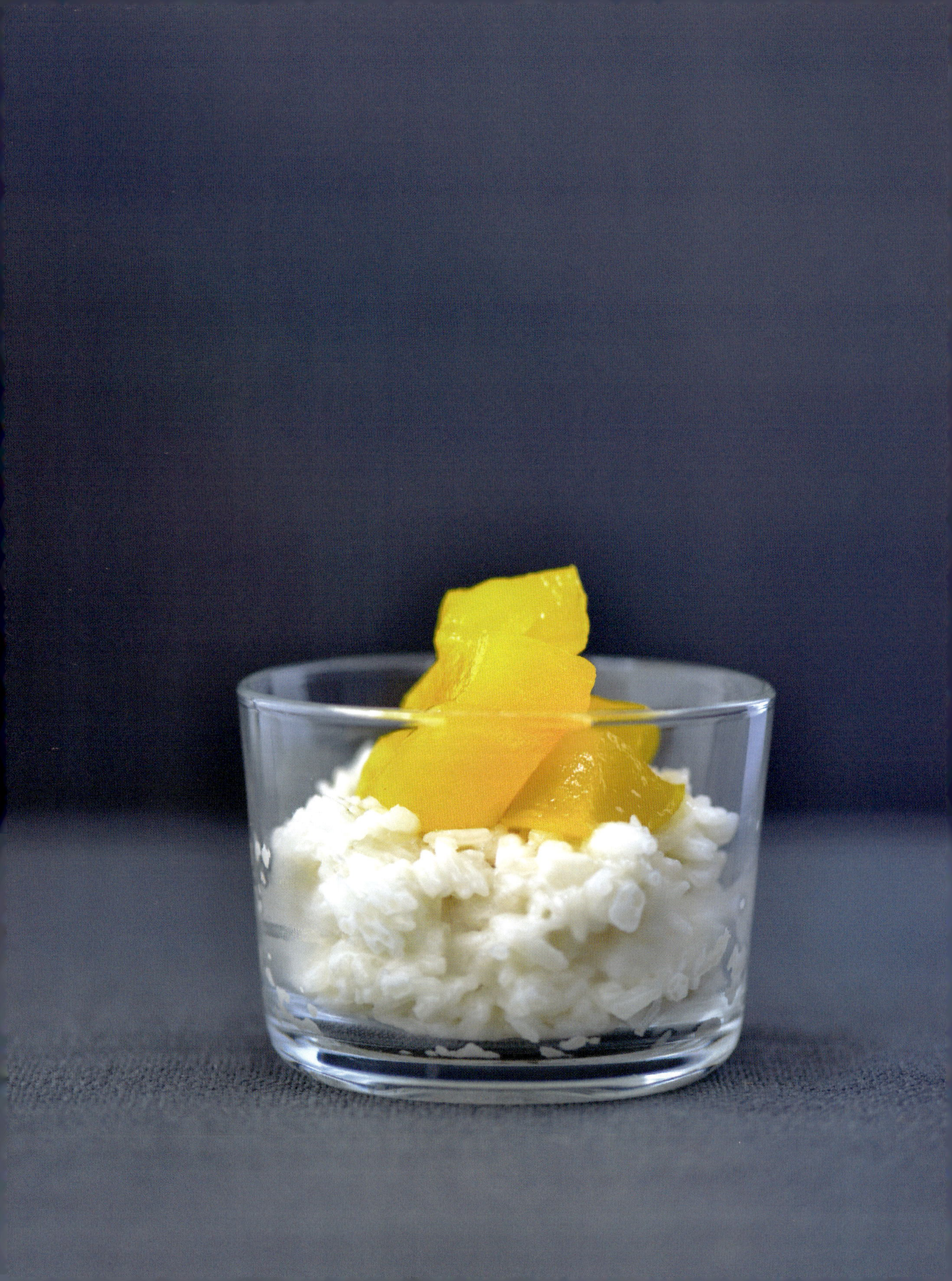

SWEET STICKY RICE WITH MANGO

Serves 1-2

- 100g Thai sticky rice
- 40ml Coconut milk
- 12g Palm sugar
- 1g fine sea salt
- 1/2 fresh, ripe mango

Soak about 100g Thai sticky (glutinous) rice in cold water overnight.

The following day drain the rice and steam in a bamboo steamer basket for 25-30 minutes until well cooked.

Warm the coconut milk, add the sugar and salt and stir to dissolve the sugar. Stir, gently, through the rice. Be careful not to turn the cooked rice into a paste! The grains should stay separate.

Peel and chop or slice the mango and serve over the sticky rice.

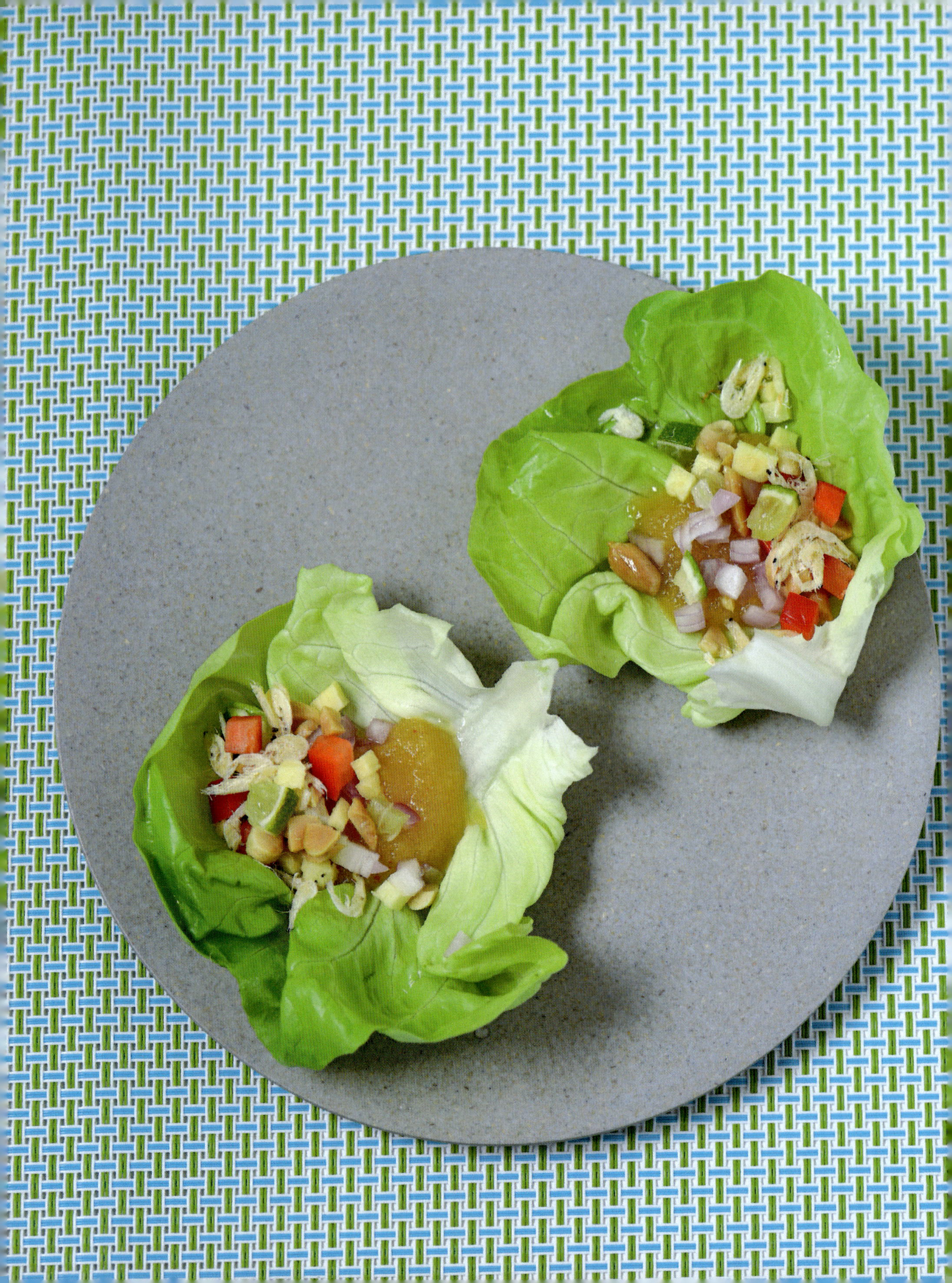

LEAF WRAPS WITH PINEAPPLE CHUTNEY

LEAF WRAPS

Betel leaves or round lettuce leaves

Dried shrimp

Shallot, chopped

Ginger, peeled and chopped

Roasted peanuts

Red pepper

Lime with skin

PINEAPPLE CHUTNEY

200g peeled and chopped pineapple or mango (fresh or frozen)

40g chopped shallot

1 fat clove of garlic, peeled

2cm piece of peeled ginger

40ml water

50g palm sugar

Fresh red chilli to taste (if not sure, cut the chilli in half rather than in small pieces and remove when the required heat is reached)

Salt to taste

Betel leaves are the traditional wrap for this dish but are hard to source in the UK and have an astringent taste that is not to everyone's liking. Lettuce is actually more popular and learners at the school love making these whilst we do introductions. It's a great way to start the Thai workshop and good fun to make at home too! Just prepare individual bowls of the ingredients and let people help themselves.

TO MAKE THE WRAPS: Chop everything, except the Betel leaves, the same size, about 3mm, and set aside.

TO MAKE THE CHUTNEY: Place all the ingredients in a small pan, bring to the boil and simmer until the fruit is soft. Liquidise to a smooth paste (add a little water if the mix is too thick). Chill before use.

TOP TIP

For a less intense chutney remove the chilli before blending. Excess chutney freezes well.

TO SERVE: Place all the chopped ingredients and the chutney in little bowls with a teaspoon in each one. Let your guests help themselves to a lettuce leaf and spoon a little of each ingredient onto their leaf. Fold each leaf into a little parcel so that the filling is completely enclosed and eat in one bite.

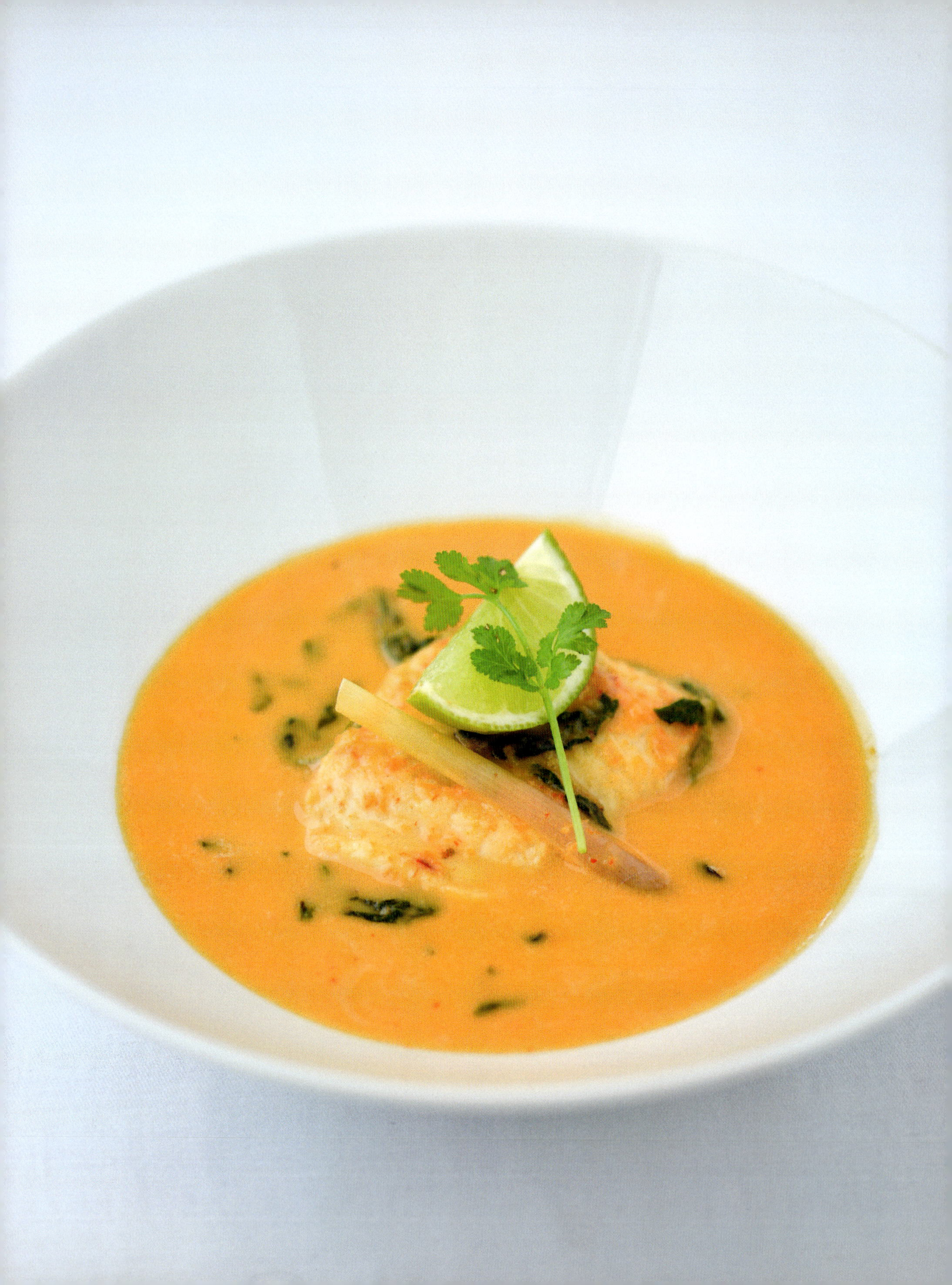

FISH RED CURRY

Serves 2 with some curry paste left over

CURRY PASTE

16 large dried red chillies, de-seeded and soaked for 20 minutes in hot water, draining before use

1/2 teaspoon salt

2 teaspoons coriander seeds

2 strips lime peel

1 stalk lemongrass

1 3-4cm piece galangal

Finger root: 4 fingers (or 2cm ginger)

2 round shallots

2 cloves garlic

FISH CURRY

1 tin coconut milk (400ml)

2 x 100g fillets of firm white fish (I like to use two nice pieces of fish rather than chunks)

2 kaffir lime leaves

Fish sauce

Fresh lime juice

Palm sugar

Fresh coriander and Thai basil

TO MAKE THE CURRY PASTE: Chop everything as finely as you can by hand and pound all of the ingredients in batches (in the order below) in a pestle and mortar until smooth:

Pound the coriander seeds and salt first. When this is finely ground, add the lime peel and lemongrass. Pound until smooth. Next add the chillies and pound until completely smooth.

Follow with the galangal and finger root / ginger and pound again until smooth, then finish by pounding the shallot and garlic.

TO FINISH THE CURRY: Take two tablespoons of coconut milk (make sure it is from the top of the tin, so it's nice and thick) and heat in a saucepan until the fat separates out and it starts to spit.

Fry a generous teaspoon per person of curry paste in this oil and cook, stirring for a couple of minutes. Add the rest of the coconut milk and the lime leaf and cook the curry sauce for a few minutes. Taste and season with fish sauce, palm sugar and lime juice aiming for a balance of hot, sour, salty and sweet. If the curry is too mild add more paste or fresh chilli.

Add the fish and simmer gently to cook until the fish just starts to flake — don't overcook.

Taste again before serving, the fish will draw out some of the seasoning.

If you want to add more vegetables do so now, along with the herbs, and serve.

TOP TIP

Serve with steamed or sticky rice and add more vegetables to the curry if you wish, bean shoots, baby corn, pak choy etc., add these at the last minute so they don't overcook.

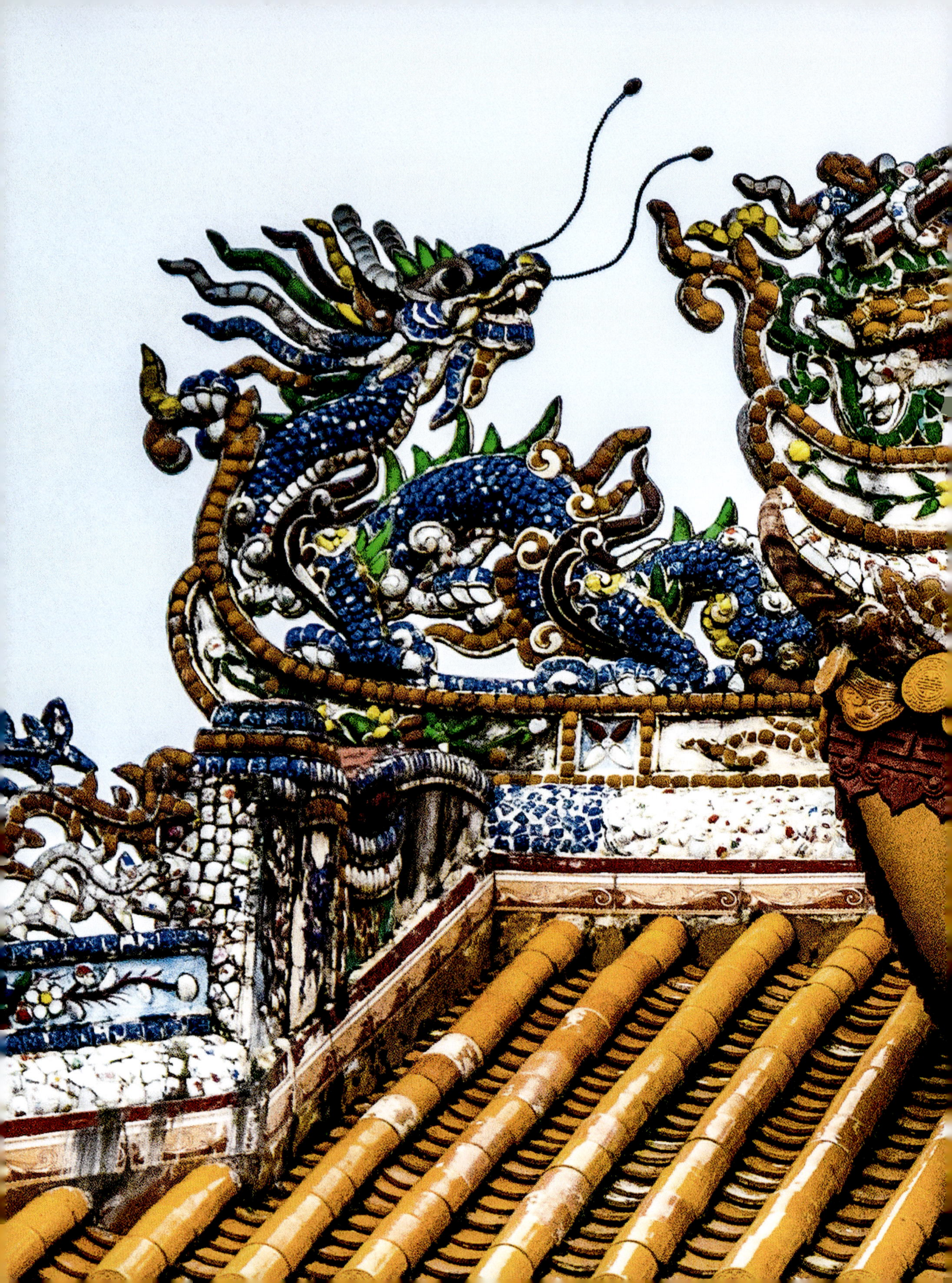

TASTE OF CHINA

I must be honest; I have a love / hate relationship with Chinese food. When it is cooked properly it is without doubt one of the great cuisines of the world, but the average high street Chinese in the UK leaves me feeling deeply disappointed. It is a long time since I was in Hong Kong, but the excitement of the food and the markets is a fond memory.

When I started in recipe development, my first project was developing Chinese ready meals for a leading retailer. They didn't send me to China unfortunately, but I did get to spend time working at the Michelin-starred Oriental restaurant at the Dorchester Hotel and also discussed a collaboration (which sadly didn't happen) with Hakkasan in London. We decided that braised chicken feet were perhaps not mainstream enough for the UK market(!), but I did have the best steamed bao with char sui pork in my life. I tried to limit myself to one (they are quite filling) but in the end I scoffed the lot — about four, I think! Dipped into crispy chilli oil, they are incredibly moreish!

It is fascinating watching Chinese chefs at work. In a classical French style kitchen, we use a multitude of pots and pans, which all need repeated washing during service time, as well as the 'right' knife for the 'right' job. Chinese chefs have one pan each (a wok) and one knife (a cleaver), and that's it. Such economy of utensils makes the life of the kitchen porter so much easier!

Working at a different food manufacturer I had responsibility for developing chilled stir fry sauces for all of the UK retailers, bar one. Once again, no trip to China, but I did get to go home each day with a whiff of the Orient about me!

On the Chinese workshop we steer well clear of gloopy sauces and tinned pineapple. Chinese food is so complex and varied and I try to offer a snapshot of that. Ants Climbing Trees is a favourite, not least for the name. The Chinese are highly inventive when it comes to naming dishes. The 'ants' are little pieces of minced pork and the 'trees', mung bean starch (or glass) noodles, so called for their transparency. I love them for their texture and ease of use. They can be bought as a large bundle, but it is much easier to look for the bags of mini packs. One pack equals one serving. Trying to separate a big bundle is like trying to pull apart tangled wire and bits break off and shoot everywhere. As there are Chinese supermarkets in the UK now, many ingredients are much easier to come by.

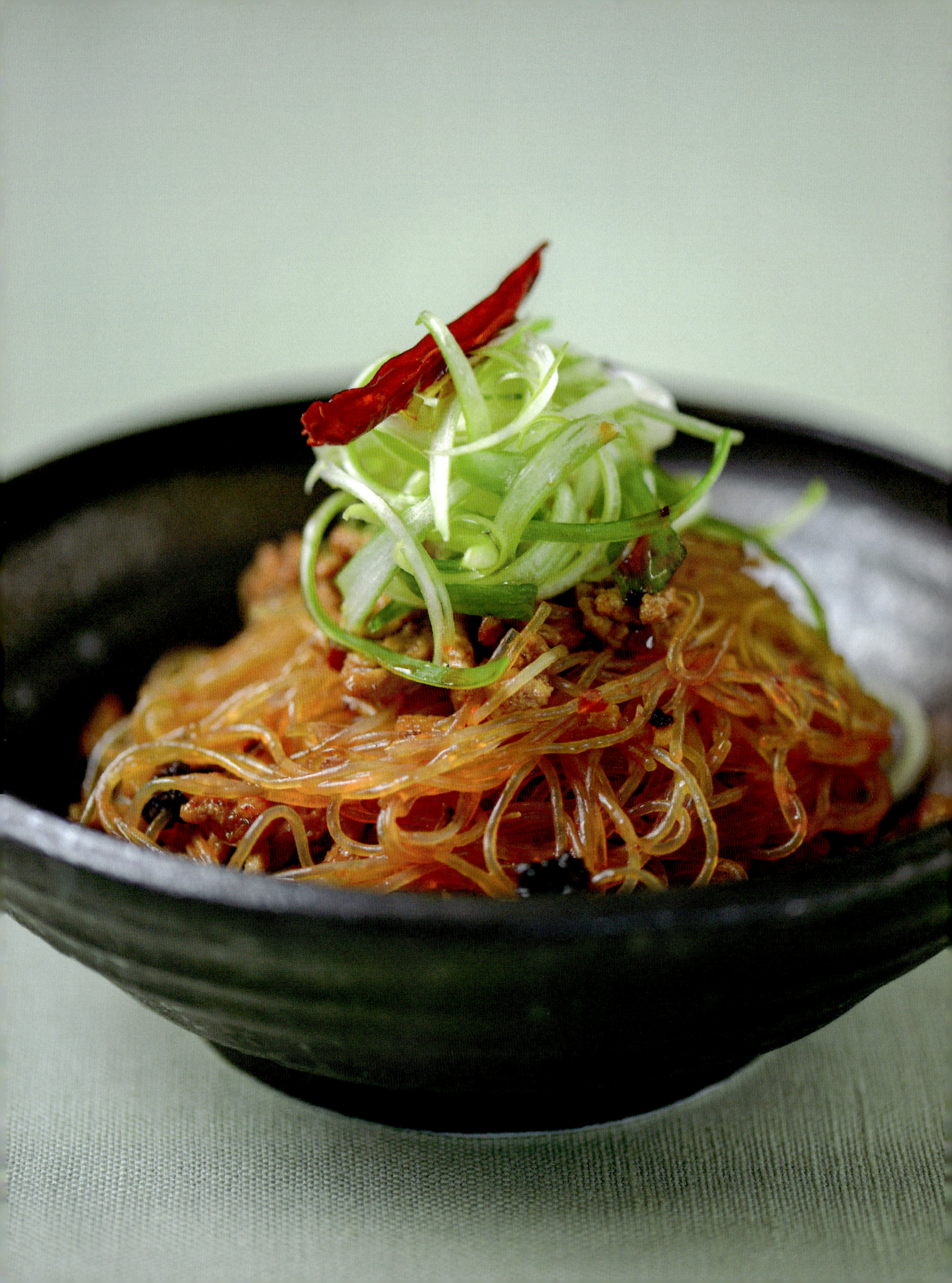

ANTS CLIMBING TREES

Serves 1

- 60g bean thread noodles (1 small pack)
- 80g minced pork
- 1/2 tablespoon oil
- 2 spring onions
- 1/2 tablespoon finely chopped ginger
- 1 garlic clove finely chopped
- 1 tsp chilli bean paste
- 1/2 tablespoon soy sauce
- 1/2 tablespoon Shaoxing rice wine
- 1/4 teaspoon sugar
- 1/4 teaspoon roasted sesame oil
- 50ml chicken stock (a stock cube is fine)

Pour boiling water over the noodles, leave for 5 minutes, then drain and reserve.

Finely chop the white part of the spring onion and cut the green into shreds.

Heat a wok or frying pan until very hot, add the oil and stir-fry the meat until golden brown. Push to one side of the pan and add the white spring onion, ginger, garlic, chilli bean paste and stir-fry for a few seconds. Mix together with the meat.

Add soy sauce, rice wine, sugar, sesame oil and chicken stock. Stir together. Then add the noodles and boil the mix until most of the liquid has reduced, the dish should be nearly dry.

Serve topped with the shredded green part of the spring onion.

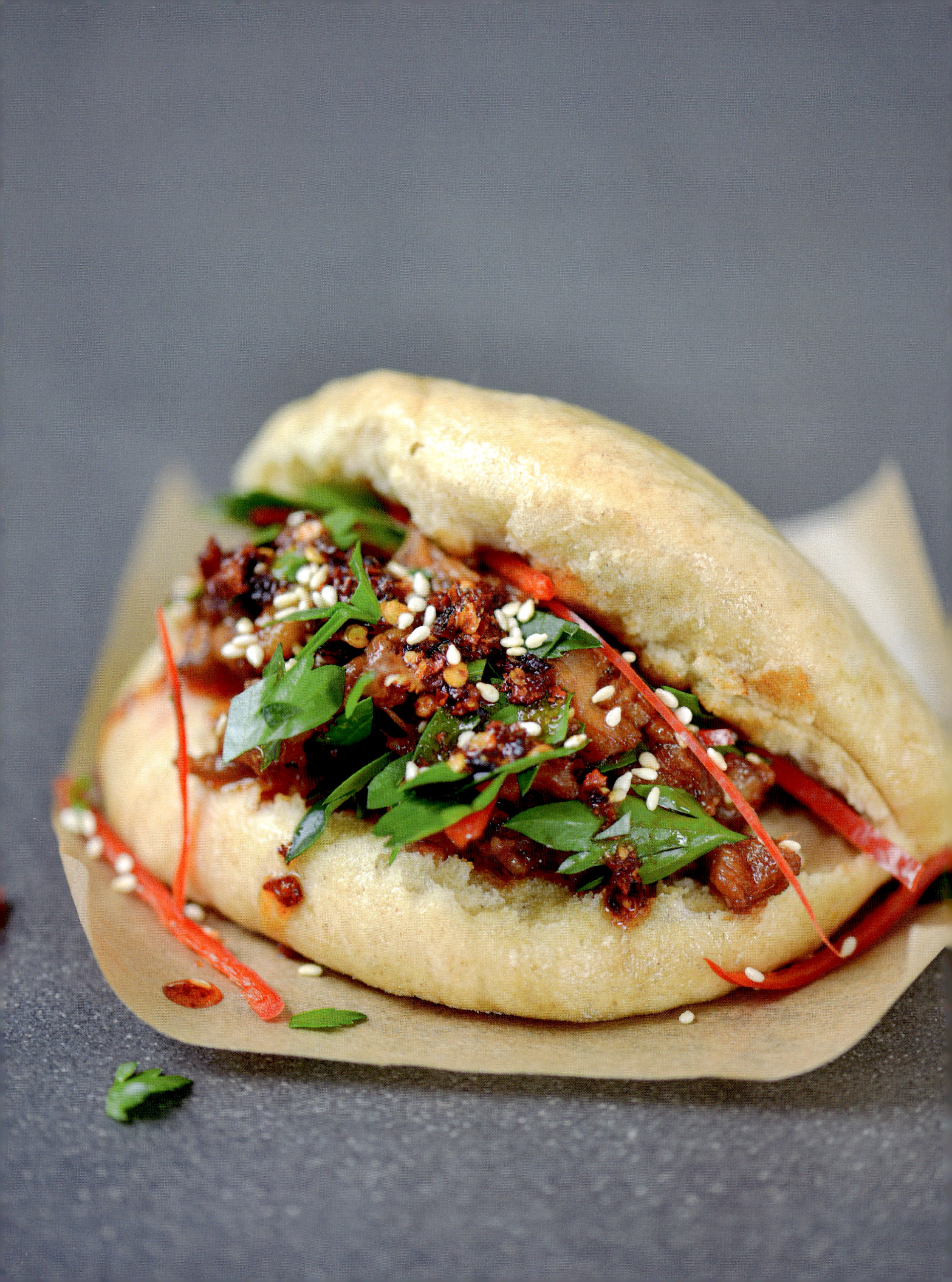

CHAR SIU BAO

Serves 2

- 25g hoisin sauce (buy or use the recipe below)
- 150 - 160g pork belly
- 175g plain flour
- 2g yeast
- 2g baking powder
- 30g sugar
- 10g cold lard (or butter)
- 100ml water
- Soy sauce or crispy chilli sauce for dipping

TOP TIP

Don't over-crowd. You may only be able to cook one or two at a time, so just keep them warm as you go.

Preheat the oven to 160°C

TO MAKE THE CHAR SUI PORK: Mix the pork belly and hoisin together and place in an ovenproof dish, then cover with tin foil and bake for 90 minutes, or until very tender. Allow to cool, and dice finely. There should just be enough sauce left to keep everything moist. Reserve.

TO MAKE THE DOUGH: Mix together the flour, yeast, baking powder and sugar. Rub the lard into the flour mix, add the water and mix to a soft dough. Cover and leave to prove until doubled in size.

Divide into 4 and roll each piece out to an oval about 5mm thick. Then flour well and fold loosely in half. Place each bao onto a piece of parchment, cover with a piece of oiled cling film, or a tea towel, and leave to prove again for 30 minutes. Steam for 10 minutes in a bamboo steamer basket.

TO SERVE: Once cooked, gently prise each bun open and stuff with char siu pork. You can add some red chilli, chopped parsley, or coriander and a few sesame seeds to add colour and texture. Serve with soy sauce or crispy chilli sauce for dipping.

HOISIN SAUCE

- 4 tablespoons soy sauce
- 2 tablespoons tomato paste
- 1 tablespoon honey or brown sugar
- 2 teaspoons white or black vinegar
- 2 teaspoons sesame oil
- 1 teaspoon chilli in oil
- 1/4 teaspoon black pepper

Place all the ingredients in a small pan and heat gently until everything is nicely mixed.

BAKING

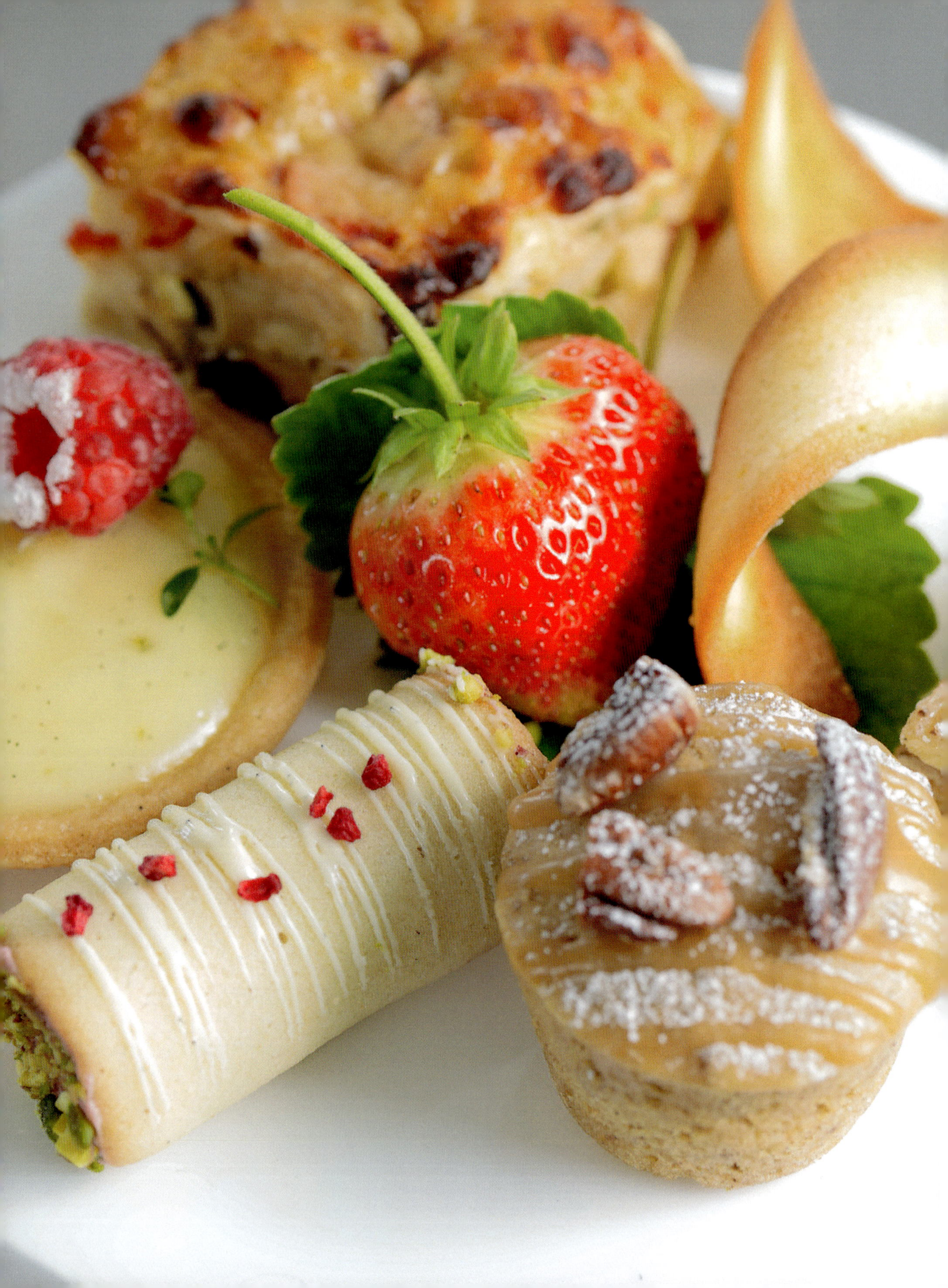

BAKING FOR AFTERNOON TEA

Tea consumption increased dramatically during the early nineteenth century and it is around this time that Anna, the 7th Duchess of Bedford, is said to have complained of 'having that sinking feeling' during the late afternoon. At the time it was usual for people to take only two main meals a day, breakfast, and dinner at around 8 o'clock in the evening. The solution for the Duchess was a pot a tea and a light snack, taken privately in her boudoir during the afternoon.

Later friends were invited to join her in her rooms at Woburn Abbey and this summer practice proved so popular that the Duchess continued it when she returned to London, sending cards to her friends asking them to join her for 'tea and a walk in the fields'.

Other social hostesses quickly picked up on the idea and the practice became respectable enough to move it into the drawing room. Before long all of fashionable society was sipping tea and nibbling sandwiches in the middle of the afternoon.

Afternoon tea has become increasingly popular over the last 10 years or so, to the point that even some pubs offer it! Afternoon tea is very profitable for restauranteurs especially since it fills an eating gap between lunch and dinner. Portion sizes seem commensurate with cost, unfortunately there is nothing delicate about large sandwiches and a huge slice of Victoria sponge. The recipes we bake on the Afternoon Tea workshop are petite — designed as two bites maximum per piece. This enables a full selection to be sampled, a little bit of everything. Which is how it should be.

My good friend Graham developed these two recipes and we made them on the first workshop that Graham and his wife Rose ran with me. I have known Graham since I was 18 or so, but we didn't work together until much later. Graham was the executive pastry chef at the Connaught Hotel. Usually when I research recipes, I adjust them to my style/taste, but these are two of only a handful of recipes I have not needed to modify!

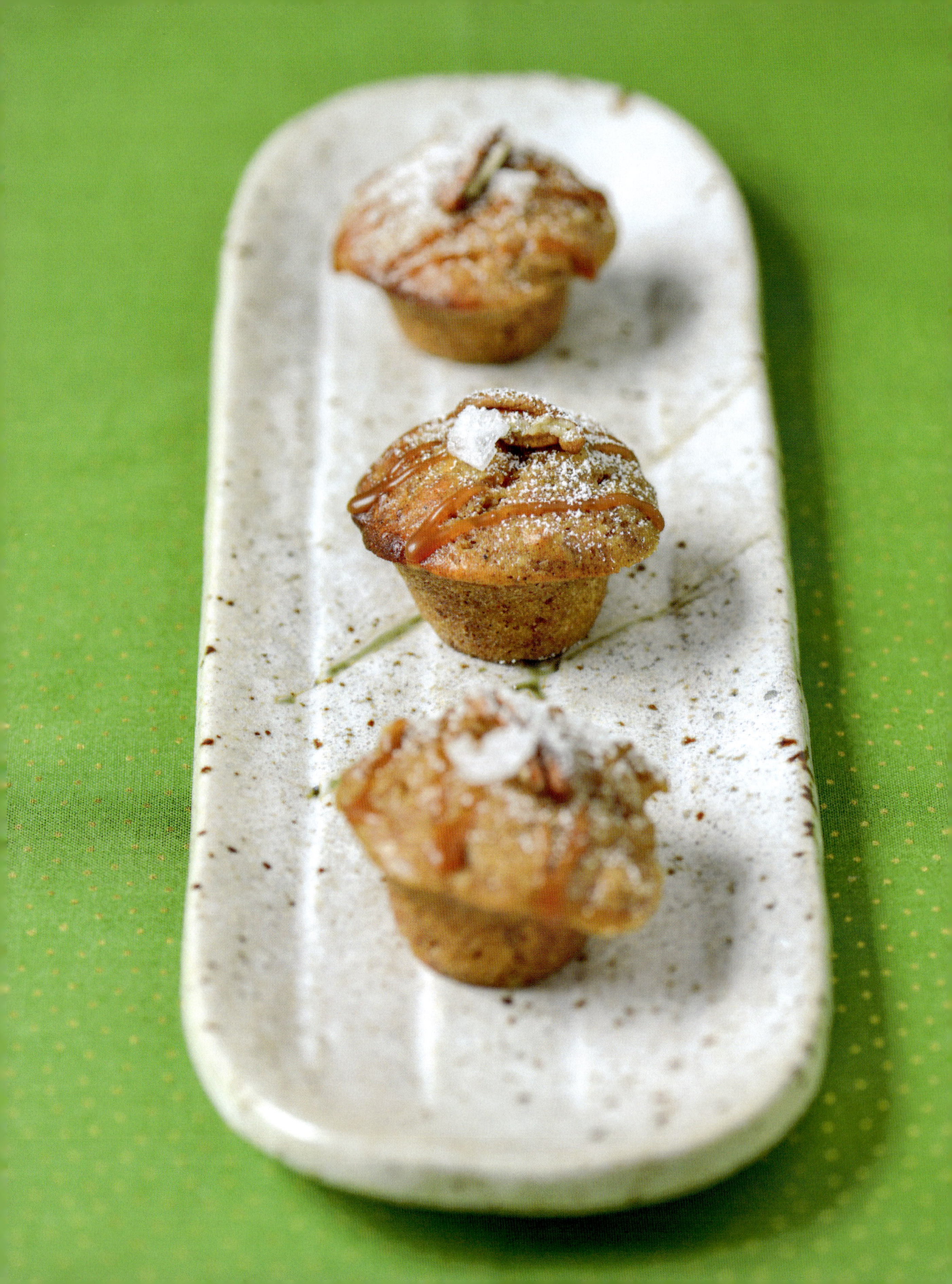

MINI PECAN & SALTED CARAMEL CAKES

Makes 8

SALTED CARAMEL

95g water

10g glucose syrup

180g caster sugar

75g unsalted butter

1/2 teaspoon sea salt

140ml double cream

CAKE BASE

15g butter

15g sunflower oil

65ml buttermilk

1 egg

1/4 teaspoon vanilla essence

40g light soft brown sugar

70g self-raising flour

1/2 - 1 teaspoon ground cinnamon

Pinch of salt

20g roughly chopped pecan nuts

Plus half a pecan to decorate each cake

TO MAKE THE CARAMEL: Combine butter, sugar, water, salt, and glucose syrup in a medium sized pan. (The mix will rise when the cream is added during the next stage, so make sure your pan is big enough). Place over a low heat to melt the butter and then turn up to a medium heat, stirring constantly with a whisk, until the mixture thickens. Then use a wooden spoon, keep stirring until the mixture has turned a deep golden brown. Immediately remove the pan from the heat and add the cream in 3 stages, stirring until combined (if you add the cream in one go it will boil over). Transfer the caramel to a bowl to cool.

Preheat the oven to 170°C. Grease 8 small baking moulds — mini muffin tins are just right.

TO MAKE THE CAKES: Whisk together the oil, buttermilk, egg and vanilla in a bowl, then melt the butter and add that as well. Whisk in the brown sugar. Sieve the rest of the dry ingredients together and combine with the wet mixture, along with the roughly chopped pecans. Do not over mix! It doesn't matter if a few small lumps remain.

Divide the mixture evenly between the 8 moulds and bake for 10-12 minutes. Leave for 10 minutes before removing them from the moulds.

Using a small piping bag with a very small nozzle, inject a little salted caramel into the centre of each cake. Do this whilst they are still warm. Garnish with a drizzle of salted caramel and a few roasted pecans and finish with a few grains of Maldon sea salt.

> **TOP TIP**
>
> These cakes eat well when warm. They are best eaten fresh but will keep up to 5 days in an airtight container. They freeze well for up to 2 months.

CIGARETTE BISCUITS FILLED WITH GANACHE

Makes 6

CIGARETTE PASTE

50g soft unsalted butter

55g sieved icing sugar

50g plain flour

40g egg white whisked

Drop of vanilla extract

GANACHE FILLING

50g raspberry puree (frozen raspberries or fresh depending on seasonality, pushed through a sieve or blended in a liquidiser)

65g chopped white chocolate

80ml double cream

Chopped pistachio nuts, melted white chocolate and dried raspberry pieces to decorate.

NOTE: You will need to make a stencil for the cigarette paste, 11cm x 6cm oblong. (see photos below) A sheet of heavy, gloss photographic paper works well. This can be handwashed in soapy water and used again.

Preheat the oven to 180°C (fan)

TO MAKE THE CIGARETTE PASTE: Cream the butter with the icing sugar and vanilla. Add a little of the egg white and mix, then add a little flour and blend well. Add more egg white and flour alternately until you have a smooth soft paste.

Lay the stencil on a piece of greaseproof paper and spread the paste to fit the centre of the stencil. Remove the stencil, carefully place the greaseproof paper onto a baking sheet and bake for around 5 minutes until just coloured. Keep an eye on them! They must not over bake.

> **TOP TIP**
>
> Do not bake more than 2 cigarettes at a time as they cool quickly and will be too brittle to roll.

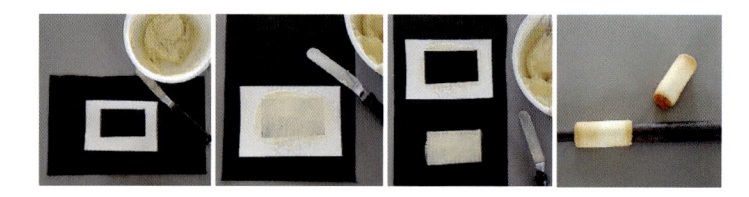

Remove from the oven and roll around a tubular form. Whilst still on the tube, press down firmly on the seam so the tubes do not try and unroll. Leave to cool until required for filling.

> **TOP TIP**
>
> At the school we use little Indian rolling pins I brought back with me from Mumbai, but short lengths of plastic plumbing pipe, approx. 15mm diameter, work well and can be cut into short lengths with a hacksaw.

TO MAKE THE GANACHE: Heat the raspberry puree until warm and add the chopped chocolate. Mix until smooth, using a little more heat if required. Do not overheat! Allow to cool completely.

Whip the cream until very thick but still smooth. Fold into the raspberry and chocolate puree and mix until very smooth.

TO ASSEMBLE: Using a piping bag fill a cigarette biscuit with the ganache filling. Dip the ends in chopped pistachio nuts and drizzle a little liquid white chocolate along the length of the cigarette. Finally sprinkle with a few dried raspberry pieces.

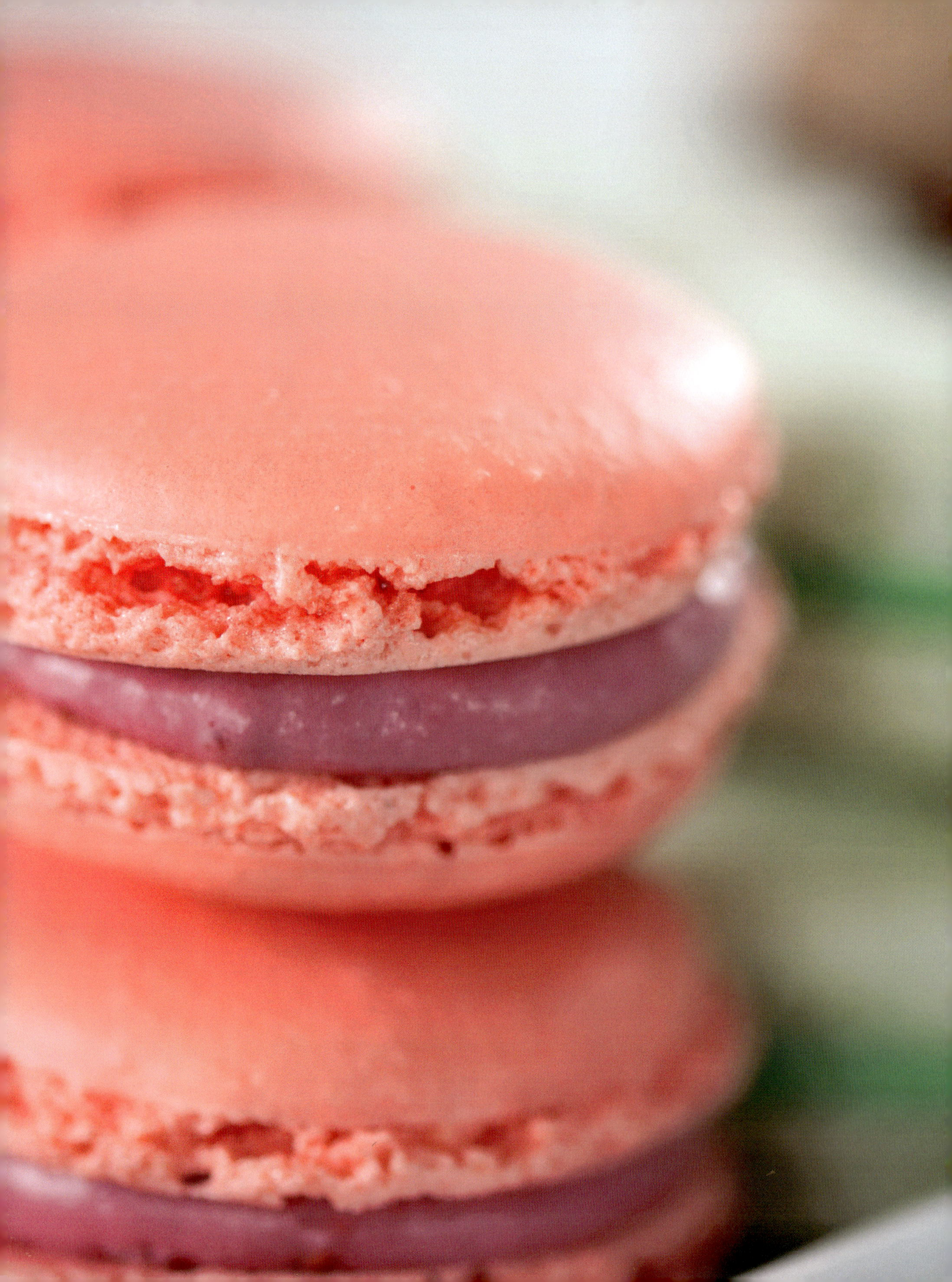

MACARONS

Tricky little devils macarons and not to be confused with macaroons which are coconut cookies and quite different. Macarons are just fancy meringues really but getting them right every time takes a little bit of know-how. It is not unusual to get learners at the school who have made them successfully only to follow-up with a batch that failed. Why?

Firstly, let's distinguish between the two methods: Italian meringue and French meringue. Italian meringue involves a cooked syrup poured gradually onto egg whites as they are being whisked. French meringues are simply whisked egg whites with caster sugar that are then baked in a low oven. This recipe uses the French meringue method which is much simpler and works better in small quantities

Secondly, the whisking. The time taken to whisk the egg whites will seem the longest nine minutes of your life (it does mine every time I demonstrate it!) but do stick with it — it works. Increasing the speed gradually builds a very thick and strong meringue which is what you need. It makes no difference adding the sugar gradually, which is why we dump it all in at the beginning. Do make sure your bowl is clean before you start though. Egg whites don't like grease (or any egg yolk), so a quick squirt of vinegar, or lemon juice, and a wipe with kitchen paper is a good idea.

Thirdly, the macronage. This is the stage of folding in the icing sugar and ground almonds into the whisked egg whites. Much of that carefully incorporated air needs to be released — but too much and your macarons will spread and be thin, not enough and they will not spread at all. Much like Goldilocks and the Three Bears, something in the middle will be just right. Some recipes refer to this texture as resembling molten lava.

The problem with molten lava, though, is that there are several types. It can flow fluidly like syrup, or hardly move at all, so this advice is not very helpful. Perhaps like thickly whipped cream before it sets, it's not runny, it still flows, but slowly. It takes practice. It is unlikely your first batch will be your best — but they always taste delicious!

Finally, they are sensitive to oven temperatures too. At the school we get best results from a longer, slower cook than most recipes suggest. Our ovens are electric, fan assisted, and the fans cannot be turned off.

Once again, practice and don't be afraid to tweak the temperature, and time, if you think it may help. Test with small batches initially. Pipe the full recipe onto two trays, not one. That way you can have a second go. The second tray will sit quite happily on the table whilst you bake the first half.

TOP TIP

Do make sure that food colouring is heat-stable. The stuff in tubes for colouring frosting is usually not and the colour will bake out. Check the pack. Dry powder food colouring is much better than liquid. Any 'inclusions' you make to the basic recipe can affect the end result and powder works much better than liquid.

RASPBERRY MACARONS WITH WHITE CHOCOLATE & RASPBERRY FILLING

Makes 10 (20 half shells)

SHELLS

46g ground almonds

92g icing sugar

58g egg white

29g caster sugar

0.7g salt

Red food colouring (powder, heat stable)

FILLING

150g raspberry jam

125g white chocolate

TO MAKE THE SHELLS: Sieve the ground almonds and icing sugar together, then using an electric whisk, whisk the egg white and caster sugar on low speed for 3 minutes. Increase the speed to medium and whisk for another 3 minutes, then increase the speed to full and whisk for final 3 minutes. At this point the egg whites will be very stiff.

Carefully fold the sieved almonds and icing sugar into the egg white. Fold in carefully — you must keep the mix as thick as possible at this stage.

Stir once, slowly and carefully, to release a little air. Repeat until you reach the required consistency (like thickly whipped, but still flow-able cream — see notes about the macronage stage above).

Make sure all the meringue is evenly mixed — bits of unmixed meringue from the top of the bowl will cause problems if they get scraped into the piping bag.

Prepare a baking sheet as detailed in the introduction.

Spoon the mixture into a piping bag fitted with a small plain 1cm tube. Be careful not to squeeze out more air from the meringue or it will become thinner. Pipe 3cm diameter discs for the shells.

> **TOP TIP**
>
> Hold the piping bag directly over the marked circles and keep at the same level. Do not lift the bag upwards as you pipe.

Put a tea towel on the table and gently tap the tray to release any air pockets in the meringues.

Some recipes suggest standing for 30 minutes to form a skin. This is not essential. It makes little difference to baking straight away. At the school, by the time we get to the second and third batches (we make three types), oven space is at a premium, so they go in as soon as piped.

Bake at 125°C (fan) for 28 minutes

Allow to cool on the tray for about 5 minutes before carefully removing to a cooling rack. Pair up evenly sized halves at the same time.

TO MAKE THE FILLING: Warm the raspberry jam in a small pan, stirring all the time. Break the chocolate into small pieces and stir into the jam until it is melted and the mix is smooth. Leave to cool before use.

TO ASSEMBLE: Pipe the filling carefully onto one shell half and gently twist the second half, down onto the filling so it spreads the filling to the edge in a neat circle.

Refrigerate for 24 hours before serving at room temperature.

TOP TIP

Silicon baking mats are useful for macarons, but not essential, greaseproof paper is fine. Likewise, the very expensive macaron mats with circles or indentations on them are not necessary. Simply take a 3cm plain piping nozzle, dip it into icing sugar and 'mark' your circles onto your lined baking sheet. Space them out! Unless your mix is too thick the macarons will spread a little and you must allow for this.

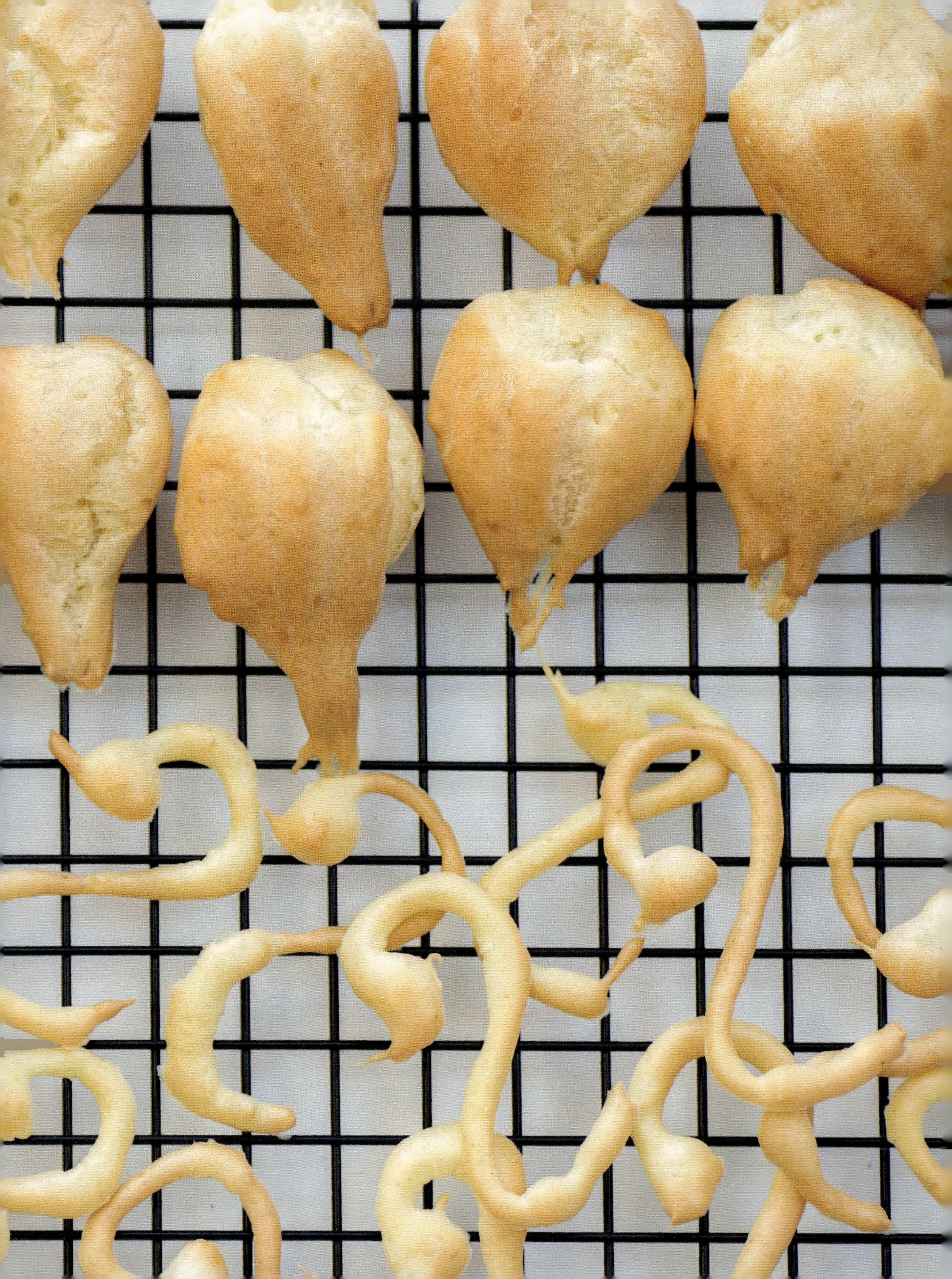

PATISSERIE

Choux pastry swans are a regular feature on the patisserie workshop, simply because they are such fun to make! Very retro, I admit, but there is quite a bit of skill involved in making and cooking the choux correctly, and filling and using a piping bag — not something that many people do at home now and very different to piping icing on a cake.

We also make a small piping bag from greaseproof paper for piping the necks and heads. You can, of course, use a normal piping bag with a very thin nozzle, but it is actually easier (with a bit of practice) to make your own and is another skill for learners to master.

I like to keep the filling to a simple whipped cream sweetened with a little sugar, but you could add a few berries too, or make a pastry cream filling. It's up to you. The initial piping and baking are usually met with some trepidation, but it is so worth it to see the joy on people's faces, as ugly ducklings are transformed into beautiful swans!

Another favourite on the Patisserie workshop is the sweet pastry pear tart, or Pear Bourdaloue. The trick to making sweet pastry is to not add any water. Some recipes do and when baked, this water evaporates, and the pastry shrinks. When you start to make this pastry, it does seem too dry — it isn't! Keep kneading gently and it will come together. The biggest problem I find learners have, is simply working too slowly and overworking the paste, to the point the butter gets too warm and you end up with a greasy paste. Work quickly and if you have warm hands, chill them in cold water and if you think the paste is getting too warm, stop and put it in the fridge for 10 minutes.

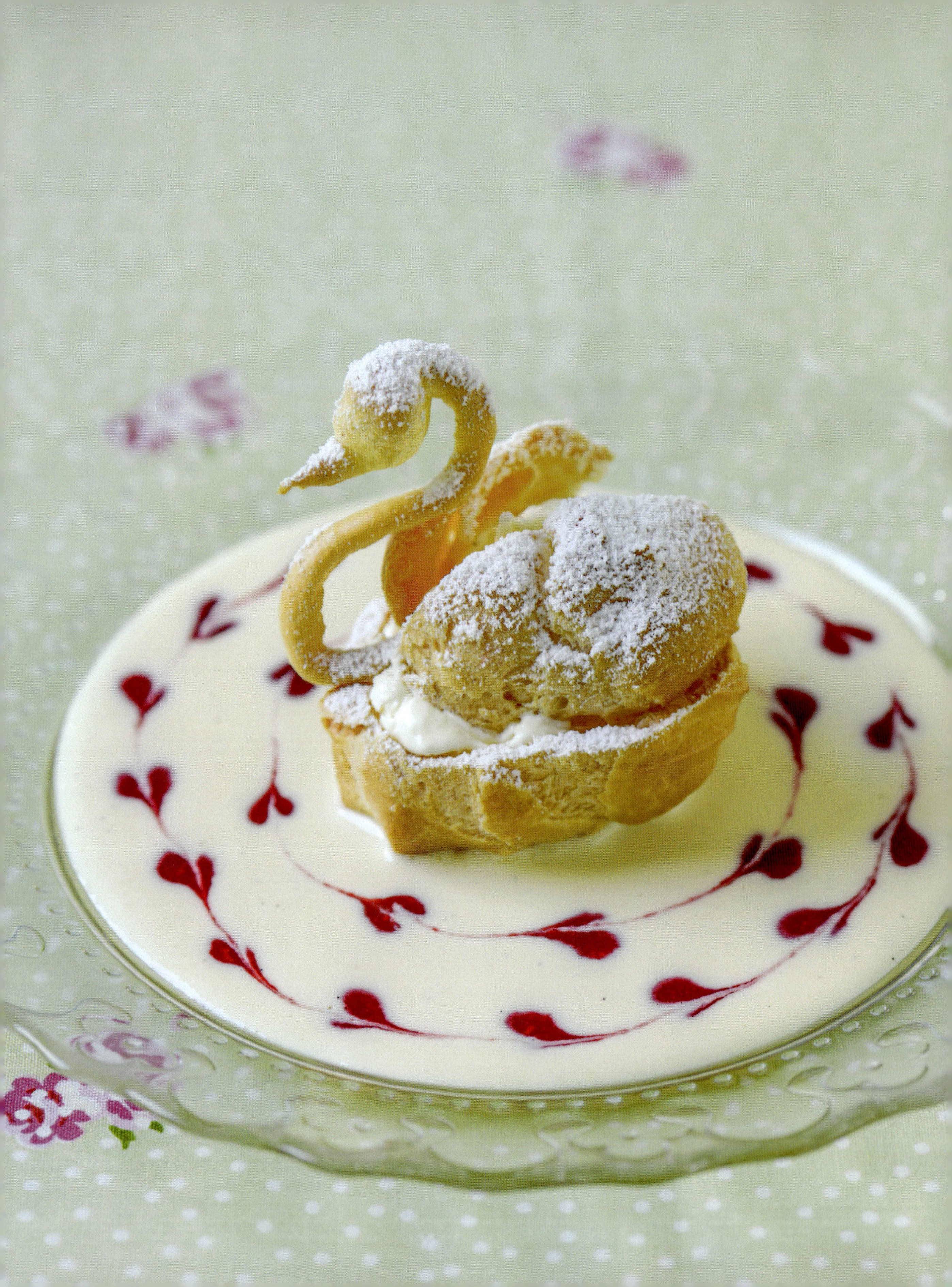

CHOUX PASTRY SWANS

Makes 8

CHOUX PASTRY

112g water (or 112ml, but must be accurate)

30g butter

1/4 teaspoon salt (1.5g)

62g plain flour (sifted)

2 medium eggs (100g)

FILLING

Whipped cream

Icing sugar to decorate

TOP TIP

The swans look very elegant floating on a pool of crème Anglaise, and a few drops of sweetened fresh raspberry puree adds a final touch.

TO MAKE THE CHOUX PASTRY: Bring the water, butter and salt to the boil in a saucepan. Tip in the flour, in one steady stream. Keep whisking until the mixture clings to the whisk. Swap the whisk for a spoon and beat well over the heat for 2-3 minutes, until the mixture is glossy and comes away from the edges of the pan. Transfer the mixture to a bowl and beat the eggs in one at a time. You are aiming for a smooth, glossy, piping consistency.

TO PIPE: Preheat the oven to 180°C (fan) and line 2 baking sheets with parchment. (A dab of paste on the underside of the parchment will stop it sliding around.)

Put a heaped teaspoon of choux paste into a small piping bag and, using a fine nozzle approx. 3mm, start by piping a small ball of paste, about 5mm across, on one lined baking sheet, for the head. Drag a little paste out from the left side of the head to form the beak. Then from the right side of the head, pipe a smooth reverse 'S', about 4-5cm long, for the neck. Repeat 8 times. Bake in the oven for about 5-8 minutes until risen and golden.

Whilst the necks are baking, pipe the bodies. Using a 10-15mm star nozzle fill a full-size piping bag with the remaining choux paste. Holding the bag vertically above the other lined baking sheet, pipe a dome about the size of a ping-pong ball and, to finish, drag your piping bag down to one side to form the 'tail'. Repeat 8 times.

Bake for 26 minutes. Do not open the door during this time! When 26 minutes have elapsed turn the oven off, open the door briefly to release excess steam, and then close the door again. Leave the bodies to cool slightly in the oven.

TO ASSEMBLE: Remove the bodies from the oven and, using a serrated knife, carefully cut across the top of the body to remove about a 1/3rd — always do this as soon as they come out of the oven. It is much easier with warm, crisp shells. Then cut each top into two pieces lengthways — these are the wings. Fill each body with some stiffly whipped cream, place the wings on top and slip the neck and head into the front. Dust with icing sugar.

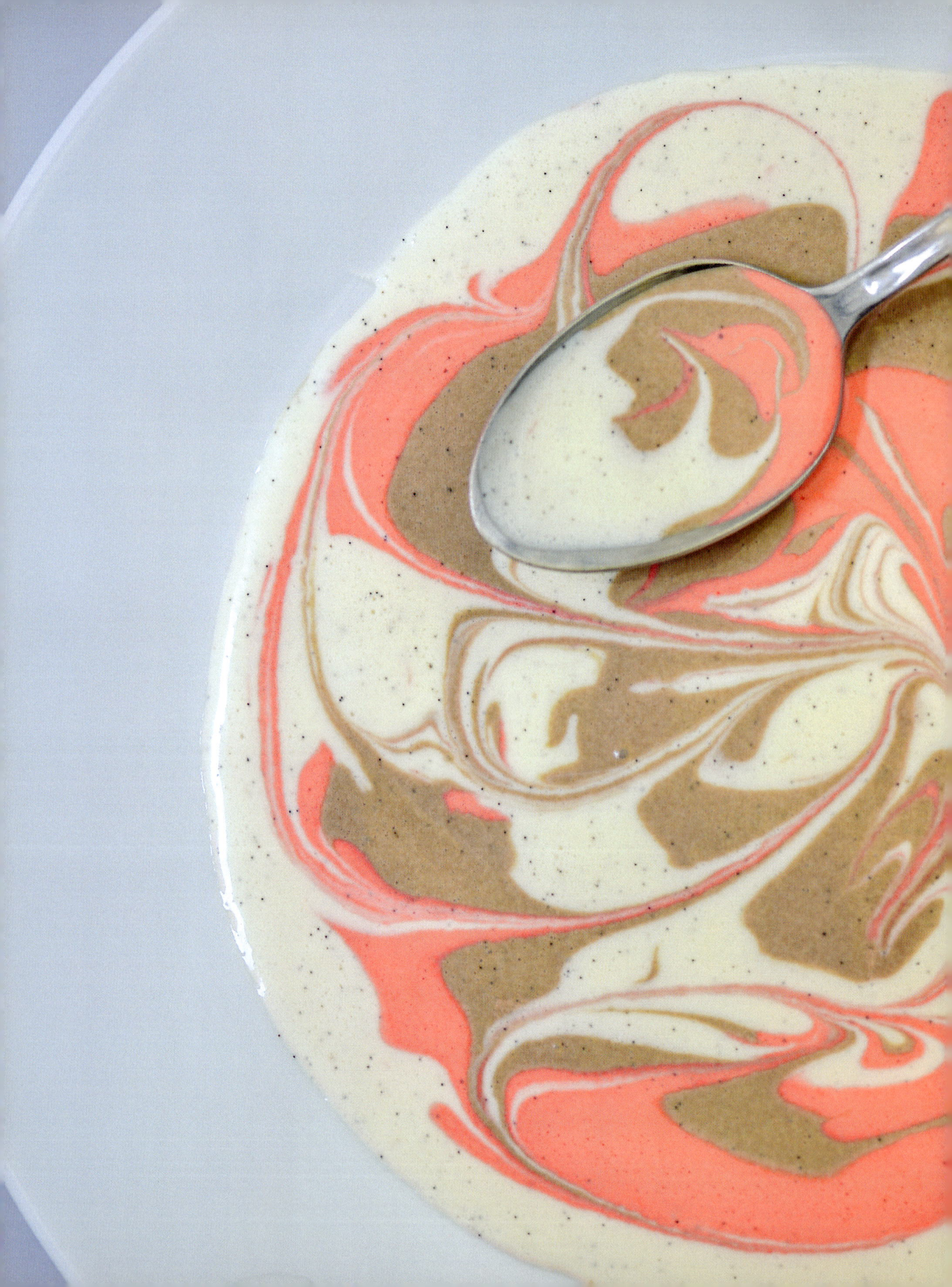

CRÈME ANGLAISE

85ml milk

85ml double cream

2 egg yolks

25g caster sugar

1/4 vanilla pod seeds

Raspberry puree to decorate

TO MAKE THE CRÈME ANGLAISE: Heat the milk, cream and vanilla seeds together. Bring to the boil and remove from the heat.

Beat the egg yolks with the sugar until light and thick. Pour the hot milk and cream onto the egg mix, whisking as you go. Return the pan to a low heat and cook gently, stirring continuously, making sure the custard doesn't catch on the bottom of the pan. Do not boil!

Keep cooking and stirring until the custard coats the back of a spoon and a finger dragged through it leaves a clear channel. Strain into a clean bowl and continue stirring as it cools.

TOP TIP

Crème Anglaise can be used for any dessert, in place of custard, for a more luxurious and elegant dish.

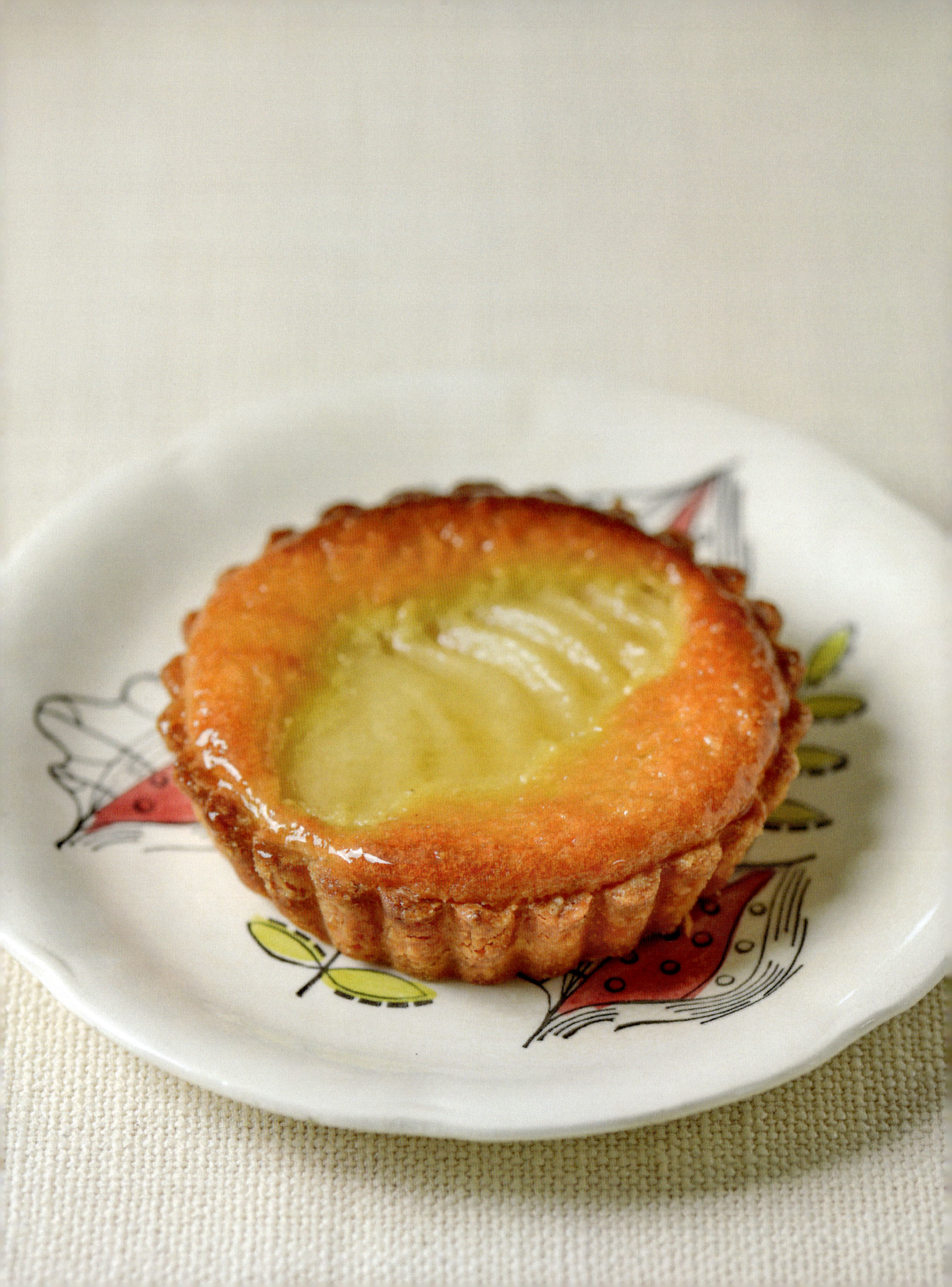

PEAR BOURDALOUE

Makes 8 small or 4 large

SWEET PASTRY:

115g plain flour

Pinch of salt

85g very cold unsalted butter

45g caster sugar

Zest of 1/2 lime

1 teaspoon vanilla essence

1 egg yolk (medium)

FRANGIPANE:

55g butter, softened

55g caster sugar

1 free-range egg

55g ground almonds

Drop of almond essence

Tinned pear halves

1 tablespoon apricot jam

TO MAKE THE SWEET PASTRY: Mix the salt into the flour. Next take a sheet of greaseproof paper, place the block of butter on one half, fold the other half of the paper on top and 'bash' with a rolling pin until the butter is flat (about 5mm), pliable, but still very cold. Quickly tear into pieces and work the flour and butter lightly between your fingertips until only small pieces of butter remain — about the size of your little fingernail is fine.

Add the sugar and lime zest and mix lightly. Make a well in the middle and add the egg yolk and vanilla essence. Cup your hands around this mix and start squeezing it together. Don't overwork it, but it must hold together. Wrap in cling film and chill for 30 minutes minimum.

Once chilled, temper the pastry before use by kneading it gently until it becomes pliable again. If it is too cold, it will crack when you try to roll it.

Roll the pastry about 3-4mm thick and line some lightly-oiled tartlet tins. Put in the freezer whilst you make the frangipane.

TO MAKE THE FRANGIPANE: Beat the soft butter, sugar and almond essence together in a bowl until pale and fluffy. Beat the egg and incorporate into the mixture. Then carefully fold in the ground almonds.

Preheat the oven 180°C (fan).

TO ASSEMBLE: Fill the tartlet cases 3/4 full with frangipane. Don't overfill the frangipane filling! This is a common mistake. It will just spill out in the oven.

Take one pear half, fan it with a sharp knife and gently press into the frangipane. Bake for 20 minutes until risen and golden. Leave to cool before removing from their tins.

Heat the apricot jam with a little water (or pear juice) and brush the tartlets to glaze.

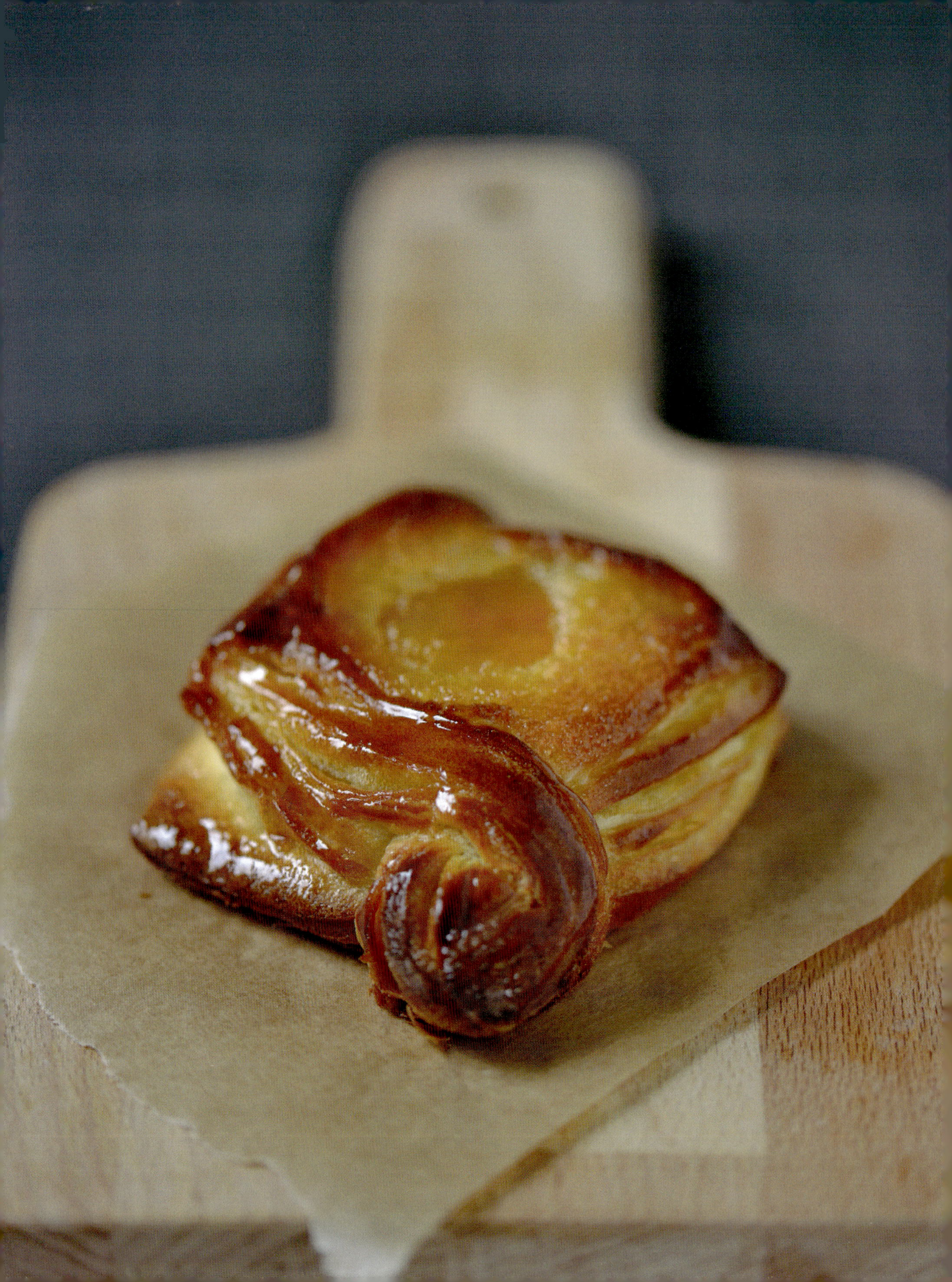

DANISH PASTRY

A Danish pastry is a laminated sweet pastry in the Viennoiserie style. This style of pastry was brought to Denmark by Austrian bakers and became a Danish speciality. It is similar to puff pastry with layers of butter (laminations) between dough, but with the addition of yeast. On the Croissant, Danish and Brioche workshop at the school we make croissants, pain au chocolate, brioche and three types of Danish; custard, apple and cinnamon, pecan and maple, and frangipane and apricot.

Because of the fat content in these pastries it is important to keep everything nice and cold when you work — within reason. Too cold and the butter can crack and split the dough, too warm and the butter works its way into the dough in a greasy mess. The trick is to work as quickly as you can and don't be afraid to stop halfway through a stage and put your dough back in the fridge if it gets too warm.

Both Danish and croissants take practice — your first attempts are unlikely to be your best. Practice makes perfect!

FRANGIPANE & APRICOT DANISH PASTRIES

Makes 10

PASTRY BASE

250g strong white flour

5g dried fast-action yeast

5g sea salt

40g caster sugar

1 medium egg

45g water

62g whole milk

125g cold, unsalted butter for laminating

FRANGIPANE

55g butter softened

55g caster sugar

1 free-range egg

55g ground almonds

Drop of almond essence

DECORATION

10 semi-dried apricots,

1 beaten egg

Apricot jam

TO MAKE THE PASTRY BASE: Mix the flour, yeast, salt and sugar together, add the egg, milk and water and knead into a smooth ball. Cover with cling film and rest in the fridge for 30 minutes minimum.

Once rested, flour the worktop and roll the dough into a square about 20cm x 20cm.

Place the butter between two sheets of greaseproof and gently pound with a rolling pin into a 10cm square. Place on the dough at a 45° angle.

Fold each side of the dough over the butter to enclose it completely – there must be no gaps at all.

Gently roll the pastry out into a rectangle 2-3 times longer than its original length (35 x 15cm).

Fold both ends into the middle and then in half again (this is called a book turn).

Wrap in cling film, and rest for 30 minutes in the fridge to keep the butter cold.

Once rested, turn 90° and roll out again as before, then fold to make one more book turn.

Rest and chill again before using, for at least 30 minutes.

> **TOP TIP**
>
> The pastry can be frozen at this stage for later use.

While the pastries are resting, make the Frangipane.

TO MAKE THE FRANGIPANE: Beat the butter and sugar together in a bowl until pale and fluffy. Crack in the egg and beat again until fully incorporated into the mixture. Add a drop of almond essence, then gently fold in the ground almonds.

TO ASSEMBLE: Once rested, roll the pastry into a rectangle 5-7mm thick. Leave for a minute or two to relax, then divide into 10 squares using a pizza wheel or knife.

> **TOP TIP**
>
> Using a ruler or set square will ensure the squares are straight and even.

Cut and shape each square following the photographs below, using a little egg wash to glue the sides into place.

Place a tablespoon of frangipane in the centre of each pastry and gently press a semi-dried apricot into the frangipane.

Place on a parchment-lined baking sheet. Space them out, remember they will double in size as they cook. Cover loosely with cling film and leave to prove at room temperature for about 90 minutes.

Preheat the oven to 180°C (fan).

Carefully egg wash the pastry, but NOT the frangipane middle, and bake in a preheated oven for 15 minutes.

Whilst they are baking, take two tablespoons of apricot jam and heat in a saucepan (or microwave), with a tablespoon or two of water. Whisk until smooth and pourable but still thick.

After baking, leave the pastries to cool for 4-5 minutes and then brush generously with this glaze.